OECD Green Growth Studies

Green Growth in Cebu, Philippines

OECD
BETTER POLICIES FOR BETTER LIVES

Please cite this publication as:
OECD (2017), *Green Growth in Cebu, Philippines*, OECD Green Growth Studies, OECD Publishing, Paris.
http://dx.doi.org/10.1787/9789264277991-en

ISBN 978-92-64-27798-4 (print)
ISBN 978-92-64-27799-1 (PDF)

Series: OECD Green Growth Studies
ISSN 2222-9515 (print)
ISSN 2222-9523 (online)

Foreword

This publication is the result of a study on urban green growth in Cebu, Philippines. It analyses the economic and environmental performance of Cebu, assesses the policies and governance practices that can promote green growth, and provides recommendations to enhance Cebu's green growth potential. Metro Cebu, the second most populated urban area of the Philippines, has been growing faster than any other city in the country. However, despite this economic growth, Metro Cebu still faces many challenges that hinder its green growth. Changing land-use patterns and a growing population have severely strained local infrastructure and the provision of basic urban services, especially water supply, which will be tackled with a special focus in this report. Metro Cebu also faces several natural disasters risks, like floods and earthquakes. Still, the implementation of appropriate policy frameworks is impaired by a lack of both vertical and horizontal co-operation in the metropolitan governance. All these challenges will need to be addressed to build a more sustainable, resilient and greener city.

This is the fourth case study in the OECD **Urban Green Growth in Dynamic Asia** project, which explores how policies and governance practices can promote green growth and competitiveness in Asian fast-growing cities. It contributes both to the *OECD Green Growth Strategy* and to the *OECD Strategy on Development*, as well as to ongoing discussions on the role of cities in tackling the urgent challenges of climate change. Five case studies have been carried out so far: Bangkok (Thailand), Hai Phong (Viet Nam), Bandung (Indonesia), Iskandar Malaysia (Malaysia) and Cebu (Philippines). The results of the case studies were published in 2016 in a synthesis report entitled *Urban Green Growth in Dynamic Asia.*

The analysis is based on a "focused comparison" strategy of case study research. This entailed asking the same questions in the different city case studies in order to discern similarities and draw general lessons. Although the analysis focuses on Asian cities, the lessons for promoting green growth will also be relevant for other OECD member countries and cities.

The publication benefited from guidance by the OECD Regional Development Policy Committee and its Working Party on Urban Policy, as well as the support of the local team. It draws on data provided by the local team and the OECD Metropolitan Database. The analytical approach draws on *Urban Green Growth in Dynamic Asia: A Conceptual Framework* (2014). The expertise and experience of OECD member countries provided relevant international benchmarks and policy examples.

As part of the *OECD Green Growth Studies* series, further case studies will be carried out in a variety of cities, chosen on the basis of criteria such as population size, speed of growth, economic structure, and the centrality of the city in the national and regional economy.

Acknowledgements

The OECD Secretariat would like to thank Governor, Province of Cebu, Hilario P. Davide III (Chair, the Metro Cebu Development and Coordinating Board (MCDCB); Mayor Michael L. Rama (Co-Chair, MCDCB; Mayor, City of Cebu); Mr. Efren B. Carreon (Vice Chair, MCDCB; Regional Director, National Economic Development Authority Region VII); Mr. Gordon Alan P. Joseph (Chair, MCDCB Research Program and Organization Development (RPOD) Executive Committee, President, Cebu Business Club); and Ms. Dominica B. Chua (Vice Chair, MCDCB RPOD Executive Committee; COO, Ramon Aboitiz Foundation, Inc. (RAFI), under whose leadership and support the study was made possible in Cebu. Our thanks also go to the local team that provided support throughout the study, including the preparation of the background report and organisation of the OECD study missions to Cebu, Atty: Mark Tolentino and Jennifer Maniwang (Province of Cebu), Evelyn Nacario Castro and Jackie Amazona Clavin (MCDCB RPOD/ RAFI – Eduardo Aboitiz Development Studies Center (EADSC), the Department of Environment and Natural Resources Region 7 Office Atty. Rose-Liza Eisma-Osorio (University of Cebu) provided professional support on local data collection and policy assessment. We also thank the members of the Philippines' central government who participated in the OECD study missions and provided valuable comments on the report. In addition, members of the MCDCB RPOD Program Management Office and RAFI EADSC staff provided valuable comments.

The OECD Secretariat would also like to gratefully acknowledge the financial support of the Province of Cebu, the government of Japan and the *Deutsche Gesellschaft für Internationale Zusammenarbeit* (GIZ) GmbH within the framework of Germany's Global Initiative on Disaster Risk Management (GIDRM). Stephan Huppertz and his team also provided valuable inputs on the report.

This project was undertaken by the Regional Development Policy Division within the OECD's Centre for Entrepreneurship, SMEs, Local Development and Tourism, led by Lamia Kamal-Chaoui (Director). This publication was prepared by Tadashi Matsumoto (Project Manager, Urban Green Growth/Knowledge Sharing, Regional Development Policy Division), Loïc Daudey, Martin Abbott, and Kwame Boye Frimpong (Consultants), directed by Joaquim Oliveira Martins (Special Advisor to the Director). It benefited from valuable comments and input from numerous colleagues: Karen Maguire, Aziza Akhmouch, Oriana Romano, Christophe Etienne and Juliana Chia.

The case study's two international peer reviewers from Spain and Canada, Ton Padullés (Metropolitan Area of Barcelona) and Heather McNell (Metro Vancouver) joined the OECD study mission to Cebu (8-12 December 2015) and provided valuable reports. Richard Carlos Worden (international environmental consultant) participated in the mission and provided valuable insights and comments on urban resilience and disaster risk management.

The publication also benefited from valuable input from the Knowledge-Sharing Platform on Urban Green Growth in Dynamic Asia and the participants of the Cebu Knowledge Sharing Workshop on Urban Green Growth in Dynamic Asia (9-10 December 2015). These include the MCDCB, City of Cebu, other local government units (LGUs) in the MCDCB, departments and agencies, international organisations and experts, subnational networks and other Asian and OECD cities. The workshop was supported by the OECD Knowledge-Sharing Alliance, in partnership with the German Federal Ministry for Economic Development and Cooperation (BMZ) and the Korean Ministry for Strategy and Finance (MOSF). Masato Hayashikawa, Chelsea Roberts, John Lloyd, Amanda Gautherin, Charles Victor and Théa Chubinidze provided the organisational support.

This publication is dedicated to the memory of Roberto Eduardo “Bobby” Aboitiz (1949-2017), who served as Co-Chair of MCDCB.

Table of contents

Tables

Figures

Acronyms and abbreviations

APEC	Asia-Pacific Economic Cooperation
ASEAN	Association of South East Asian Nations
BRT	Bus Rapid Transit
CAT-BOND	Catastrophe Bond
CAT-DDO	Catastrophe Deferred Drawdown Option
CDRRM	Cebu's Disaster Risk Reduction and Management Office
CVR	Central Visayas Region
CESET	City Environmental Sanitation Enforcement Team
CTF	Clean Technology Fund
CLUP	Comprehensive Land Use Plan
DOE	Department of Energy
DENR	Department of Environment and Natural Resources
DILG	Department of Interior and Local Government
DPS	Department of Public Services
DRRM	Disaster Risk Reduction Management
EWI	Environment and Water Programme Office
EIA	Environmental Impact Assessment Methods
EPR	Extended Producer Responsibility
FAR	Floor-Area-Ratio
FDI	Foreign Direct Investment
AFD	French Development Agency
GIDRM	Global Initiative on Disaster Risk Management
GDP	Gross Domestic Product

GRP	Gross Regional Product
HLURB	Housing and Land Use Regulatory Board
ICT	Information and Communication Technologies
IEA	International Energy Agency
ITU	International Telecommunication
IMER	Iskandar Malaysia Economic Region
JICA	Japan International Cooperation Agency
LGU	Local Government Unit
LWUA	Local Water Utilities Association
MRF	Materials Recovery Facility
MCDCB	Metro Cebu Development and Coordinating Board
MCDA	Mega Cebu Development Authority
MCIFDS	Metro Cebu Integrated Flood and Drainage System
MCLUTS	Metro Cebu Land Use and Transportation Study
MCWD	Metro Cebu Water District
NEDA	National Economic Development Agency
NWRB	National Water Resources Board
ODA	Official Development Assistance
PHP	Philippine Peso (currency)
PSA	Philippines Statistics Authority
PPP	Public Private Partnership
PPP	Purchasing Power Parity
RE	Renewable Energy
SWM	Solid Waste Management
SEZs	Special Economic Zones
TPES	Total Primary Energy Supply
WHO	World Health Organisation

Executive summary

Urban green growth policies encourage economic development while minimising either negative environmental externalities or the unsustainable consumption of natural resources and environmental assets. Cities play a critical role in national growth, but also generate negative externalities, and thus must be part of national solutions to stimulate growth and address climate change.

The Metropolitan Area of Cebu (Metro Cebu), Philippines, is located on the central-eastern flank of Cebu Province in the Central Visayas Region (CVR). In 2015, Metro Cebu was home to over 2.8 million people and is the most populous Filipino metropolitan area after Metro Manila (13 million). Metro Cebu is a key contributor to the remarkable economic growth of its region. The region's annual economic growth reached 8.5% between 2009 and 2015, which was higher than both the national average (5.8%) and that of Metro Manila (6.5%). This growth has been underpinned by the rapid expansion of the manufacturing sector. Despite this economic growth, Metro Cebu still faces many challenges that hinder its green growth potential. For example not all residents have benefitted equally from the region's success, and inequality is also rising. Changing land-use patterns and a growing population have severely strained local infrastructure and the provision of basic urban services, such as transportation, energy, water management and municipal solid waste. The metro area also faces environmental risks such as typhoons and earthquakes and is vulnerable to climate change effects such as floods.

Key findings and recommendations

Areas for action

The growth of Metro Cebu's urban population has been accompanied by an uncontrolled urban sprawl, exacerbated by poor enforcement of land-use plans and zoning ordinances which need updating for some of its 13 Local Government Units (LGUs). The absence of an integrated high capacity public transport system, coupled with increasing private vehicle use, contributes to traffic congestion and pollution. As a matter of priority, Metro Cebu needs to promote a compact city model, both to ensure the sustainable use of land resources as well as promote integrated sustainable urban mobility to support productivity, competitiveness and inclusiveness.

Waste management remains a challenge for most of the LGUs in Metro Cebu. Current consumption patterns still follow a linear trend with the end being disposal. Addressing this calls for drastic measures such as adopting a zero-waste policy, a review of waste pricing and stronger enforcement of the "no segregation, no collection" policy, aiming to impose the separation of waste for the purpose of recycling. Furthermore, as a major manufacturing centre, Metro Cebu should promote clean, energy-efficient manufacturing processes as well as greener services and products. Additionally, minimising pollution from MSMEs and large industries, ensuring compliance with environmental regulations as well as adoption of environmentally friendly approaches in production needs to be encouraged.

Metro Cebu has a good mix of energy supply for electrification (53% of power is from renewable sources). Nonetheless, more opportunities for energy production through rooftop solar panels and from waste exist and should be urgently explored.

Water security and green growth

Water security is a cornerstone of urban green growth strategies for Cebu. The entire province faces major water challenges, including increasing water demand in a context of diminishing resources, inefficiency of the water distribution network, and suboptimal coverage of the water supply and sanitation infrastructure, leading to quality issues in surface and ground water. These challenges are particularly acute for Metro Cebu, and are accentuated by rapid urbanisation, economic growth and climate change.

To address these water supply and sanitation issues, a comprehensive strategy that encompasses a long-term vision needs to be developed, including measures such as diversification of water sources, investment in green infrastructure, demand-side management tools and smart technologies. Most LGUs need to design robust disaster risk reduction and management strategies with a thorough assessment of vulnerability to floods, in particular for critical infrastructure. Water governance in Cebu is complex and is one of the main challenges for LGUs, which suffer from fragmentation of authority, and lack both a relevant scale for investment and incentives for co-operation.

Governance for urban green growth

LGUs in Cebu have faced great difficulties in undertaking sustainable growth and developing infrastructure that could foster urban green growth. The transfer of competencies to LGUs with the decentralisation laws since the 1990s has not been sufficiently supported by co-ordination, transfer of resources and capacities between the national governments and LGUs. The lack of horizontal policy co-operation, notably among the 13 LGUs making up Metro Cebu has also hindered the sustainable development of the region. The creation of the Metro Cebu Development and Coordinating Board (MCDCB), a consortium of public authorities, private sector and civil society representatives, was an attempt to address this issue. The MCDCB has played a promising co-ordinating role but has limited financial and legal power. The planned Mega Cebu Development Authority (MCDA) should be designed to effectively tackle both horizontal and vertical governance issues.

Strategies to unlock finance for urban green growth will be critical as well. The total revenues of the 13 LGUs in Metro Cebu have increased significantly but are still highly dependent on national government transfers. Public investment remains low compared to OECD countries. The LGUs should make the most of opportunities to raise their own revenue, in particular tariffs and user charges, and the central government could create a more efficient public investment framework, including specific financial channels for local green growth initiatives. Attracting private investment should be emphasised, as FDI inflows are still low in the Philippines. International co-operation can further bridge the finance gap for urban green growth: between 2002 and 2014, the Philippines has been the third-largest recipient of official development finance in Southeast Asia, with around USD 30 billion, but Cebu has not profited enough from this trend.

Chapter 1

The economic, social and environmental performance of the Cebu metropolitan area, Philippines

Chapter 1 examines Metro Cebu's economic and environmental performance. The first section introduces Metro Cebu's geographic and demographic characteristics. The second section focuses on Cebu's socio-economic growth and includes an assessment of: 1) economic performance and structure; 2) foreign direct investment and infrastructure; 3) skills and inequality; and 4) shifting sectorial employment. The third section discusses environmental trends and green growth challenges across six primary sectors. It includes an assessment of: 1) land-use and transport; 2) air pollution; 3) energy performance; 4) CO_2 emissions; 5) water supply and wastewater treatment, in addition to solid waste management; and 6) urban resilience. The final section outlines how Cebu is governed.

Key findings

- Metro Cebu is located on the central-eastern flank of Cebu Island in the centre of the Philippine archipelago. **Home to over 2.8 million people in 2015**, it is the most populous city after Metro Manila (13 million). In the 80s, Metro Cebu grew faster than comparable Filipino cities, on average at an annual rate of 4.1% before slowing down to 2.3% between 2010 and 2015, the population growth being fastest in peripheral local government units. By 2030, Cebu's population is projected to reach 3.8 million people. The demographic structure of Metro Cebu remains young and it has benefitted from significant expansion of the working age population.
- **The Central Visayas has achieved remarkable economic growth** that is faster than the national average and stronger than Metro Manila. Between 2010 and 2015, the Gross Regional Product (GRP) of the Central Visayas Region (CVR) averaged 8.35% annual growth to reach USD 35.6 billion (PHP 488.7 billion). Metro Cebu is recognised as the primary economic centre of the CVR. In 2012, the GRP of Metro Cebu was estimated to be USD 16.4 billion (PPP) (PHP 225 billion).
- **Cebu's impressive economic growth has been underpinned by the rapid expansion of the manufacturing sector**, consisting of industries such as furniture, electronics and food processing. The CVR's secondary sector grew on average by 11% yearly from 2010 to 2014. The tertiary sector remains the mainstay of the regional economy and while it expanded by 7.1% between 2010 and 2014, its comparative share of GRP declined to 54.6%. Nonetheless, service industries remain by far Metro Cebu's largest employer thanks to the burgeoning Business Process Outsourcing (BPO) companies and the tourism industry.
- While Cebu has benefited from the strong economic growth during the last 5 years, **not all residents have benefitted to the same extent as inequality is rising**. This is mainly demonstrated by a rising GINI co-efficient (0.47 in 2012) in the CVR.
- **Changing land-use patterns and a growing population have severely strained local infrastructure and the provision of basic urban services, such as transportation, energy, water management and municipal solid waste (MSW).** Vehicle numbers almost doubled between 2003 and 2012, contributing to traffic congestion and high air pollution levels. Also, less than half of Metro Cebu's households have access to piped water services. The volume of MSW produced daily has rapidly increased, although only 65% of the household waste is collected.
- **While 46.40% of energy for electricity in the Visayas is generated from geothermal plants, there is still a heavy reliance on fossil fuels (45.27%).** Overall, the transportation sector is the largest energy consumer followed by the industrial sector. However, the industrial sector emits more GHG emissions than the transportation sector.
- **Metro Cebu is exposed to acute disaster risks.** It regularly experiences severe flooding, especially during the wet season from June to November and annual tropical storms. In 2013, Cebu City experienced a magnitude 7.2 earthquake which affected 870 000 people and damaged nearly 1 000 houses, local infrastructure and community facilities.

The Metropolitan Area of Cebu: Location and characteristics

The Metropolitan Area of Cebu (Metro Cebu) is located on the central-eastern flank of Cebu Island and covers an area of 1 163 square kilometres (km^2) (Figure 1.1). It extends along a narrow 70 kilometre coastal strip of territory which is sandwiched between rugged mountain ranges that traverse the island's north-south spine and the Strait of Cebu. The City of Cebu lies at the centre of this metropolitan area and is the capital of the Province of Cebu, which is largely focused on the Island of Cebu, and covers an area of 4 944 km^2.

The OECD (2012) methodology that would normally be employed to delineate the Functional Urban Area (FUA) of the Philippines has not been utilised due to a lack of detailed commuting data. While Metro Cebu as delineated by the Metro Cebu Development and Coordinating Board (MCDCB) is the primary unit of analysis, the Province of Cebu is also considered for the purposes of this report. In situations where information pertaining to the metropolitan area is unavailable, the study utilises data covering the Province of Cebu, the Central Visayas Region, the City of Cebu and the other highly urbanised cities located in Metro Cebu.

Though its definition in terms of composition has expanded, Metro Cebu has existed in the regional planning of the Central Visayas Region (Region VII) since the early 1980s (Mercado, 1998). Prior to the formation of the MCDCB in 2011, there was no formal basis for metropolitan planning and development. Today, Metro Cebu has evolved from four local government units (LGUs) (Cebu, Mandaue, Talisay and Lapu Lapu) to 13 LGUs (Figure 1.1).[1]

Figure 1.1. **Locations of the Province of Cebu and Metro Cebu**

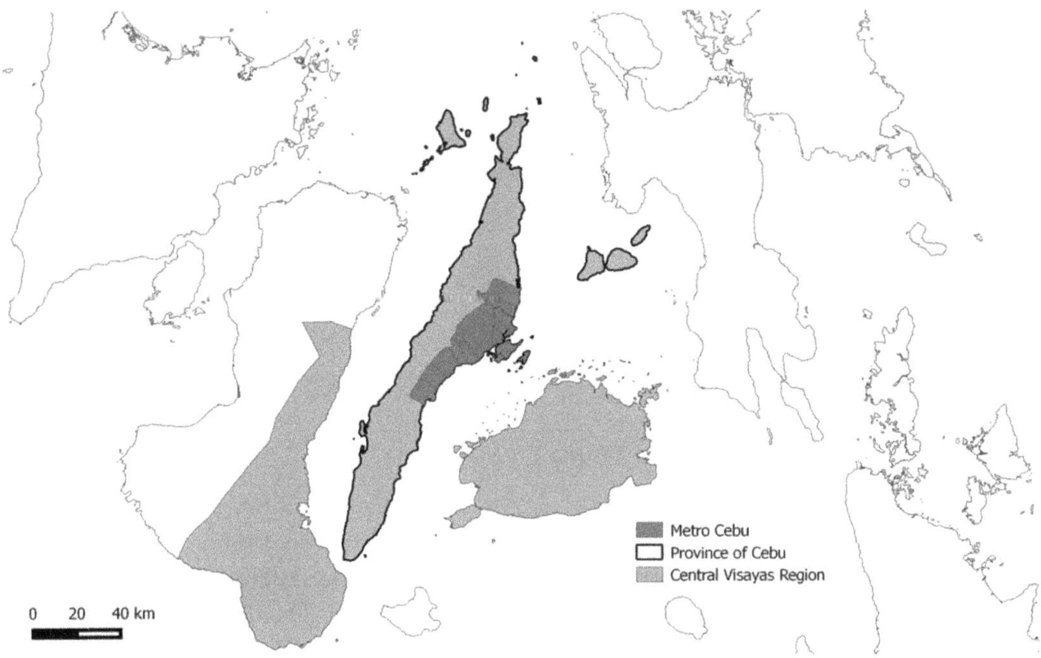

Source: Global Administrative Boundaries (2016), available at: www.gadm.org/country.

Between 2000 and 2010, Metro Cebu has experienced rapid expansion that was characterised by three different patterns (Figure 1.2). Firstly, a densification of the urban core of Cebu City, and an extension towards the municipalities of Mandaue and Consolacion was observed. The urban fabric also seems to have grown along the coast, probably due to the mountainous hinterland, stretching as far as the study zone, which extends from Danao in the north to San Fernando in the south. Furthermore, the cities of Lapu-Lapu and Cordova have experienced very strong developments, which concentrated on the coast of Mactan Island facing the city of Cebu. In 2010, urban population comprised 93% of Cebu City's population, whereas it constituted only about 50% for municipalities like Danao and Compostela (2010 Census on Population and Housing). In the Central Visayas region as a whole, the urbanisation trend has also been strong even if less pronounced than in Metro Cebu, with an annual rate of urbanisation of 8% between 2000 and 2016. However, as of 2016, 56% of the CVR population still remained rural.

Figure 1.2. **Metro Cebu expansion between 2000 and 2010**

Source: OECD based on World Bank PUMA, https://puma.worldbank.org/intro/

Demographic characteristics of Metro Cebu

Metro Cebu's population has grown rapidly in the last three decades. As of 2015, it was home to over 2.8 million people, compared to 1.5 million in 1990 (Table 1.1), and is expected to reach 3.8 million people by 2030 and 5 million by 2050 (JICA and MCDCB, 2015). Metro Cebu is the second largest metropolitan area in the Philippines after Metro Manila which was home to 13 million people in 2015. The Philippines' third largest metropolitan area, Metro Davao, was home to 2.3 million people in 2015. The Province of Cebu's population has grown slightly more slowly and was home to 4.6 million people in 2015, an increase of 1.9 million people since 1990. By 2030, the Province of Cebu's population is expected to reach 5.1 million people and 7.4 million by 2050 (JICA and MCDCB, 2015).

Table 1.1. **Metro Cebu's growing population**

Local Government Unit	2000 Population	2010 Population	2015 Population	Annual population growth 2000-2010	Area (km²)	Density (2015)
Metro Cebu	1 930 100	2 551 100	2 849 213	2.8%	1 163	2 450
City of Carcar	89 200	107 300	119 664	1.9%	116.8	1 025
City of Cebu	718 800	866 200	922 611	1.9%	315.0	2 929
City of Danao	98 800	119 300	136 471	1.9%	107.3	1 272
City of Lapu-Lapu	217 000	350 500	408 112	4.9%	58.1	7 024
City of Mandaue	259 728	331 320	362 654	2.5%	25.2	14 391
City of Naga	80 200	101 600	115 750	2.4%	102.0	1 135
City of Talisay	148 100	200 800	227 645	3.1%	39.9	5 710
Municipality of Compostela	31 400	42 600	47 898	5.5%	53.9	889
Municipality of Consolacion	62 300	106 600	131 528	5.5%	147.2	894
Municipality of Cordoba	34 000	50 400	59 712	4.0%	17.2	3 482
Municipality of Liloan	65 000	100 500	118 753	4.5%	45.9	2 586
Municipality of Minglanilla	77 300	113 200	132 135	3.9%	65.6	2 014
Municipality of San Fernando	48 200	61 000	66 280	2.4%	69.4	955

Note: Density is defined as the number of people per square kilometre.

Source: Philippine Statistics Authority (2015a), *2015 Philippine Statistical Yearbook*, https://psa.gov.ph/sites/default/files/2015%20PSY%20PDF.pdf; Philippine Statistics Authority (2016a), "Total Population by Province, City, Municipality and Barangay: Region VII – Central Visayas", http://psa.gov.ph/content/highlights-philippine-population-2015-census-population.

Metro Cebu's population expanded the fastest between 1980 and 1990, on average by 4.1% per year (Figure 1.3). Since then, it has continued to expand quickly, by 2.9% per year during the following decade and 2.8% between 2000 and 2010. Metro Cebu's annual population growth rate was significantly higher than in Metro Manila which expanded by 1.8% between 2000 and 2010, and was above the national average (1.9%) during the same time period. The Province of Cebu's population also grew more quickly than both the metropolitan areas and the national average (Figure 1.4). The lure of employment and educational opportunities has fuelled significant migration from outlying rural areas and largely explains Cebu's rapid metropolitan growth.

Figure 1.3. **Fast-growing metropolitan areas (population size)**

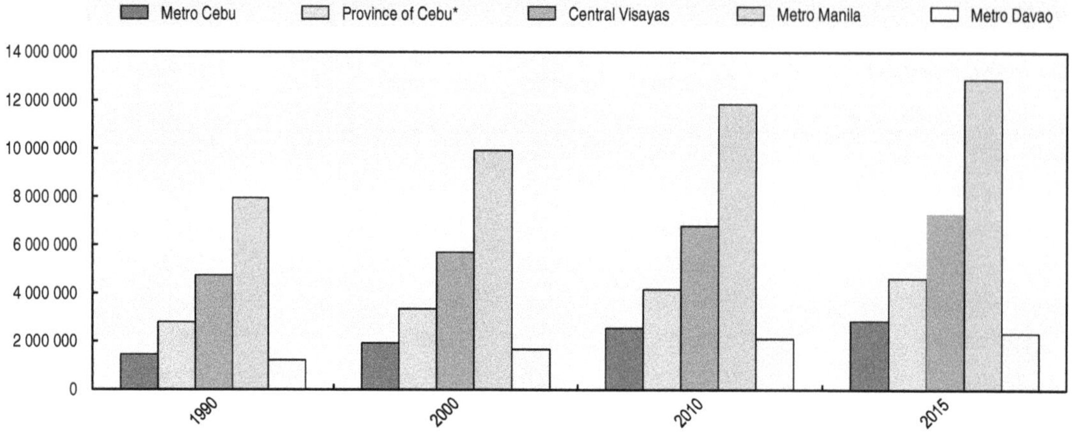

Note: *Province of Cebu includes the City of Cebu, City of Lapu-Lapu and City of Mandaue.

Source: Philippine Statistics Authority (2015), *2015 Philippine Statistical Yearbook*, https://psa.gov.ph/sites/default/files/2015%20PSY%20PDF.pdf (accessed 8 June 2016); Philippine Statistics Authority (2016), "Total Population by Province, City, Municipality and Barangay: Region VII – Central Visayas", http://psa.gov.ph/content/highlights-philippine-population-2015-census-population.

The expanding Metro Cebu dominates Cebu Province's overall population growth which has been primarily concentrated in the suburban areas that surround the City of Cebu, especially in the northeast. Between 1980 and 1990, the City of Cebu grew by 3.1% per year, 1.65% during the following decade and by 1.9% annually between 2000 and 2010 (Table 1.1). In contrast, the population of the Municipality of Consolacion, which is located to the north of the City of Cebu, grew by 6% per year between 1980 and 1990, 4.2% per year during the following decade and by 5.5% annually between 2000 and 2010 (Table 1.1). A similar trend has been observed in the Bandung and Bangkok Metropolitan Areas where populations are expanding fastest on the urban periphery (OECD, 2016b).

Figure 1.4. **Average annual population growth**

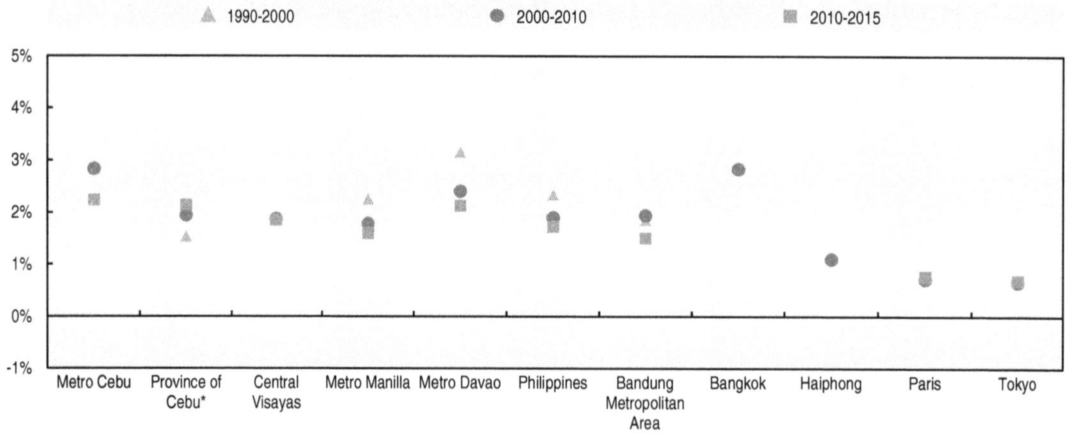

Note: *Province of Cebu includes the City of Cebu, City of Lapu-Lapu and City of Mandaue.

Source: Philippine Statistics Authority (2016), Population and Housing, http://psa.gov.ph/statistics/census/population-and-housing; OECD (2016b), *Green Growth in Bandung, Indonesia*, OECD Publishing, Paris, http://dx.doi.org/10.1787/9789264264113-en.

The demographic structure of Metro Cebu remains young, although it has aged substantially since 2000. The benefit to Metro Cebu has been the significant expansion of the working age population (15 – 64 years of age) which reached 65% according to the 2010 census. The large youth population (under 15 years of age) stood at 31.6% of the population (Figure 1.5). Metro Cebu's population in 2010 reflected a slightly higher number of females (50.3%) than males (49.7%).In the time between 2000 and 2010, the share of Cebu Province's working age population rose substantially from 59.2% to 62.8%, while the youth population declined from 36.6% to 32.7%. In contrast, the proportion of Cebu City's working age population remains higher and rose substantially from 63.8% in 2000 to 66.8% in 2010. While Cebu City's demographic structure is similar to that of the other highly urbanised cities, it differs from Metro Cebu and the Province of Cebu, having a higher share of working age population.

Figure 1.5. **Demographic structures of selected cities and regions (2010)**

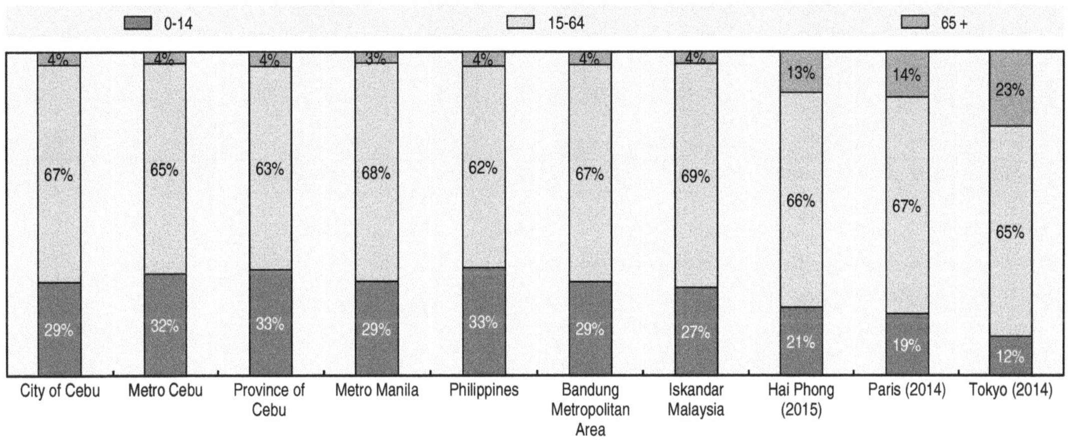

Source: City of Hai Phong (2015), "Answers to the OECD case study questionnaire", internal document, unpublished; Department of Statistics Malaysia (2011), "Population Distribution and Basic Demographic Characteristics; Population and Housing Census of Malaysia", Government of Malaysia, Petaling Jaya; Philippine Statistics Authority (2014), "Statistical Tables on Sample Variables from the results of 2010 Census of Population and Housing Cebu", https://psa.gov.ph/content/statistical-tables-sample-variables-results-2010-census-population-and-housing-cebu; Philippine Statistics Authority (2015a), *2015 Philippine Statistical Yearbook*, https://psa.gov.ph/sites/default/files/2015%20PSY%20PDF.pdf; Statistics West Java (2015), "Jawa Barat Dalam Angka/West Java in Figures", http://jabar.bps.go.id/new/website/pdf_publikasi/Jawa-Barat-Dalam-Angka-2015.pdf; OECD Metropolitan Database, https://stats.oecd.org/Index.aspx?DataSetCode=CITIES#.

Metro Cebu's socio-economic structure

The metropolitan area has achieved impressive growth

Cebu continues to achieve remarkable levels of economic growth[2]. The Gross Regional Product (GRP) of the Central Visayas Region (CVR) in terms of purchasing power parity (PPP) grew on average by 8.35% annually in constant 2000 prices, as it increased from USD 22 billion (PHP 301.9 billion) in 2009 to USD 35.6 billion (PHP 488.7 billion) in 2015. This ranks the CVR among the top four performing regional economies (out of 16) in the Philippines, in terms of the growth rate. In comparison, the average rate of growth of the CVR was substantially higher than in Metro Manila (6.5%) and the national (5.8%) growth rate as well (Figure 1.6). Overall however, the relative economic share of the CVR vis-a-vis the Philippines' Gross Domestic Product (GDP) has declined since 2004 when it accounted for 7% of the nation's GDP, compared to 6.1% in

2014 (Philippines Statistics Authority, 2006 and 2016d). Metro Manila dominates the Philippines' economy and in contrast to Metro Cebu, the share it contributes to national GDP has increased substantially from 31.3% in 2004 to 37.4% in 2015. All the selected cities from Southeast Asia that have served as case studies in this Urban Green Growth in Dynamic Asia project have seen an economic growth much superior to OECD cities such as Paris and Tokyo, which underlines the dynamism of this region.

Figure 1.6. **Average annual GRP growth**

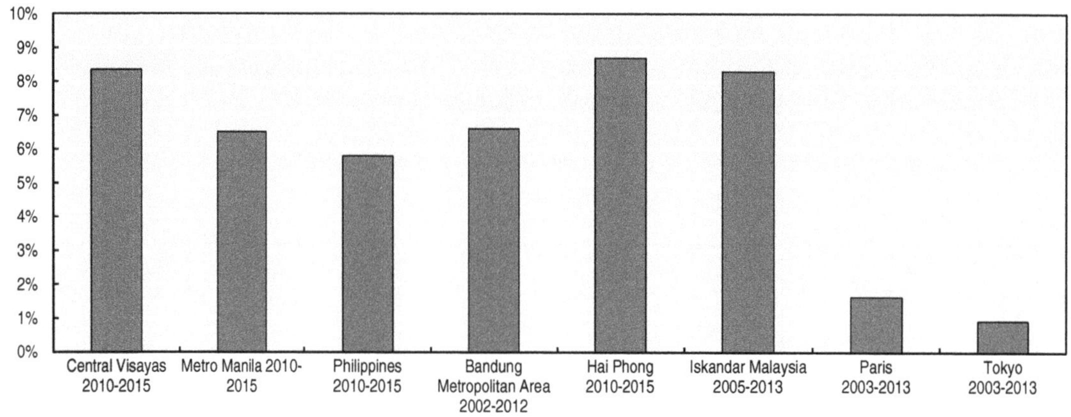

Source: Philippine Statistics Authority (2016d), GRDP Tables, https://psa.gov.ph/regional-accounts/grdp/data-and-charts; OECD Metropolitan Database, https://stats.oecd.org/Index.aspx?DataSetCode=CITIES#.

Cebu's impressive GRP growth is underpinned by Metro Cebu, which is recognised as the primary economic centre of the Central Visayas Region and the central Philippines. In 2012, the GRP of Metro Cebu was estimated to be USD 16.4 billion (PPP) (PHP 225 billion in constant 2000 prices) which accounted for more than half (56%) of the regional economy of the Central Visayas (JICA and MCDCB, 2015). In the coming decades, it is anticipated that the Metro Cebu economy will grow at a faster pace in comparison to both the regional and national economy. By 2030, it is estimated that Metro Cebu's GRP will reach USD 50.3 billion, equivalent to a 71% share of the regional economy at this time.

Per capita GRP (PPP) growth has also been strong in the in the Central Visayas, however, it still remains significantly below the Philippines' per capita GDP and Metro Manila's per capita GRP. The Central Visayas' per capita GRP (PPP) grew on average by 5.3% annually in constant 2000 prices, increasing from USD 3 645 (PHP 49 966) in 2010 to USD 4 730 (PHP 64 858) in 2015 (Figure 1.7). This compares sharply with Metro Manila's per capita GRP which increased during the same time period by an average of 6.2% per year from USD 11 840 (PHP 162 321) to USD 15 981 (PHP 219 114). While the Philippines' overall per capita GDP averaged 5.1% annual growth between 2010 and 2015, rising from USD 4 245 (PHP 58 199) to USD 5 454 (PHP 744 770) (Philippines Statistics Authority, 2016d). Thus, the CVR's per capita GRP remains less than one-third of Metro Manila's GRP and about 13% lower than its national counterpart.

In contrast, it was estimated that Metro Cebu's per capita GRP was equivalent to USD 5 084 (PHP 69 700 in constant 2000 prices) in 2012 (JICA and MCDCB, 2015). This amount is 24% higher than the equivalent per capita GRP of the CVR, although it remains slightly less than one third that of Metro Manila's per capita GRP of USD 14 816

(PHP 203 132). In comparison to other Southeast Asian cities, Metro Cebu's per capita GRP (PPP) is lower than the Bandung Metropolitan Area which was equivalent to USD 7 490 (IDR 10.69 million) and Bangkok (USD 29 540) although above the GRP of Hai Phong (USD 3 940) (Figure 1.6). It is projected that by 2050, Metro Cebu's per capita GRP will grow to more than USD 20 000 (JICA and MCDCB, 2015).

Figure 1.7. **Per capita GRP (PPP) in constant 2000 prices**

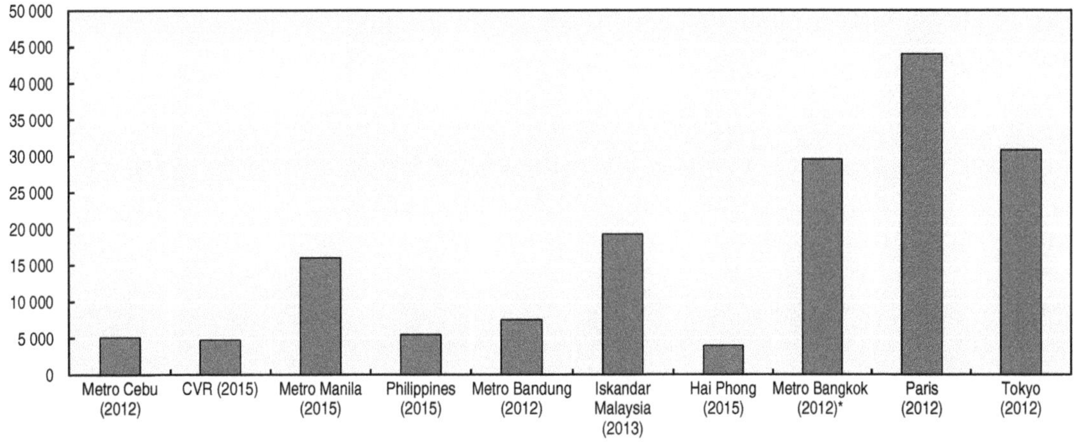

Note: * Constant 2005 prices.

Source: Philippine Statistics Authority (2016d), "GRDP Tables", https://psa.gov.ph/regional-accounts/grdp/data-and-charts.

Services dominate but manufacturing is driving economic growth

The impressive economic growth of recent years in the Central Visayas has been underpinned by the rapid expansion of the secondary sector. It expanded its GRP share of the Central Visayas Region to 35% in 2016, a rise of 5 percentage points since 2008 (Figure 1.8). The sector is dominated by the manufacturing and construction industries which accounted for 63% and 30% respectively of the sector's economic output in 2015. During the 4 years to 2014, the sector grew on average by 11% per year, but saw a slight downturn of about 2% between 2014 and 2015 due to a prominent decline of the construction industry. Overall, manufacturing represents more than one-fifth of the region's economic output and its strong growth may be attributed to the establishment of several special economic zones (SEZs) in Metro Cebu which have attracted light industry and manufacturers of electronic products, garments, furniture, and marine-based products (JICA and MCDCB, 2015).[3] Electronics and optical manufacturers have clustered in the Mactan industrial zone in close proximity to the airport. The growth of the construction industry is partly explained by strong housing demand in Metro Cebu.

The tertiary sector has also grown strongly and remains the mainstay of the Central Visayas' regional economy. Its comparative share of GRP was 58.3% in 2016, a decline of 1.7 percentage points since 2008 (Figure 1.8). This decline can be explained by an average annual growth rate of 7.1% between 2010 and 2014 which was significantly lower than that of the secondary sector. Financial services grew the most rapidly, by 9.4% on average between 2008 and 2015. It is worth pointing out that the tertiary sector is more diversified than the secondary sector as no single industry dominates it in the same way as the manufacturing industry. In 2015, wholesale and retail trade contributed the largest economic share of 32%, while the other services and real estate, renting and business each contributed to 20% of the sector's output. In comparison, Metro Manila derived four-fifths (82%) of its economic output from the tertiary sector in 2015.

Despite the substantial number of people still living in rural areas of the CVR and the Province of Cebu, the GRP share of the primary sector has declined from 10% in 2008 to 6.7% in 2016 (Figure 1.8). Moreover in 2014, the sector contracted by 2.6% due to a reduction in agricultural production and the fishing industry but recovered slightly between 2014 and 2015. There is a growing policy need to address these structural changes in the rural economy, especially in the context of promoting integration of urban and rural areas.

Figure 1.8. **Sectoral economic structures (GRP share)**

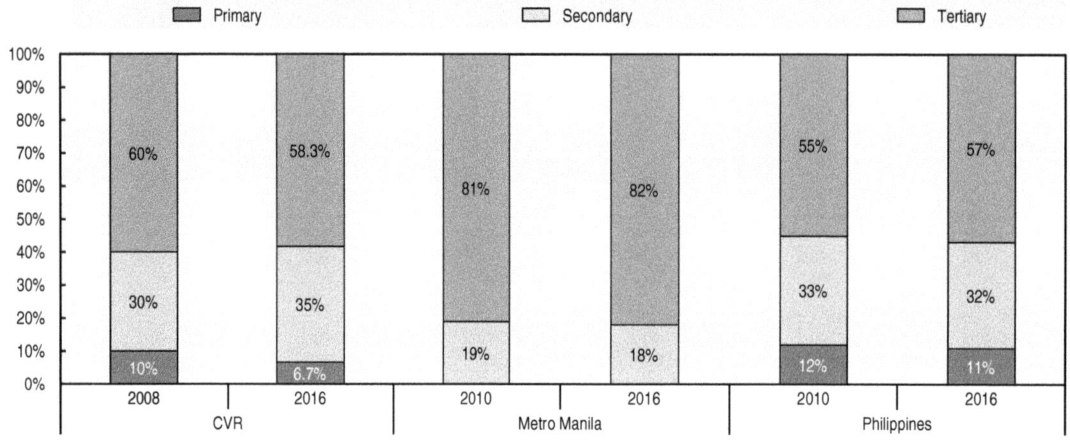

Source: Philippine Statistics Authority (2016d), "GRDP Tables", https://psa.gov.ph/regional-accounts/grdp/data-and-charts.

The Central Visayas economic development is the product of local economic policy that has prioritised a shift from agriculture-based and services-led economic growth to a more pervasive and sustainable development catalysed through industrial upgrading since 2013 through government initiatives such as the Industry Roadmapping Project, the Manufacturing Resurgence Program, and the formulation of the Comprehensive Industrial National Strategy (Department of Trade and Industry, 2014). The increasing value added by the secondary sector to GRP in the CVR is a trend that is evident in other Southeast Asian metropolitan areas, such as Iskandar Malaysia. This implicitly signals that there are a series of urban green growth challenges associated with meeting the rising energy and green manufacturing needs of the metropolitan area in contrast to cities with more dominant tertiary sectors, such as Metro Manila or Bangkok. Hence, it appears Metro Cebu needs to address these challenges as it grows with more manufacturing-based urban economy.

Nonetheless, service industries will still remain by far Metro Cebu's largest employer. The burgeoning tourism sector welcomed 2.6 million visitors in 2013 which makes it one of the key domestic holiday destinations in the Philippines (Figure 1.9). Forty-four per cent of these visitors (1 152 821) were foreign tourists which is sharply in contrast to Bandung City where 95.6% of the 3.9 million tourists arrivals (3 763 500) in 2014 were domestic holidaymakers (Statistics Bandung City, 2015). Between 2003 and 2013, the number of tourist arrivals averaged 11.3% growth per year, with foreign tourist arrivals growing by 14.6%. This is strongly supported by the International Airport located on

Mactan Island. It is anticipated Cebu will welcome somewhere between 6 and 13 million visitors by 2030, at least double the number of arrivals in 2013 (JICA and MCDCB, 2015), even though a new international airport currently under construction on Bohol Island, south east of Cebu Island, may attract some of Cebu's holidaymakers. Cebu is widely known for its white sand beaches as well as its rich cultural history, as the island where the Spanish first arrived in 1521. The tourism industry will remain an important contributor to the local economy, and in order for Cebu to maintain the sector's remarkable growth and competitive advantage over the long-term, proper consideration for the white sand beaches, local environment and water quality must be preserved and enhanced. Also showing great prospects in Cebu is medical tourism, which is promoted by the Department of Health and has the potential to provide employment to the medical workforce and trickle down to other sectors.

Figure 1.9. **Tourist arrivals in the Province of Cebu**

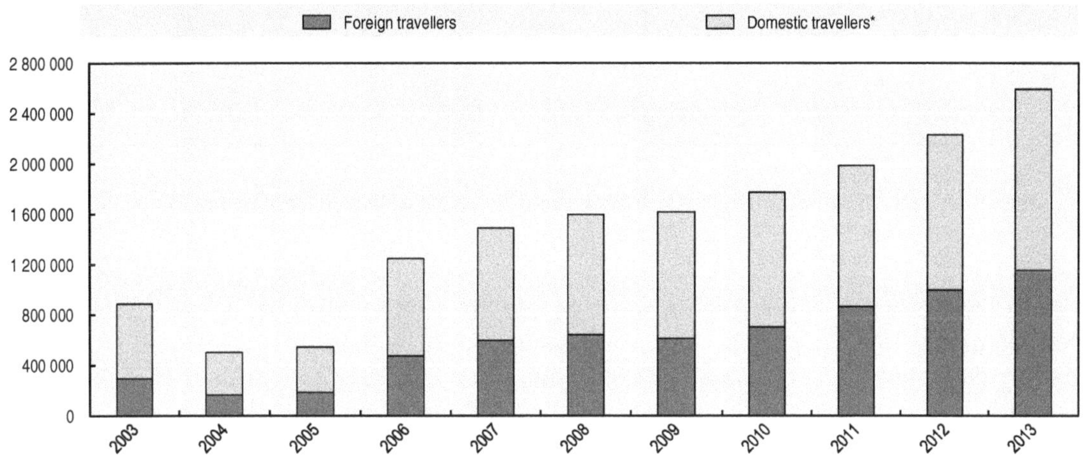

Note: * Includes domestic travellers and overseas Filipinos.

Source: Philippine Statistics Authority (2016b), "The Countryside in Figures: Statistical Profile of the Province of Cebu 2000-2015", http://nap.psa.gov.ph/countryside/#.

Employment structure in Metro Cebu

The sectorial employment structure and labour force participation in the CVR and Metro Cebu are developing swiftly as the number of people employed has increased across all employment sectors, particularly in the manufacturing and service industries (JICA and MCDCB, 2015). In 2007, the labour force participation rate (LFPR) of the CVR was 63.9%, whereas in 2016 it had increased to 64.6% (Philippines Statistics Authority, 2016c). There is a marginal difference between the percentage of people in formal employment in the CVR and Philippines' national LFPR, which decreased slightly from 64% to 63.3% (2007-16).

Nonetheless, there remain sectors which are heavily reliant on informal sector workforce participation. The informal economy consists of independent, self-employed small-scale producers and distributors of goods and services who are mostly not covered by labour laws. In 2008, it was observed that nearly half of informal workers in the Philippines were working in agriculture, 30% in wholesale and retail trade, 10% in transportation and 5% in the manufacturing industry (Philippines Statistics Authority, 2008). Pertinent examples of informal employment in Metro Cebu include street vendors and privately-owned jeepneys or three-wheelers inside the city and farming outside. These informal workers do not pay income tax to the government which results in a substantial loss of revenue to the state and lack of access to social protection to the workers.

Figure 1.10. **Sectorial employment projections in Metro Cebu**

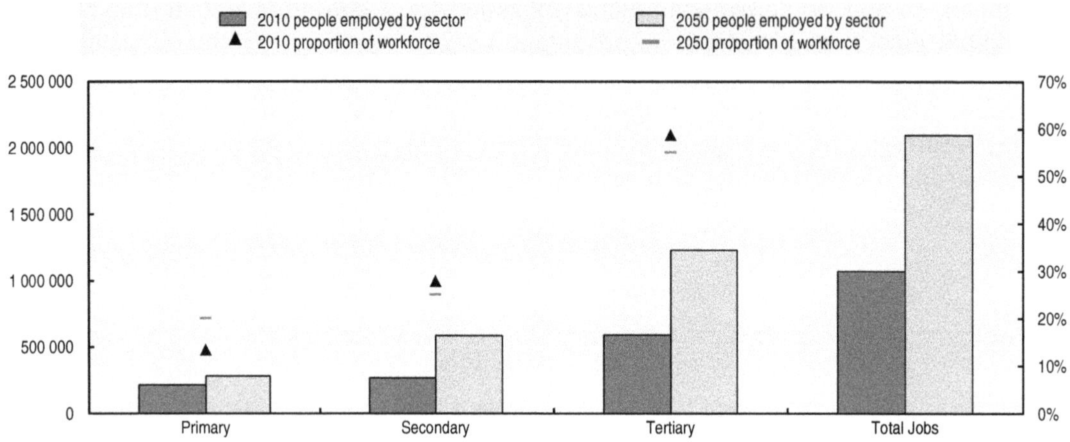

Source: JICA and MCDCB (2015), "The Roadmap for Sustainable Urban Development in Metro Cebu", http://open_jicareport.jica.go.jp/pdf/12235529.pdf.

In the Central Visayas Region most people are employed in the tertiary sector and less than one-fifth work in the secondary sector. In 2016 there was a total of 3 335 000 people employed, an increase of 758 000 jobs since 2007. More than half (55%) of this workforce is employed in the tertiary sector (Philippines Statistical Authority, 2016c). Despite the secondary sector's rapid growth in recent years, the number of people employed increased by 2.3% per year between 2007 and 2016 to reach 634 000 people. Equally surprisingly, employment in the manufacturing sector declined by 1.2% to per annum to 317 000 people during the same time period, although it remains the largest employer by industry. In contrast, employment in the primary sector which makes a much smaller contribution to GRP, expanded by 2.6% annually between 2007 and 2011 and employed 31% of the population (906 000 people). This is similar to sectorial employment structure of the Philippines with the exception of the secondary sector which provides employment to 16% of the population nationally.

In Metro Cebu, half of the workforce of 1 072 000 people are employed in the tertiary sector in 2010. More precisely, it was estimated that 589 000 (55%) of Metro Cebu's workforce were employed in the tertiary sector, while 268 000 (25%) people were working in the secondary sector (Figure 1.11), despite the rapid expansion of the secondary sector and in particular manufacturing. By 2050, it is anticipated the tertiary sector's share will increase further to 59% (641 000 people), while the proportion of people employed in the secondary sector will increase marginally to 28% (585 000 people). In 2050, it is anticipated that employment will be driven principally by urban service industries (JICA and MCDCB, 2015). This sectorial employment structure undergirds Metro Cebu's core position within the regional economy.

Figure 1.11. **Sectorial employment structure**

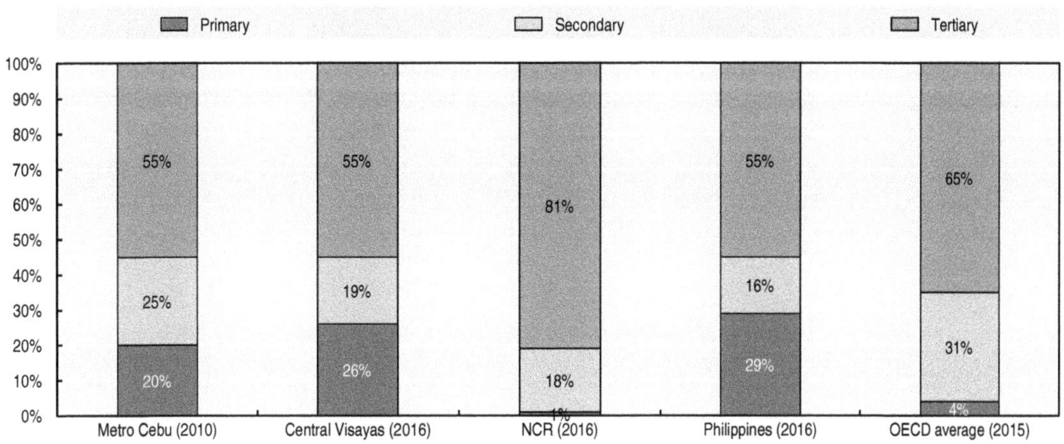

Source: Philippine Statistics Authority (2016c), January 2016 Labour Force Survey, https://psa.gov.ph/content/january-2016-labor-force-statistical-tables; OECD Regional Database, http://stats.oecd.org/Index.aspx?datasetcode=REG_DEMO_TL2.

The rate of unemployment in the Central Visayas is relatively low. Although it has fluctuated, there was an overall steady decline from 6.5% in 2007 to 5.6% in 2016. Moreover, it was lower than both the rates of Metro Manila (7.6%) and the national rate of unemployment (5.8%) in 2016 (Figure 1.12). It is also considerably lower than the Bandung Metropolitan Area's unemployment rate (8.4%). At the same time, female unemployment in the CVR is lower than the male average (Philippines Statistical Authority, 2016c). It is also important to note that the lower female unemployment rate may be the result of the greater proportion of women in the informal workforce (about 76% unpaid jobs are carried out by women, who are more likely to work in the informal economy, according to ADB, 2015), and this is not accounted for in the official labour force surveys.

Figure 1.12. **Unemployment rate 2007-2016**

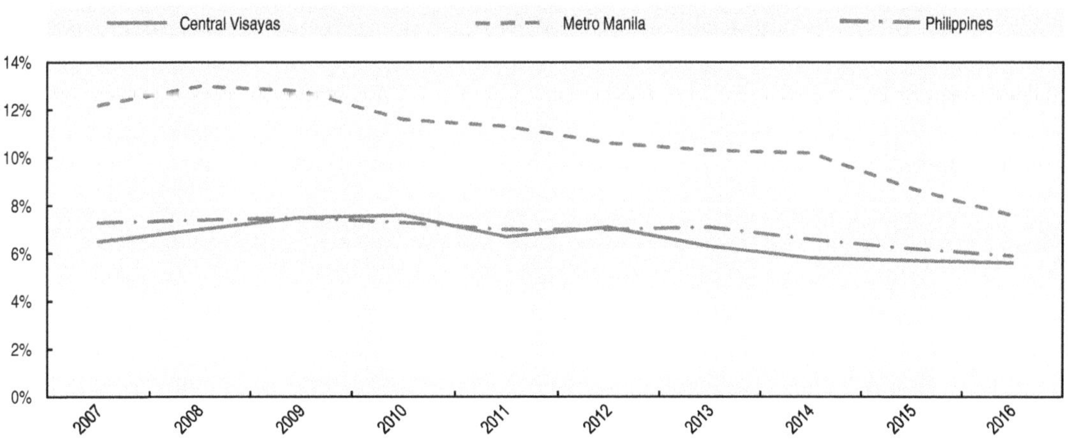

Source: Philippine Statistics Authority (2015a), *2015 Philippine Statistical Yearbook*, https://psa.gov.ph/sites/default/files/2015%20PSY%20PDF.pdf; Philippine Statistics Authority (2016c), "January 2016 Labour Force Survey", https://psa.gov.ph/content/january-2016-labor-force-statistical-tables.

Education attainment level remains behind

With regards to levels of education as of 2016, the CVR lagged behind in higher levels of educational attainment compared to the national rates (Figure 1.13). Metro Manila's rate (47%) of employed persons with a post-secondary education exceeded that of the CVR (27%). With regards to tertiary education, Metro Cebu has 80 institutions which have been instrumental in the training of its labour force, such as the University of San Carlos, University of San Jose Recoletos, University of the Philippines, the University of Cebu, Cebu Institute of Technology University, Cebu Doctors University, among others.

Figure 1.13. **Educational attainment (of employed persons) in 2016**

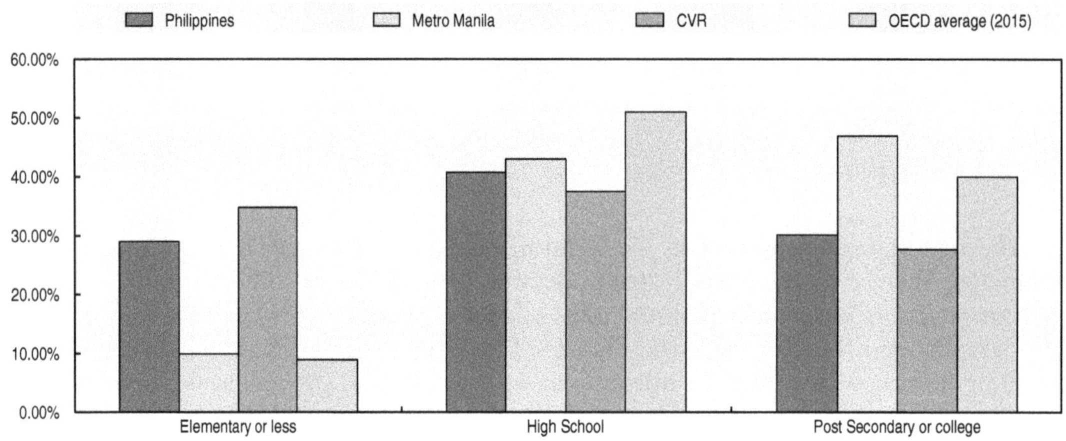

Source: Philippine Statistics Authority (2016c), January 2016 Labour Force Survey, https://psa.gov.ph/content/january-2016-labor-force-statistical-tables; OECD Regional Database, http://stats.oecd.org/Index.aspx?datasetcode=REG_DEMO_TL2.

Challenges to a more inclusive Metro Cebu

Metro Cebu has recorded impressive levels of economic growth during recent years which have markedly improved the collective wealth of residents. However, not all Cebuanos have benefitted equally and as a result inequality is rising. This is mainly demonstrated by an increasing GINI co-efficient. Furthermore, it is important to underscore that a large proportion of people living in poverty are concentrated in the nation's major cities, namely Metro Manila, Metro Cebu and Metro Davao (ADB, 2009).

The GINI co-efficient of the CVR, a widely used indicator that represents the income distribution in a city or region, grew slightly from 0.469 in 2000 to 0.471 in 2012 (Figure 1.14). Data is not available for Metro Cebu nor for the Province of Cebu, which makes direct comparisons between other metropolitan areas difficult. In contrast, Metro Manila's GINI co-efficient has decreased from 0.445 in 2000 to 0.403 in 2012, while nationally, the GINI coefficient dropped from 0.482 to 0.461 during the same time period. However, in some other regions such as Central Luzon the GINI coefficient increased significantly although it is still lower than that of CVR. In comparison, the Bandung Metropolitan Area's GINI coefficient remains substantially lower that of the Central Visayas even though it experienced an upward adjustment from 0.29 to 0.36 between 2008 and 2013.

Figure 1.14. **GINI coefficient in selected cities and countries**

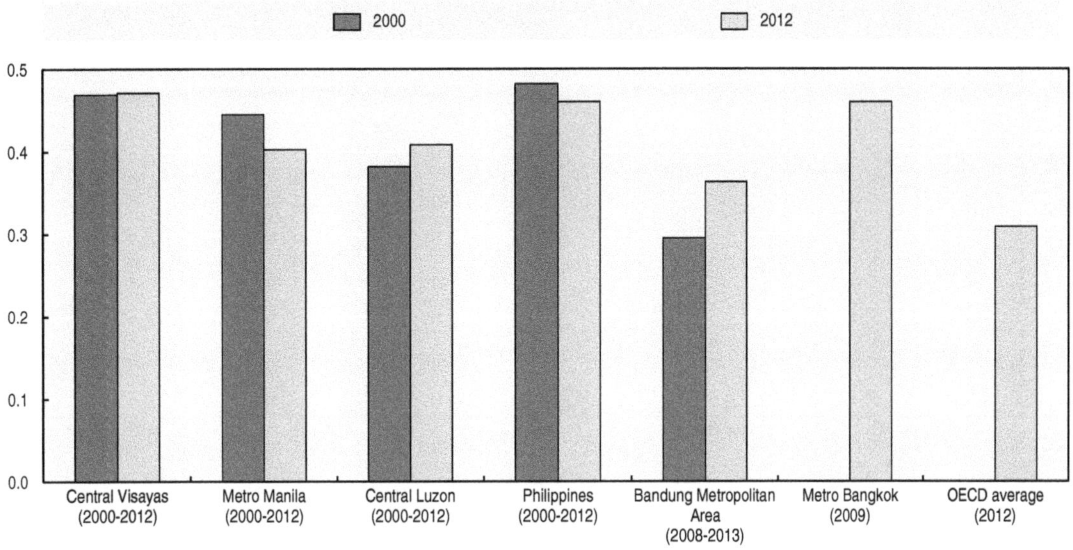

Source: Philippine Statistics Authority (2015a), *2015 Philippine Statistical Yearbook*, https://psa.gov.ph/sites/default/files/2015%20PSY%20PDF.pdf; OECD (2016a), *Urban Green Growth in Dynamic Asia*, OECD Publishing, Paris, http://dx.doi.org/10.1787/9789264266360-en; OECD Regional Database, http://stats.oecd.org/Index.aspx?datasetcode=REG_DEMO_TL2.

Nevertheless, the Province of Cebu has been rather successful in reducing the proportion of Cebuanos living in poverty. In 2006, the incidence rate of poverty among families was 25.6% whereas in 2012, it had fallen to 18.9% (Figure 1.15). This compares favourably to the national poverty incidence rate among families which stood at 19.7% in 2012, although in Metro Manila it is only 2.6%. However, despite the large strides that the Province has made, little has changed in absolute terms since the turn of the millennium. In 2012 there were 185 603 families living in poverty as compared to 187 359 in 2000 which is less than 1% improvement (Philippines Statistics Authority, 2016b). Moreover, these estimates may in fact underestimate the true numbers of people living in poverty because families with no formal address may not be included, nor wish to participate in government surveys for many different reasons (ADB, 2009). Such considerations are important in ensuring effective provision of basic urban services such as water, sanitation and municipal waste management. In Metro Cebu, for example, there were 35 217 informal settler families in 2012 and four-fifths were concentrated in the City of Talisay (50%) and the City of Cebu (32%) (JICA and MCDCB, 2015).

The Government continues to focus on poverty alleviation as part of overall development goals, although more Filipinos live in poverty than before (Philippines Statistics Authority, 2015b). In 2012, there were 19 million poor urban households and 24.3 million people living below the poverty line (Philippines Statistics Authority, 2015b).[4] This indicates an increase in absolute terms since 2006 when there were 18.3 million households and 23.2 million people in poverty.

Figure 1.15. **Incidence rate of poverty among families**

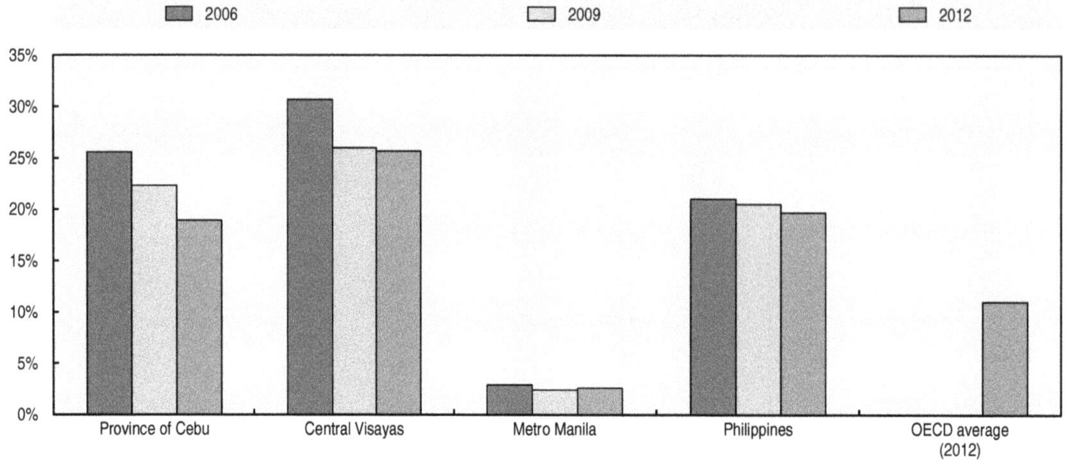

Source: Philippine Statistics Authority (2015b), *2015 Philippine Statistical Yearbook*, https://psa.gov.ph/sites/default/files/2015%20PSY%20PDF.pdf; OECD Regional Database, http://stats.oecd.org/Index.aspx?datasetcode=REG_DEMO_TL2.

Environmental trends and challenges

Metro Cebu continues to grapple with several urban green growth challenges that have emerged as a result of the metropolitan area's rapid population growth and economic development. For one, this places increasing strain on existing urban infrastructures and natural resources and is leading to congestion in some parts.

Land use and transport

The Island of Cebu lies more or less in the centre of the Philippine archipelago. It is surrounded by limestone plateaus, rolling hills and rugged mountain ranges reaching 900 meters above sea level. The island is equally characterised by long and narrow coastal plains (it is 196 km long, 32 km across at its widest point and covers an area of 4 500 km²). In the City of Cebu, these low lying areas extend a few kilometres inland from the coast and represent about 8% or 25 km² of the total land area. Despite the small area, this land hosts approximately two-thirds of the city's population (Cebu City, 2010). This pattern appears to be repeated across the breadth of Metro Cebu's 12 other LGUs. Cebu is further surrounded by another 170 islands, the largest being Mactan Island which is located in close proximity to the east of Cebu City LGU and connected via two large bridges (the construction of a third bridge is anticipated to begin soon to alleviate traffic congestion).

There is growing pressure on land use in Metro Cebu because land that is suitable for development is limited – 76% of the land is considered as hazardous and thus not suitable for urban development (JICA and MCDCB, 2015). Almost all existing industrial land in the special economic zones (SEZs) is utilised and it is becoming increasingly challenging to obtain space for new development projects. There is a need for a 9-fold increase in the current land area dedicated to the SEZs by 2020 in order to sustain the manufacturing sector's strong growth (JICA and MCDCB, 2015). In addition, the population of Metro Cebu will double by 2050 with space required to accommodate residential and commercial real estate.

Cebu's motorisation rate is rapidly increasing. The number of vehicles has more than doubled on the roads of the Province of Cebu in ten years, rising from 208 416 motor vehicles in 2003 to 432 436 in 2012 (Figure 1.16). Vehicle ownership is dominated by motorcycles, with over 18% of the households owning one or more; about 10% owning a bicycle and less than 3% owning a car. There are an estimated 8 300 public utility jeepneys[5] (PUJs), 5 800 taxis and 950 buses and mini-buses operating in Cebu City (World Bank, 2014). On the other hand, the road infrastructure investment in the Province of Cebu has not kept pace with the expanding number of vehicles. Most are two lane roads and there are few four lane roads. In Metro Cebu, almost half (46%) the roads are not paved, and most of which are looked after by the barangay local governments. This has resulted in heavy traffic congestion in major roads and streets in the Province (Figure 1.17), mainly on the main arteries of the urban core centre, such as Governor Mariano Cuenco Avenue and Osmeña Boulevard, or on the bridges linking Mactan Island to Mandaue, or more generally on the principal roads between Talisay and Cebu. Another problem is enforcement of traffic rules and parking regulations. For example, tricycles often disrupt traffic flows in highways and cause serious traffic problems, although they are not supposed to operate on national highways.

Figure 1.16. **Total registered motor vehicles in the Province of Cebu**

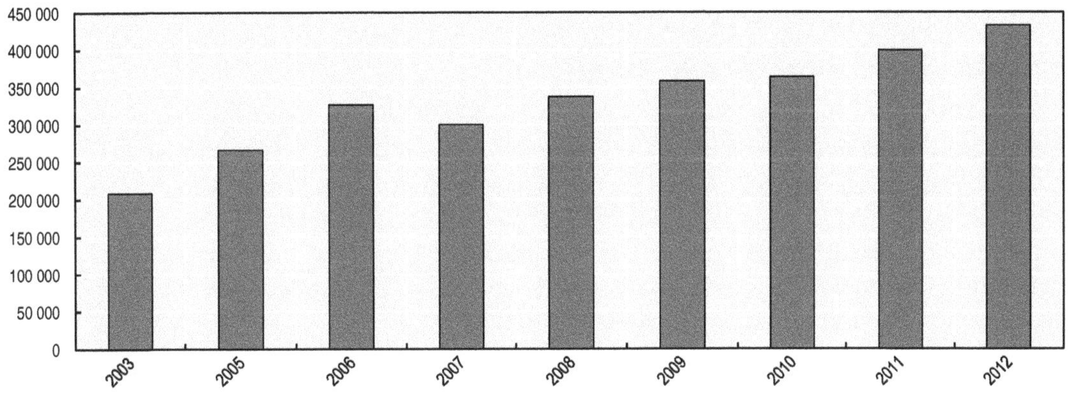

Source: Philippine Statistics Authority (2016b), The Countryside in Figures: Statistical Profile of the Province of Cebu 2000-2015, http://nap.psa.gov.ph/countryside/#.

Metro Cebu lacks a formal public transport although plans are underway for the construction of a Bus Rapid Transit. The public transport is almost exclusively road-based (mostly PUJs, tricycles and pedicabs) and provided by private entities. There is no rail network. Shorter trips are often served by tricycles or three-wheelers, which are regulated by LGUs. In terms of the transport modal split within Metro Cebu (Figure 1.17), jeepneys account for the highest share of 35%, followed by motorcycles (22%), walking (13.10%), and pedicabs and tricycles (10.80%) (JICA and MCDCB, 2015). Many residents use buses to travel longer distances outside of Metro Cebu and there are two terminals located in the north and south. The modal share in Metro Cebu shows a reliance on low capacity private vehicles. For example, the share of motorcycle (22%) is higher compared to bicycle (2%) or buses (3.7%) (Figure 1.17). This in part contributes to the traffic congestion and air pollution in the metropolitan area.

Figure 1.17. **Modal share of trips, Metro Cebu**

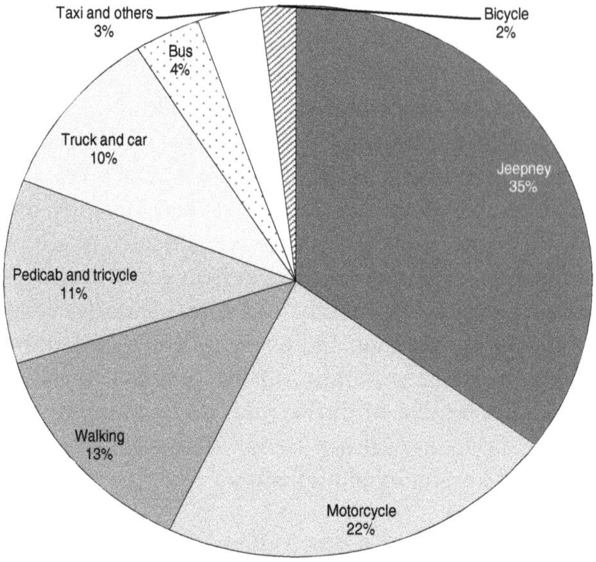

Source: Calculation based on JICA and MCDCB (2015), "The Roadmap for Sustainable Urban Development in Metro Cebu", http://open_jicareport.jica.go.jp/pdf/12235529.pdf.

Water supply and wastewater treatment

Metro Cebu's water supply is managed and operated either by an LGU or water district. The Metro Cebu Water District (MCWD) is a government-owned and controlled corporation (GOCC) that operates in eight out of the 13 LGUs in Metro Cebu (Table 1.2). MCWD is the principal water utility, serving 57% of Metro Cebu's population. The rest of Metro Cebu's water is provided by independent suppliers that sell piped potable water from private wells (World Bank, 2013). Groundwater is MCWD's main source of water and accounts for 59.6% of the total supply, while surface water represents 0.8% (MCWD, 2016).

Table 1.2. **Existing water sources and rated production in Metro Cebu, 2016**

Sources	Actual supply (cube meter/day)	Ratio (%)
a) MCWD Service Area	216 222	87.5
Groundwater	147 285	59.6
Surface water	2 049	0.8
Bulk supply (Private supplier)	61 563	24.9
Desalination (Mactan Rocks)	5 326	2.1
b) Non-MCWD Service Area	18 273	7.4
Northern Areas-Danao	5 541	2.2
Southern Areas	12 732	5.1
Minglanilla (Miwasco)	2 690	1.1
Naga (Abejo)	1 200	0.5
San Fernando (LGU)	1 271	0.5
Carcar (Water District)	7 571	3.1
Total Rated Production (cube meter/day)	247 228	100

Source: Metropolitan Cebu Water District (forthcoming), *MCWD Databook 2016*, Cebu City. *Note*: In Metro Cebu as well as in the Philippines in general, only 40% of households have their own faucet linked to a community water system, while around 18% share a faucet linked to a community water system, and more than 30% of the water supply comes from wells (Figure 1.18). This contrasts with the situation of Metro Manila where 80% of households have their own faucet.

Figure 1.18. **Source of household water supply**

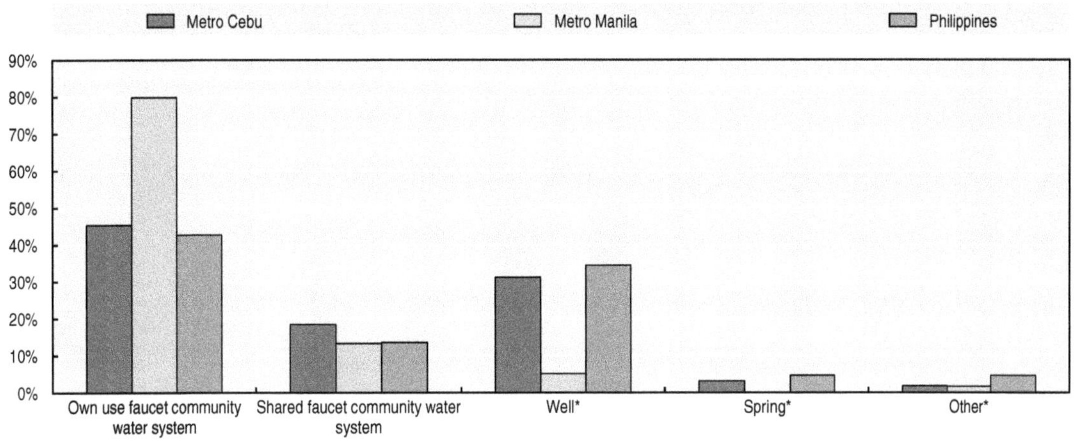

Note: *Well includes own use tubed/piped deep well, shared tubed/piped deep well, tubed/piped shallow well and dug well; *Spring includes protected and unprotected springs; *Other includes lake, river, rain, peddler and others.

Source: Metro Cebu Development and Coordinating Board (2016), "Answers to the OECD case study questionnaire", internal document, unpublished.

A series of water crises have affected Metro Cebu. In recent years, these concerns have grown more acute as sea level rise and unsustainable levels of groundwater extraction have combined to further deplete underground freshwater reserves and led to saltwater intrusion. In addition, contamination brought about by the inadequacy of the sanitation system and from improper dumping of solid and liquid wastes into local water bodies further threatens potable water supplies. Their combined effect makes Metro Cebu more susceptible to threats posed by natural hazards, such as storms and typhoons, as well as to slow-onset of climate change impacts from continued sea level rise and changing precipitation patterns leading to longer droughts and more intense rainfall. These issues have negative impacts not only on the environment and public safety, but also on long-term economic development.

Overall, these critical conditions underscore the need for government to prioritise water issues and find lasting solutions to them. Key water and sanitation issues are summarised as follows: i) saltwater intrusion; ii) nitrate and Escherichia coli (E. coli) contamination; iii) peripheral urbanisation of watershed areas; iv) wastewater treatment and v) unimproved access to water sources and sanitation[6] by the poor.

Municipal solid waste

According to a JICA study, 1 113 tonnes of solid wastes were generated daily in Metro Cebu on average between 2010-13 (Table 1.3). The average volume per capita was 159 kg/year (0.436 kg/day) in 2010. This is far below the OECD average and among the lowest compared to some selected cities as seen in (Figure 1.19). However, it should be noted that considerable amount of municipal solid waste is not collected but disposed privately by households. In Metro Cebu, only 65% of household waste generated is collected, implying that 35% of households self-dispose their waste, mostly burning it (23%) or dumping in an individual pit (8%) (Figure 1.20). In contrast, Metro Manila has a collection rate of about 95%.

Figure 1.19. **Solid waste generations in selected cities**

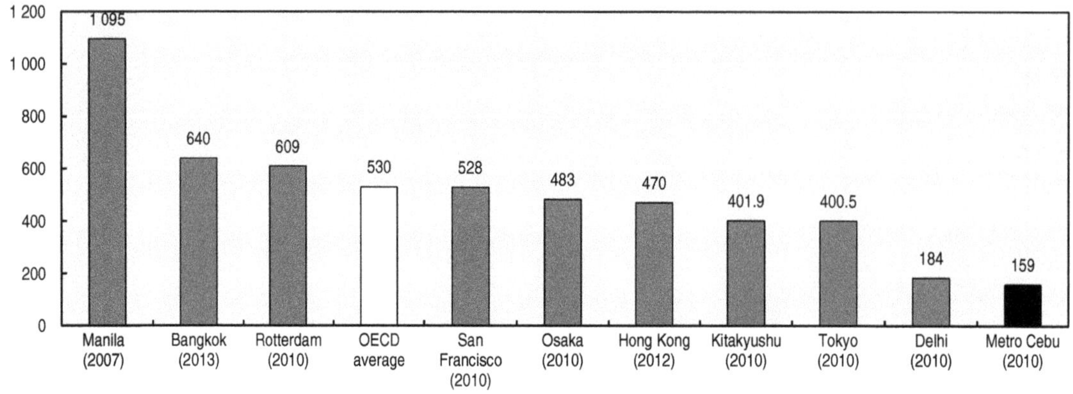

Source: UN-Habitat (2010b), "Solid Waste Management in the World's Cities, Water and Sanitation in the World's Cities 2010", UN-Habitat, New York, https://issuu.com/unhabitat/docs/solid_waste_management; BMA (2014a), "Statistical Profile of Bangkok Metropolitan Administration 2013", Bangkok Metropolitan Administration, Strategy and Evaluation Department, Bangkok, www.bangkok.go.th/main/backoffice/upload_editor/file/stat2013%28eng%29.pdf; Hoornweg, D. and P. Bhada-Tata (2012), "What a waste: A global review of solid waste management", *Urban Development Series Knowledge Papers*, No. 15, World Bank, Washington, DC, http://siteresources.worldbank.org/inturbandevelopment/resources/3363871334852610766/what_a_waste2012_final.pdf; Waste Atlas, www.atlas.d-waste.com; Hong Kong Council of Social Service (n.d.), "Social indicators of Hong Kong", www.socialindicators.org.hk/en/indicators/environmental_quality/23.10; JICA (2015), "The Roadmap for Sustainable Urban Development in Metro Cebu", http://open_jicareport.jica.go.jp/pdf/12235529.pdf.

Table 1.3. **Solid Waste Generation per capita per day**

LGUs	Population (2010)	Solid Waste Generation (2010-13, average)	
		Generation (tons/day)	Rate (g/capital*day)
Cebu City	866 171	423	488
Lapu-Lapu	350 467	175	499
Mandaue	331 320	185	543
Talisay	200 772	80	400
Danao	119 252	45	377
Carcar	107 323	30	280
Naga	101 571	21	207
Compostela	42 574	15	352
Consolacion	106 649	35	328
Cordova	50 353	20	400
Liloan	100 500	34	338
Minglanilla	113 178	45	400
San Fernando	60 970	9	148
Total	**2 551 100**	**1 113**	**436**

Source: JICA and MCDCB (2015), "The Roadmap for Sustainable Urban Development in Metro Cebu", http://open_jicareport.jica.go.jp/pdf/12235529.pdf.

Figure 1.20. **Household waste disposals**

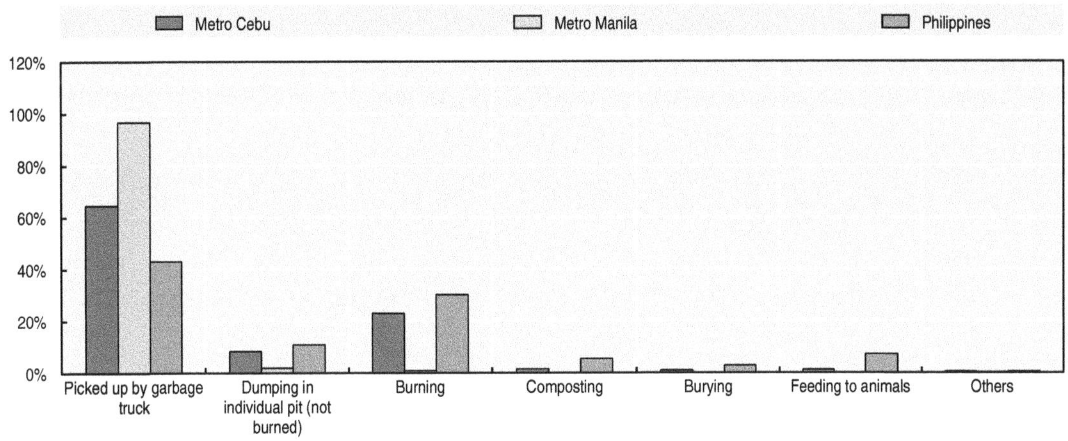

Source: Metro Cebu Development and Coordinating Board (2016), "Answers to the OECD case study questionnaire", internal document, unpublished.

In 2010, solid waste in Metro Cebu comprised of 65% organic waste, 15% plastic, 5% paperboard and wood and 15 % of other waste (Cebu Department of Public Services, 2010). Due to the high organic content, composting is a common practice in Cebu, be it at the barangay level (composting centres at the old Inayawan landfill and in other barangays) or at the household level (World Bank, 2013).

Air pollution and greenhouse gas emissions

NOx and SO2

Ambient NO2 concentration at the centre of Cebu City in 2009 recorded a yearly average of 73 ppb, standing below the standard value of 80 ppb as set by the Philippine Clean Air Act, but measures consistently exceeded this threshold during the year. Similarly, SO2 recorded an average of 47 ppb, a value way below the standard of 70 ppb (Sinogayal, 2009). Spatial variations of NO2 concentration show that the urban sites, where most if not all industries and motor vehicles are located, have relatively high NO2 levels compared to the remote areas. The SO2 concentration shows temporal variation which could be attributed to the variation of the emission of primary SO2 from vehicular and industrial sources as well as the influence of meteorological factors such as wind speed and wind direction.

With regards to fine particles, the levels of PM10 (atmospheric particulate matter with diameter less than 10 µm) in Cebu has been generally above WHO standards and higher than some selected Southeast Asian cities (Figure 1.21).

Figure 1.21. **Annual average ambient PM10 levels**

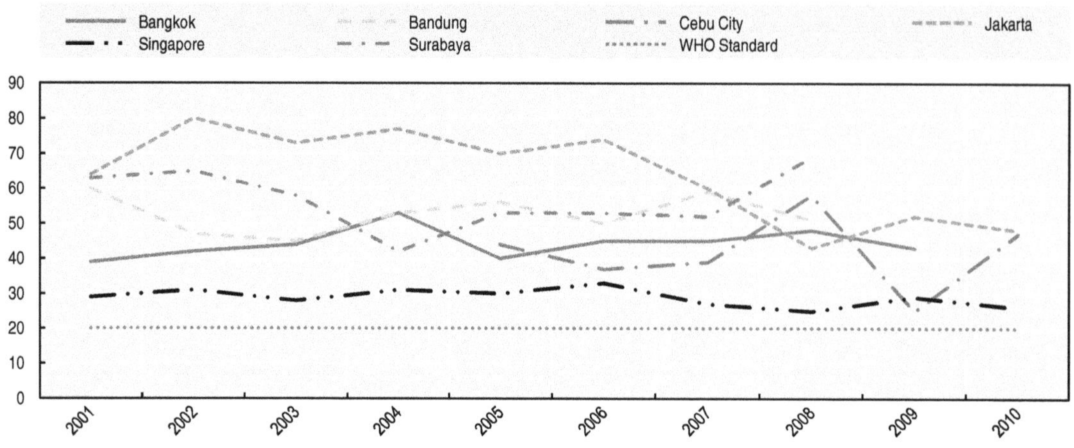

Source: Clean Air Asia- Cities ACT (2016), *Country and City database*, http://citiesact.org/data/countries-and-cities/#.

Energy consumption and GHG emission

The transport and industry sectors are the two largest energy consumers in Cebu. In Cebu City, transportation accounts for 51% of the total final energy consumption, and the industrial sector for 36%, while the part of the residential sector is considerably smaller with only 7% (World Bank, 2013). In the Philippines, transport is the largest energy consumer (34%), followed by the industry and residential sectors with 27% and 25% respectively (IEA, 2014). Data on energy consumption was not available at the metropolitan scale.

The data on the energy generation mix for Visayas and that of the Philippines in 2016 demonstrates that Visayas has a high share of geothermal (46.40%) in its energy mix compared to the national (12.20%) (Figure 1.22).[7] The geothermal energy generated in Visayas is sourced from the power plants in Negros Island and Leyte Island (JICA and MCDCB, 2015). That notwithstanding, coal (40.93 %) is still prominent in the energy mix of the Visayas. In the region, hydro power is a minor source of energy accounting for 0.49% in the energy mix (8.90% at the national level) whilst oil-based (4.33%), biomass (2.14%) and solar and wind energy (4.07 and 1.62% respectively) account for the residual. In all, renewable energy sources form 54.73% of Visayas energy generation mix.

Figure 1.22. **Power sources in Visayas and the Philippines (2016)**

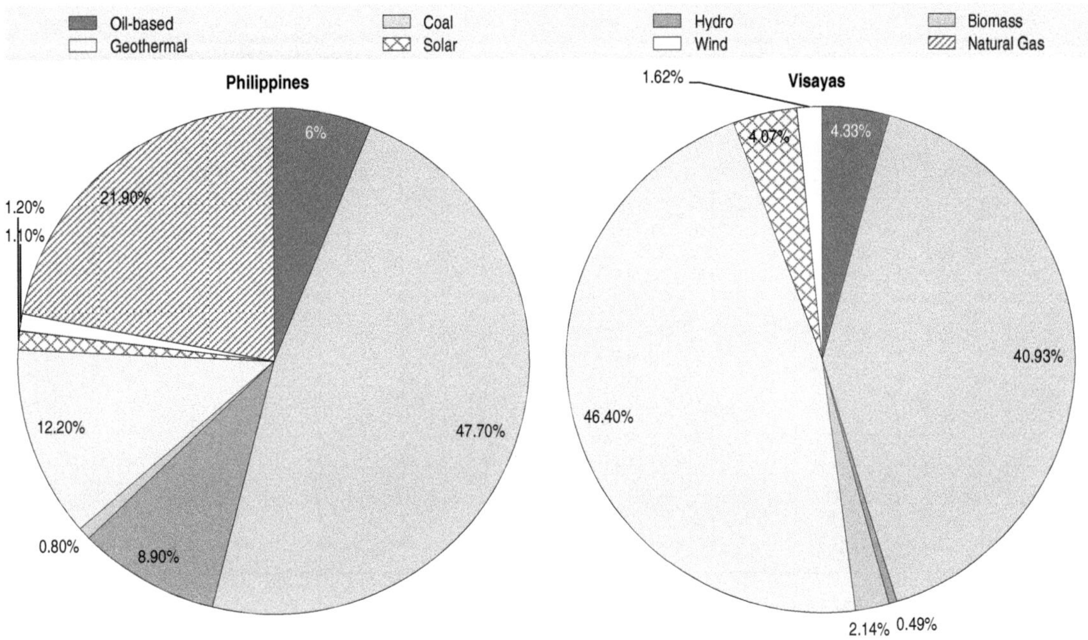

Source: Department of Energy, 2015; IEA, 2014.

Nearly 1.8 million tons of carbon dioxide equivalent were emitted in Cebu City in 2010. GHG emissions in Cebu City are chiefly caused by the transportation and industry sectors (Figure 1.23), which account for 39% and 38% of the total emissions respectively. In terms of fuel sources, oil and electricity (of which 50% is generated by geothermal and hydro sources and the other half mainly by coal are responsible for 31% and 26% respectively whereas 39% of the total emissions can be explained by gasoline and diesel, which are used solely by the transport sector. The transport sector is thus the biggest energy consumer, but proportionally to its consumption emits less than the industry sector, which uses 36% of the city's energy production but is accountable for 38% of the GHG emissions (World Bank, 2013).

Figure 1.23. **Cebu City GHG emissions by end use and fuel source, 2010**

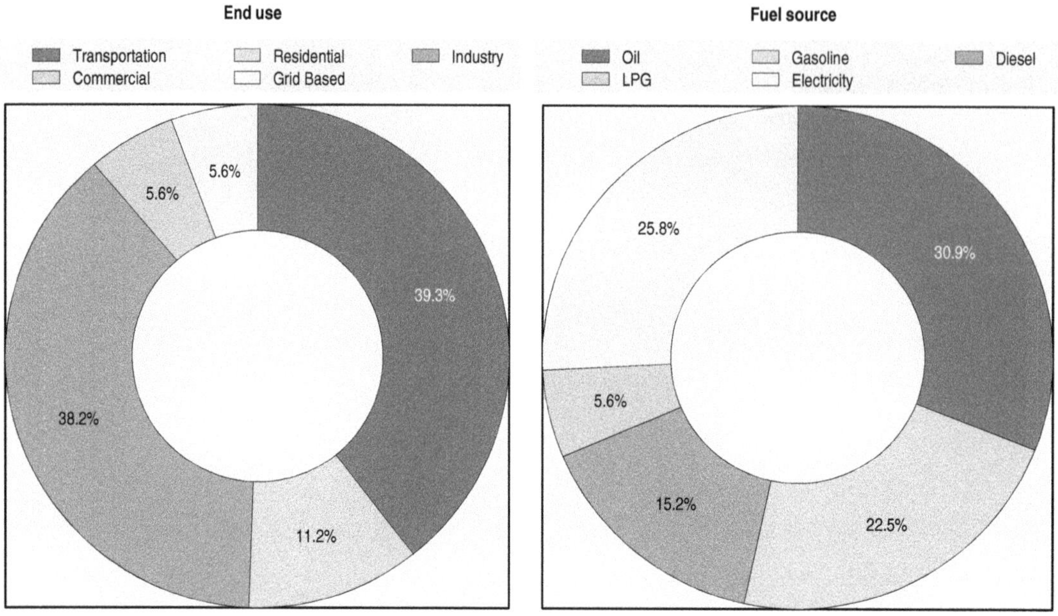

Source: World Bank (2013), *Energizing Green Cities in Southeast Asia*, http://dx.doi.org/10.1596/978-0-8213-9837-1.

Urban resilience

The Philippines is situated in an acutely high risk area and is consistently ranked among the three most vulnerable countries in the world according to the World Risk Report (UNU, 2015). For example, between 1995 and 2015, 274 disasters afflicted the country, the fourth highest total globally after the USA (472), China (441) and India (288) (UNISDR, 2015). Metro Cebu, located on an island which lies in the centre of the Philippine archipelago, is surrounded by limestone plateaus, rolling hills and rugged mountain ranges and is afflicted by geophysical (earthquakes) and climate related natural hazards (typhoons and flooding), and is characterised by a tropical climate of dry and monsoonal seasons.

Metro Cebu regularly experiences severe flooding, especially after heavy precipitation during the wet season from June to November and seasonal tropical storms. On one hand, Metro Cebu's topography is undulating and mountainous with heights reaching 900 meters above sea level. However, on the other hand, as already mentioned, low-lying coastal land extending a few kilometres inland hosts a large proportion of the population. The challenge the local geography imposes, in combination with heavy precipitation, leads to severe flooding in low lying areas and landslides in steeply sloping zones as well, such as at the 'foot' of the Mananga Watershed (Marvette, 2014). It should be noted that Cebu faces longer-term, 'slow-onset' climate change impacts including heat waves, sea level rise, water and food security issues, and saltwater intrusion into coastal aquifers and water wells.

Cebu is also subjected to occasional typhoons. In 1990, Typhoon Ruping (Mike) hit Cebu City directly. Typhoon Ruping killed nearly 750 people in the Philippines (UNDHA, 1990). In November 2013, Super Typhoon Haiyan (Yolanda), a Category 5 typhoon, the strongest ever recorded at the time, with wind gusts in excess of 300 kilometres per hour and an associated storm surge that reached as high 3.5 metres along some coastlines with more vulnerable coastal bathometric profiles (NDRRMC, 2013)[8] struck. In Cebu, it made landfall twice in the north of Cebu Island with as many as 1 million people evacuated beforehand (UNISDR, 2016). As a country, more than 1.1 million houses were damaged, half of which were completely destroyed. It also killed over 6 300 people, left more than two million homeless, and affected over 13 million people in the Philippines (NDRRMC, 2013). In total, over USD 12-15 billion in damages were recorded. Nonetheless, the Typhoon Haiyan damage bill amounted to about 5% of the Philippines' total GDP in 2013 (Financial Times, 2013). An equivalent level of damage to the United States of America's economy in terms of GDP would amount to USD 850-900 billion, or more than four times the financial impact of Hurricane Katrina in 2005, the worst natural disaster in US history.

The metropolitan area also lies in close proximity to three fault lines including the North Bohol Fault which in addition to soft soil composition in certain quarters, exacerbate the metropolitan area's vulnerability to disaster that would otherwise be reduced if one of these two factors were not present (Silva, 2015). In 2013, Cebu City experienced a magnitude 7.2 earthquake. Although the metropolitan area was not at its epicentre, it caused USD 2 billion in damages and affected 870 000 people (NDRRMC, 2013). In the broader region of Cebu, the earthquake also damaged nearly 1 000 houses, in addition to local infrastructure and community facilities.

Governance of Metro Cebu

Metro Cebu is comprised of 13 different local government units (LGU): 3 Independent Cities (City of Cebu, City of Mandaue and City of Lapu-Lapu); 4 Component Cities (City of Carcar, City of Danao, City of Naga, and City of Talisay); and 6 Municipalities (Municipality of Compostela, Municipality of Consolacion, Municipality of Cordova, Municipality of Liloan, Municipality of Minglanilla, Municipality of San Fernando) (Figure 1.24).

Figure 1.24. **Metro Cebu's local government units**

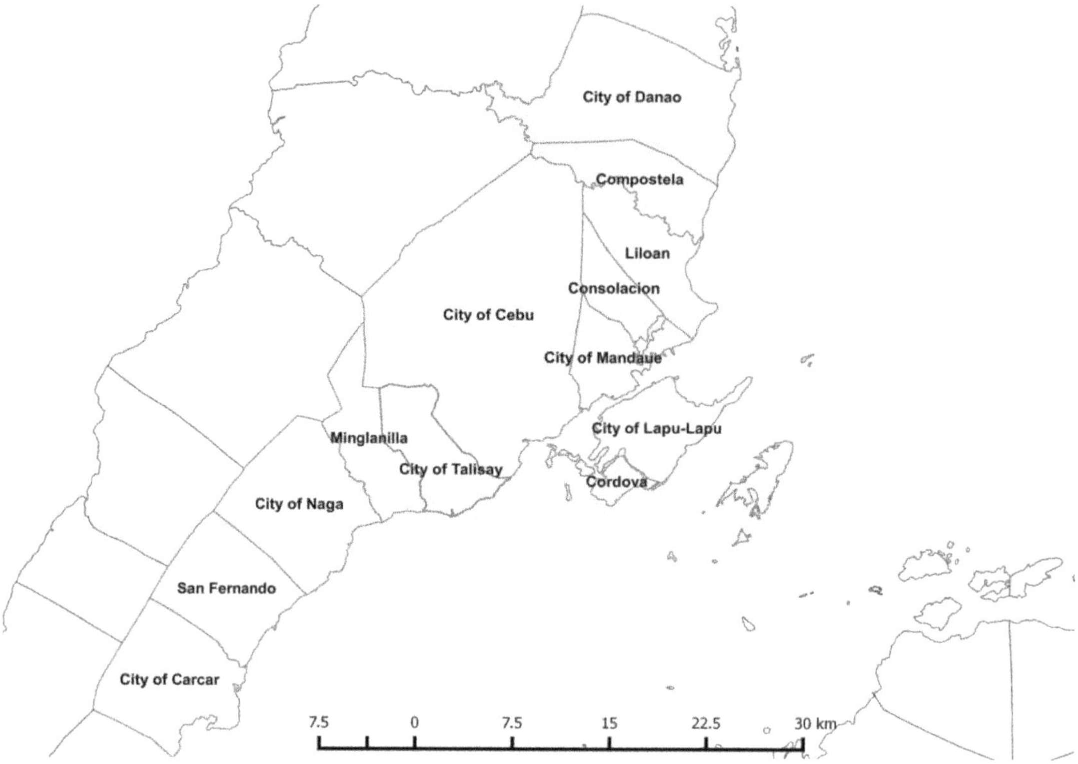

Source: Global Administrative Boundaries (2016), available at www.gadm.org/country.

In general, local governance in the Philippines is complex. Although all LGUs are governed by respective municipal charters, in addition to the *Local Government Code* of 1991 which set out a framework for increasing local autonomy and service provision, there are substantial and important differences between these three types of LGUs. For example, Metro Cebu's "Independent Cities" do not fall under the jurisdiction of the Province of Cebu but of the national government, while component cities and municipalities are under provincial authority (Figure 1.25). At the same time, both city types receive more direct fiscal transfers from the central government (see Chapter 4 for more detailed information). In contrast, all the LGUs in MetroManila are Independent Cities.

Established in 2011, the Metro Cebu Development and Coordinating Board (MCDCB) is a public-private consortium led by the Province of Cebu in addition to the 13 local government units (LGUs) of Metro Cebu, several regional government agencies, private and civil society organisations. MCDCB provides a sense of unity for the LGUs at a metropolitan scale. In partnership with its stakeholders, MCDCB acts at a metropolitan scale to promote long-term and co-ordinated planning targeting trans-LGU issues of concern. Their goal being to discuss common challenges, discuss options for addressing them, and reach consensus-based decisions and collaborative actions that will make the region more sustainable, inclusive, and resilient. The Mega Cebu programme spearheaded by MCDCB envisions a vibrant, equitable, sustainable and competitive environment that embraces Cebu's creativity and its cultural, historical, and natural resources, with strong citizen participation and responsive governance.

Figure 1.25. **Local Governance in Metro Cebu**

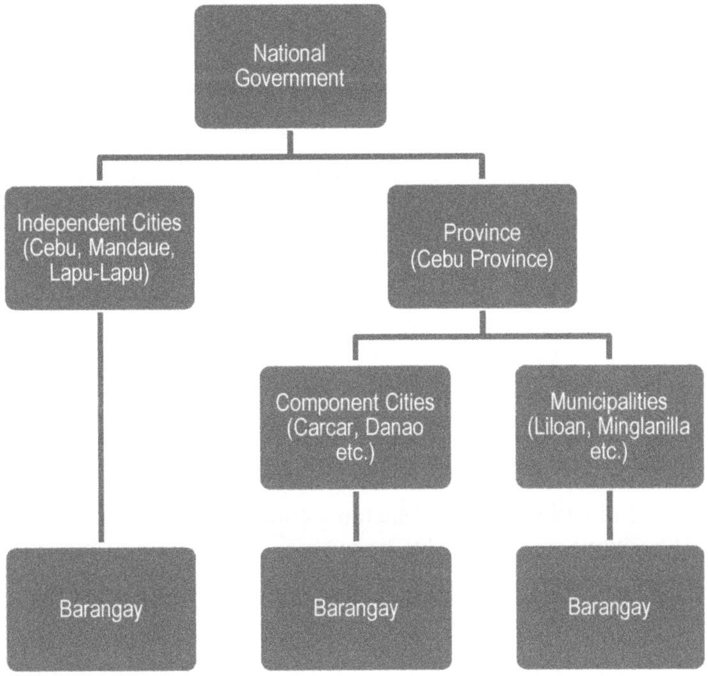

Note: Specific information about Cebu Province is given in brackets.

Source: Metro Cebu Development and Coordinating Board (2016), "Answers to the OECD case study questionnaire", internal document, unpublished; Yilmaz S. and V. Venugopal (2010), Local government discretion and accountability in Philippines, Journal of International Development, Wiley Online Library, http://onlinelibrary.wiley.com/doi/10.1002/jid.1687/abstract (accessed 26 May 2016).

Notes

1. i) City of Carcar; ii) City of Cebu; iii) City of Danao; iv) City of Lapu-Lapu; v) City of Mandaue; vi) City of Naga; vii) City of Talisay; viii) Municipality of Compostela; ix) Municipality of Consolacion; x) Municipality of Cordova; xi) Municipality of Liloan; xii) Municipality of Minglanilla; xiii) Municipality of San Fernando

2. For the purposes of Section 1.2, the Central Visayas Region is utilised owing to the lack of official data at the metropolitan and provincial level.

3. i) Cebu Light Industrial Park, ii) Mactan Economic Zone, iii) Mactan Economic Zone II, iv) MRI Ecozone, v) New Cebu Township, vi) West Cebu Industrial Park.

4. This is calculated using Philippines Statistics Authority (2015b), 2012 population projection.

5. Jeepneys are jeeps that have been customised and converted into taxis; they have become the most popular means of public transportation in the Philippines

6. For MDG monitoring, an improved sanitation facility is defined as one that hygienically separates human excreta from human contact and an improved drinking-water source as one that, by nature of its construction or through active intervention, is protected from outside contamination, in particular from contamination with faecal matter (WSS JMP, UNICEF and WHO)

7. Data on the energy sources for electricity in Metro Cebu is not available as it taps into the single power grid in Visayas.

8. *A bathometric profile* refers to the steepness of the surf zone, or near-coastal area, which can impede or accentuate damage from a storm surge.

References

Asian Development Bank (2015), *Women in the Workforce an Unmet Potential in Asia and The Pacific*, www.adb.org/sites/default/files/publication/158480/women-workforce-unmet-potential.pdf.

Asian Development Bank (2009), *Poverty in the Philippines: Causes, constraints and opportunities*, www.adb.org/sites/default/files/publication/27529/poverty-philippines-causes-constraints-opportunities.pdf.

BMA (2014a), "Statistical Profile of Bangkok Metropolitan Administration 2013", Bangkok Metropolitan Administration, Strategy and Evaluation Department, Bangkok, www.bangkok.go.th/main/backoffice/upload_editor/file/stat2013%28eng%29.pdf.

Cebu City (2010), "About Cebu City", https://www.cebucity.gov.ph/home-new/about-cebu-city, (accessed 5 July 2017)

City of Hai Phong (2015), "Answers to the OECD case study questionnaire", internal document, unpublished.

Clean Air Asia- Cities ACT (2016), "Country and City database", http://citiesact.org/data/countries-and-cities/#.

Department of Statistics Malaysia (2011), "Population Distribution and Basic Demographic Characteristics"; Population and Housing Census of Malaysia, Government of Malaysia, Petaling Jaya.

Financial Times (2013) "The economic cost of Typhoon Haiyan", http://blogs.ft.com/the-world/2013/11/the-economic-cost-of-typhoon-haiyan/?mhq5j=e1 (accessed 5 July 2017).

Global Administrative Boundaries (2016), www.gadm.org/country.

Hoornweg, D. and P. Bhada-Tata (2012), "What a waste: A global review of solid waste management", *Urban Development Series Knowledge Papers*, No. 15, World Bank, Washington, DC, http://siteresources.worldbank.org/inturbandevelopment/resources/336387-1334852610766/what_a_waste2012_final.pdf.

IEA (International Energy Agency) (2014), *Statistics on the Philippines for the Year 2014*, www.iea.org/statistics/statisticssearch/report/?year=2014&country=philippine&product=balances.

JICA (Japan International Cooperation Agency) and MCDCB (Metro Cebu Development and Coordination Board) (2015), "The Roadmap for Sustainable Urban Development in Metro Cebu", http://open_jicareport.jica.go.jp/pdf/12235529.pdf.

Marvette, A.D. (2014), "DENR-7: 14 barangays prone to landslide, flood", News article on the Freeman, www.philstar.com/cebu-news/2014/08/21/1360054/denr-7-14-barangays-prone-landslide-flood.

Mercado, R. G. (1998) Metropolitan Cebu: The Challenge of Definition and Management. Discussion Paper Series No. 98-15 (Revised), Philippine Institute for Development Studies. http://dirp4.pids.gov.ph/ris/dps/pidsdps9815.pdf.

Metro Cebu Development and Coordinating Board (2016), "Answers to the OECD case study questionnaire", internal document, unpublished.

Metropolitan Cebu Water District (forthcoming), *MCWD Databook 2016*, Cebu City (forthcoming).

NDRRMC (2013), "NDRRMC report on 2013 Bohol Earthquake", http://www.ndrrmc.gov.ph/attachments/article/1330/FINAL_REPORT_re_Effects_of_Magnitude_7_2_Sagbayan_Bohol_Earthquake_15OCT-04NOV2013.pdf

OECD (2016a), *Urban Green Growth in Dynamic Asia*, OECD Publishing, Paris, http://dx.doi.org/10.1787/9789264266360-en.

OECD (2016b), *Green Growth in Bandung, Indonesia*, OECD Publishing, Paris, http://dx.doi.org/10.1787/9789264264113-en.

OECD (2012), *Redefining "Urban": A New Way to Measure Metropolitan Areas*, OECD Publishing, Paris, http://dx.doi.org/10.1787/9789264174108-en.

Philippines Department of Trade and Industry (2014), "The Roadmap for Region VII (Central Visayas)", http://industry.gov.ph/roadmap-localization-region-vii/.

Philippine Statistics Authority (2016a), "Total Population by Province, City, Municipality and Barangay: Region VII – Central Visayas", http://psa.gov.ph/content/highlights-philippine-population-2015-census-population.

Philippine Statistics Authority (2016b), "The Countryside in Figures: Statistical Profile of the Province of Cebu 2000-2015", http://nap.psa.gov.ph/countryside/#.

Philippine Statistics Authority (2016c), "January 2016 Labour Force Survey", https://psa.gov.ph/content/january-2016-labor-force-statistical-tables.

Philippine Statistics Authority (2016d), "GRDP Tables", https://psa.gov.ph/regional-accounts/grdp/data-and-charts.

Philippine Statistics Authority (2016e), "Household Population 15 Years Old and Over and Employment Status, Philippines: January 2014 – January 2016", https://psa.gov.ph/sites/default/files/attachments/cls/Tab4_1.pdf.

Philippine Statistics Authority (2015a), *2015 Philippine Statistical Yearbook*, https://psa.gov.ph/sites/default/files/2015%20PSY%20PDF.pdf.

Philippine Statistics Authority (2015b), "Gross Regional Domestic Product: 2014 Gross Regional Domestic Product Highlights", www.nscb.gov.ph/grdp/2014/reglHighlights.asp.

Philippine Statistics Authority (2014), "Statistical Tables on Sample Variables from the results of 2010 Census of Population and Housing Cebu", https://psa.gov.ph/content/statistical-tables-sample-variables-results-2010-census-population-and-housing-cebu.

Philippine Statistics Authority (2009), "Gender Factsheet on Unemployment", https://psa.gov.ph/old/data/sectordata/factsheets/5unemployed.pdf.

Philippine Statistics Authority (2008), "Informal Sector Survey", http://psa.gov.ph/content/informal-sector-operators-counted-105-million-results-2008-informal-sector-survey.

Philippine Statistics Authority (2007), "Regional Accounts: 2006 Gross Regional Domestic Product Highlights", http://nap.psa.gov.ph/grdp/2006/default.asp.

Philippine Statistics Authority (2006), "Regional Accounts: 2004 Gross Regional Domestic Product (GRDP), Highlights", http://nap.psa.gov.ph/grdp/2004/default.asp.

Premakumara (2011), "Establishment of the Community-Based Solid Waste Management System in Metro Cebu, the Philippines", https://pub.iges.or.jp/system/files/publication_documents/pub/discussionpaper/2596/Cebu_Note%5BEnglish%5D%5Bfinal%5D.pdf.

Silva V. (2015), "Mapping of fault lines in Cebu done this year", http://cebudailynews.inquirer.net/58039/mapping-of-fault-lines-in-cebu-done-.

Sinogayal, J. et al. (2009), "Assessment of Air Quality As Initiative For Climate Change Mitigation In Metro Cebu, Philippines", www.researchgate.net/profile/jonnifer_sinogaya/publication/255609531_assessment_of_air_quality_as_initiative_for_climate_change_mitigation_in_metro_cebu_philippines/links/5530a3060cf27acb0de8712b.pdf.

Statistics Bandung City (2015), *Bandung in Figures Year, 2015*, Bandung, Indonesia.

UNDHA (1990), "UNDRO situation report on typhoon Mike", http://reliefweb.int/report/philippines/philippines-typhoon-mike-nov-1990-undro-situation-reports-1-6.

UNISDR (2015), "Global Assessment Report on Disaster Risk Reduction", *Making Development Sustainable: The Future of Disaster Risk Management*, www.preventionweb.net/english/hyogo/gar/2015/en/gar-pdf/GAR2015_EN.pdf.

UN-Habitat (2010b), "Solid Waste Management in the World's Cities, Water and Sanitation in the World's Cities 2010", UN-Habitat, New York, https://issuu.com/unhabitat/docs/solid_waste_management.

UNU (2015), "World Risk Report 2015", http://collections.unu.edu/eserv/unu:3303/wrr_2015_engl_online.pdf.

World Bank (2014), "Cebu Bus Rapid Trasnsit (BRT) Project", http://projects.worldbank.org/P119343/cebu-bus-rapid-transit-brt-demonstration-project?lang=en&tab=overview (accessed 06 February 2016).

World Bank (2013), *Energizing Green Cities in Southeast Asia*, http://dx.doi.org/10.1596/978-0-8213-9837-1.

Yilmaz S. and V. Venugopal (2010), "Local government discretion and accountability in Philippines", *Journal of International Development*, Wiley Online Library, Vol. 25/2, http://onlinelibrary.wiley.com/doi/10.1002/jid.1687/full (accessed 27 June 2017).

Chapter 2

Opportunities for green growth in Cebu, Philippines

Chapter 2 reviews current policies in Cebu in the following four thematic areas: land use and transport, solid waste management, green manufacturing and energy. Water resource management will be discussed in depth in Chapter 3. The analysis focuses on the following: 1) Current policies in each area. This will give more precise information on the actions taken by various authorities and the policy instruments and tools used to reach goals in each of these areas. It helps to identify gaps between existing opportunities and policy responses. 2) Policy outcomes. Where data were available, the impact of each policy is analysed to assess its effectiveness and to identify options for improvement. 3) Policy synergies and complementarities. To strengthen the impact of urban green growth policies, it is important to assess the extent to which Cebu has integrated areas of opportunity into coherent and effective policy packages. The results present several clear opportunities for green growth and call for urgent policy actions.

The statistical data for Israel are supplied by and under the responsibility of the relevant Israeli authorities. The use of such data by the OECD is without prejudice to the status of the Golan Heights, East Jerusalem and Israeli settlements in the West Bank under the terms of international law.

Key findings

- Metro Cebu's growth has been accompanied by an uncontrolled urban sprawl. This is further exacerbated by land-use plans and zoning ordinances of some LGUs being outdated and needing revision to bridge the gap between what is planned and what is built. Considering the geographical conditions which naturally limit the availability of Metro Cebu's developable land (25% of total land area), LGUs have to prioritise managing their land resources sustainably through a compact city model to ensure that Metro Cebu remains productive, competitive and inclusive.
- The absence of an integrated metropolitan-wide, high capacity public transport threatens the long-term growth and effective functioning of the urban system in Metro Cebu. Increasing vehicle ownership and use of private vehicles is contributing to traffic congestion and pollution. Although the bus rapid transit system (BRT) is being developed, integration between the BRT and other modes is needed. At the same time, clean transport such as rail systems, ferries, E-jeepneys and shared-bike schemes need to be encouraged with the supporting infrastructure.
- An effective waste management is crucial in enabling Cebu grow sustainably. Current consumption pattern still follows a linear trend with the end fixated on disposal as opposed to a circular consumption pattern where resources are continuously reused. The "no separation, no collection" policy encouraging waste segregation is a laudable strategy but suffers from a number of implementation challenges which urgently needs to be addressed. Similarly, several opportunity areas could be further pursued to strengthen the overall waste management both up-stream and down-stream especially reviewing waste pricing and enhancing access to collection services.
- As a major manufacturing centre, Metro Cebu needs to promote clean, energy efficient manufacturing process. In Cebu City, industries account for about 36% of energy consumption and 38% of GHG emissions. Energy efficiency is being encouraged in the metro area, nonetheless minimising pollution from SMEs and ensuring compliance with environmental regulations also need to be strengthened.
- Metro Cebu sources 52% of its power from renewable energy mainly geothermal. However, a high share of power (41.3%) is also sourced from coal powered facilities. More opportunities for renewable energy exist especially from waste-to-energy sources and rooftop solar PV energy which can be encouraged through incentives and regulations.
- Greening buildings in Metro Cebu offers an opportunity for the metro area to move closer towards sustainable urbanisation. Implementing the national building code through local legislative instruments such as green building ordinances has been slow but could be expedited.

Making Cebu's land use more efficient with integrated transport

Like most other cities in Southeast Asia, Metro Cebu is experiencing unprecedented population growth along with challenges to environmental sustainability. Land use and traffic congestion are among the most serious issues that policymakers need to tackle. This section has analysed land-use and transport policy. A key lesson-learned indicates it is unlikely that m^{2}aking more land available to accommodate the increasing population and the increasing traffic will solve the transport and spatial challenges. Sustainable solutions will require diversified policy instruments, particularly addressing land-use efficiency.

Harmonise land use planning across LGUs: Cebu's integrated land use planning initiatives shows promise but requires capacity building

The spatial planning process of the LGUs in Metro Cebu is guided by the national, regional and provincial frameworks. The Philippines National Framework for Physical Planning (NFPP), 2001-2030 provides perspective for allocating and managing land and physical resources anchored on sustainable growth with social equity. The National framework provided direction for the regional framework known as the Central Visayas Region Physical Framework Plan 2003-2030, which aims to promote growth of urban centres, facilitate economic and physical integration of provinces and protect the environment while reducing vulnerability to natural hazards. Cebu Province similarly develops its physical framework plan based on which LGUs prepare their Comprehensive Land Use Plans (CLUP) to be implemented through zoning ordinance as stipulated in section 20(c) of RA 7160 (Local Government Code) for a ten year period. In 2014, a CLUP guide book was released to assist LGUs in the updating and development of their plan. It can be seen that the Philippines has a laudable planning framework which provides an enabling environment for a holistic economic, social and spatial development. However much attention needs to be given to how this is translated into practice and how government action is synergised with it.

The Metro Cebu Development and Coordinating Board (MCDCB) is responsible for metro wide planning and development, and more importantly for the harmonisation of the land use plans of the 13 LGUs making up Metro Cebu into a single spatial plan. However, planning and development are still lodged separately in each and every LGU with reference to their respective and independent ordinances. In 2012, the MCDCB along with the Japan International Cooperation Agency (JICA) and the City of Yokohama (Japan) jointly initiated the first of a two-phase project which includes the 'Metro Cebu Vision 2050' and 'Roadmap Study for Sustainable Urban Development in Metro Cebu'. The primary focus of the initiatives has been the production of a blueprint to guide the city's sustainable economic development. Land use forms a critical pillar of the plan which aims to introduce and seek approval for spatial plans in each of Metro Cebu's 13 LGUs. At this stage, it is uncertain how many of Metro Cebu's 13 LGUs have approved their respective spatial plan (Table 2.1). It is equally unclear the extent to which these local administrations will influence the development of their relevant comprehensive land use plans (CLUPs) based on the JICA roadmap land-use plan. Although all of Metro Cebu's 13 LGUs are responsible for developing land-use maps, most would need additional support and capacity to update existing ones which have not been properly enforced.

The latest guidelines (DILG Memorandum Circular 2010-112) require LGUs to update their CLUPs by virtue of the Local Government Code and Executive Order No. 72 (1993), and encourages Provinces in particular to ensure that these city/municipal CLUPs will take into consideration topical plans, such as Disaster Risk Reduction and Management/Climate Change Adaptation (DRRM/CCA) and mainstreaming of sectoral/thematic plans such as General Management Plans, Coastal Resource Management Plans using the Ridge to Reef Framework. Several LGUs in Metro Cebu have failed to update in accordance with these current national guidelines. An apparent hindering factor is the lack of technical capacities by LGU personnel to complete their updated CLUPs. Additionally, no enforcement is possible to force the LGUs to implement the CLUP guidelines. Observations indicate that there is an over-reliance on regulatory approaches rather than outreach, collaboration, and capacity building for LGUs. The current state of urbanisation requires that LGUs in Metro Cebu do not only develop but strongly enforce their land use and zoning plans to guide developments and avoid any further intrusion or unwarranted land conversion of environmental areas such as forest, agricultural, parks and watersheds areas. Unplanned and unregulated land conversion is an important issue that was flagged in the Philippines National Urban Assessment (ADB, 2014). Moreover, Metro Cebu would also need to consider harmonisation of all land use plans in its jurisdiction as proposed by the JICA roadmap land-use plan. Besides, Barcelona's urban planning experience in having been constrained by similar topographic conditions as Metro Cebu could be an inspiration for the latter (Box 2.1).

Table 2.1. **Status of CLUPs in Metro Cebu**

LGU	Planning period
Danao	2017-27
Compostela	1995-2004
Liloan	2009-18
Consolacion	2001-10
Lapulapu	2010-20
Cordova	2005-14
Mandaue	2015-24
Cebu City	2006-16
Talisay	2000-10
Minglanilla	1999-2009
Naga	2017-26
San Fernando	2011–20
Carcar	2008-17

Source: Metro Cebu Development and Coordinating Board (2016), "Answers to the OECD case study questionnaire", internal document, unpublished.

Box 2.1. **Barcelona urban land use planning**

Barcelona has two main plans regulating land-use, one approved in 1976 called the "Pla General Metropolità de Barcelona" (PGM), and another created in 2010 which encompasses a larger area called the "Pla Territorial Metropolità de Barcelona" (PTMB). In 2013, the Area Metropolitana de Barcelona (AMB) began drafting a new metropolitan plan, heir to the PGM and called PDU (Pla Director Urbanístic Metropolità,) which reflects the future of the metropolitan city and takes into consideration concerns of institutions, communities and citizens (AMB, 2014). The plans which have contributed to the success of the city focused on:

- **Establishing a clear land typology**: the master plan defines urban limits by establishing which land has to be protected from urbanisation because of its environmental or agricultural values, as well as for risk management issues. The PGM established three different categories: urban land, potentially urban land and rural land. Within these three land categories, the PGM also specifies subtypes with their own characteristics (maximum density, green spaces, etc…).
- **Increasing urban density in existing cities**: the PTMB has got three different specific regulations regarding open spaces, settlements and infrastructures. In terms of settlement regulations, it determines where densification is needed, or where there is a lack of green spaces or public facilities, as well as identifies where priority development areas are, both at the local and metropolitan scales.

Box 2.2. **Barcelona urban land use planning** *(continued)*

- **Designing a rational and efficient urban structure enhancing sustainable mobility**: the master plan creates on the one hand a balanced hierarchal urban structure increasing sustainable mobility, not only of the road network but also the public infrastructures, and on the other hand promotes actions to enforce this structure, such as widening primary streets (either for cars or pedestrians). The PTMB combines the road network, railway, port and airport strategies with those of logistic areas and open spaces structure, emphasising the connections between the latter.
- **Preserving and protecting natural and agricultural spaces**: the master plan promotes natural and agricultural space protection. This could be included either in the master plan itself, or in several specific protection plans, in the same way that it has been done recently in Barcelona: in 2015, the "Pla especial de protecció del Parc Agrari del Baix Llobregat" was approved, and AMB is developing right now a similar protection plan for Collserola park, the most important green open space in Barcelona metropolitan region.
- **Promoting flexibility and mixed-use in new urban developments**: land use planning should be flexible and capable to re-accommodate new requirements. Residential, commercial, production and public facilities all together creates a valuable urban characteristic.
- **Redistributing urban development profits to the community**: land-use planning systems create profit expectancies depending on what is permitted by the land-use plan. For instance, the value of an agricultural plot of land rises dramatically if it receives a building permit. The key point is that this urban profit is created discretionally depending only on land-use planning criteria. Therefore, this added value should not go into the hands of the private sector but be redistributed and used for the public good. In Catalonia's urban system, there is a minimum public participation in the urban profits, established by law. Concretely, the following rules apply, however, it should be noted that all these rules are minimum percentages, and higher standards can be required by the regulating plans:
  - Potentially-urban land: developing plans must give to the public administration a minimum of 10% of the land for green spaces and 5% for public facilities. Green spaces and streets with all its infrastructures systems needed (sanitation, electricity and water supply) are built and paid by real estate developers. In addition, the public administration will receive a portion of land where it will be able to build up to 10% of the permitted square meters, free of charges.
  - Urban land: developing plans must establish an amount of land for green spaces and public facilities (in case it has not been established by general planning already).
  - Finally, it is mandatory that residential developments keep 30% of total amount of dwellings for both social housing (20%) and price-controlled housing (10%).

Source: AMB (2014), "Presentation of the new PDU", www.amb.cat/web/territori/urbanisme/pdu/presentacio; OECD (2015b), 2015 Report of the 5th OECD Knowledge Sharing Workshop on Urban Green Growth in Dynamic Asia , unpublished internal report.

Manage urban sprawl and promote mixed land use

Out of Metro Cebu's land area of 1 163.40 km^2, about 15% of the land is used for urban purposes (Figure 2.1). Physical development of the metropolitan area has been concentrated to a narrow stretch along the coastal areas whilst a major part of the hinterland for various reasons has remained undeveloped. Data on available land supply for urbanisation provided by the JICA study indicates that 76% of land area is hazardous, particularly characterised by steep slope lands over 18 degrees and vulnerable low lands below two meters from the sea level. The high steep slopes and hazardous nature of the terrain, along with environmental reserves such as forest and water shed- particularly to the west, discourage inland urban expansion. That notwithstanding, urban growth has been multi-dimensional stretching along the north and south eastern corridors of the coast as well as upland, as seen in Figure 1.1 (Chapter 1). The cities of Naga, San Fernando and Minglanilla have slopes with very high gradients few meters from the sea hindering the southern expansion, whilst Carcar possesses a relatively flat stretch of land extending inland before gradually experiencing an elevating slope. These geographical conditions naturally limit Metro Cebu's spatial expansion, requiring it to manage its scarce land judiciously to meet the increasing urban needs.

Figure 2.1. **Land use in Metro Cebu (2014)**

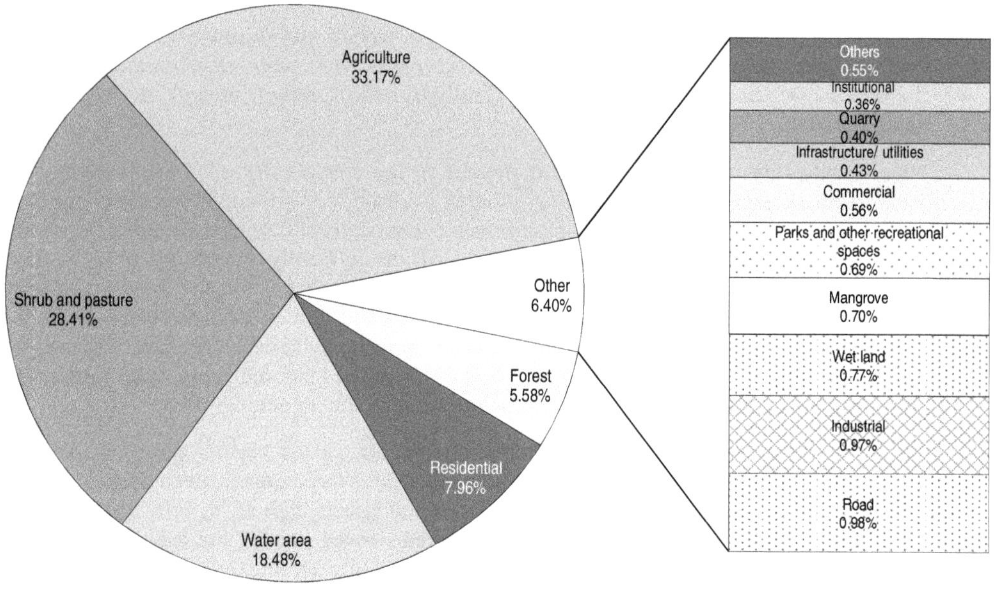

Source: Metro Cebu Development and Coordinating Board (2016), "Answers to the OECD case study questionnaire", internal document, unpublished.

Metro Cebu's land use policy needs to ensure efficiency and ward off a "lock-in" which could place the metropolitan area in a vulnerable development pattern that will be costly to reverse in the long run. A multi core urban structure connected by good transport with each core functioning independently and efficiently should be promoted. The development of polycentric compact poles provides a guiding vision to ensure Metro Cebu has a clearly delineated urban structure that allows for proper functioning of the urban system. To achieve the above, land-use planning instruments would need to be strictly enforced and coherent regulations put in place to delimit urban expansion and intrusion into land not suitable for development. The JICA report laid out a three category approach of work, play and green buffer for the polycentric development recommendation. This is important but Metro Cebu needs to adopt a flexible approach to its implementation, ensuring equal distribution of spatial opportunities. At the same time, it must be noted that traditional planning instruments are necessary but not sufficient to achieve inclusive growth and environmental sustainability. As such it is important to align fiscal policies such as taxes with desired spatial development objectives (OECD, 2017).

Revising zoning plans to accommodate mixed land uses is critical to sustainable land use. For example, the land use/zoning categorisation of Cebu City does not indicate any mixed land use. Arguably, it can be stated that some properties are not developed in their designated zones. These circumstances create confusions and problems in transparency for private developers. As a key green growth principle and to promote liveability of the various communities, mixed land use should be factored into the land use and zoning plans. This means balancing land uses to establish complementary linkages among residential, commercial and recreational areas in given neighbourhoods. By placing origins and destination in close proximity, the need for individual motorised transport can be reduced while healthy lifestyles, carbon foot print reduction and social interaction promoted. Proper mixed use zoning is a means to create dense lively neighbourhoods and reduce the need for long commute in Metro Cebu.

Another worrying concern in Cebu is the lack of focus on high-density housing developments. The population density in Metro Cebu was 2449 per km2 in 2015 which is not very high compared with other Asian Cities (Chapter 1). Given the trend of urbanisation however, Cebu needs to improve the efficiency of land use to accommodate its population and economic activities in the limited land area. According to the CLUP guidebook Volume 3 (2014), Residential 1 (R1-Z) and Residential 2 (R2-Z) are for low and medium residential uses respectively whilst Residential 3 (R3-Z) to Residential 5 (R5-Z) are for medium to very high density on that scale. Only R1-Z and R2-Z are designated in Cebu city, and no medium to high density zones are used. This is not to say that high rise buildings are absent, a number of high rise buildings can be seen across the skyline of the city which further buttresses the discrepancy between actual land use and land zoning. In general, there is clearly a need to encourage more medium to high scale residential buildings. Most of residential dwellings in Metro Cebu are detached houses, averaging 1-2 storeys, with no courtyard or limited spaces between them. To meet the housing needs of Metro Cebu's 2050 population and beyond, there is a need for densification by shifting to new residential dwelling typologies. High-density developments offer opportunities for Cebu to reduce the per capita cost of infrastructure and service provision, while offering an alternative for the metro area to judiciously use its scarce land resource and contain development within the planned area. With the rapid expansion of the city and growth target to reach 5 million inhabitants by 2050, high density developments integrated with a transit oriented development will ensure developments do not transgress the urban limit. The horizontal growth of Cebu in contrast to a vertical growth threatens the metro's long term economic potential. High density development without diversity of land uses and green open spaces also appears counterproductive; hence there is a need to link with mixed land use and adequate infrastructure developments. In addition, affordable housing will also need to be promoted in urban centres to lure in residents who otherwise would have been attracted to low cost housing in suburban areas.

Central to the recommendations on reducing urban sprawl and mixed land use is the need to guide spatial growth through a compact city model supported by a transit-oriented development. A compact city model (Box 2.2) is defined as a spatial urban form characterised by "compactness" while a transit oriented development is seen as an urban development designed to maximise access to mass-transit systems. Such neighbourhoods often consist of a centre with a public transit station, surrounded by high-density mixed-use development with gradually lower density development spreading outward from the centre (OECD, 2012).

Box 2.2. **Concepts of "compact city" and "transit-oriented development (TOD)"**

Throughout its long history, the compact city has evolved and enlarged its scope and policy objectives. From a simple urban containment policy to protect the local natural environment or agricultural land from urban encroachment, it has gradually acquired new policy objectives: energy savings, quality of life and liveability, etc. It has come to imply a multi-dimensional policy approach with a wide range of urban sustainability goals and indeed a mainstream policy approach to achieving urban sustainability. An important distinction must be made between density, which refers only to the number of residents per square kilometre of urbanised land, and compact cities, which encompasses a wider set of characteristics: i) dense and proximate development patterns, ii) urban areas linked by public transport systems and iii) accessible local services and jobs.

Compact urban form is correlated with economic, environmental and social benefits. Economic benefits take the form of increased labour productivity, reduced infrastructure costs, and more efficient use of land resources. Environmental benefits include lower air pollution and CO_2 emissions from transport, reduced transport energy consumption, and conservation of farmland and ecosystems. Social benefits include greater access to services and improved health.

Transit-oriented development (TOD) is a prominent example of policy complementarities for compact city development. It can reduce traffic congestion and rationalise densification by facilitating the use of public transport. At the same time, densifying areas near transit stations can increase ridership, which ensures the health of the public transport system. From the compact city point of view, TOD should especially be promoted in existing built-up areas. Although TODs for suburban greenfield development are important as viable alternatives to auto travel, urban expansion can generate additional demand for development on land not served by the new public transport systems and eventually lead to auto-dependent urban sprawl.

Vancouver (Canada) and Portland (United States) offer excellent examples of TOD in existing built-up areas. Metro Vancouver's "frequent transit network (FTN), defined as bus service every 15 minutes or less, 7 days a week, and "frequent transit development corridors" is a concept to shape land use in support of frequent transit. In Metro Vancouver, 97.7% of the population lives within 400 metres of bus stations and more than 40% lives within 400 metres of the FTN. Portland's TOD with streetcars has stimulated brownfield redevelopment in the centre of the metropolitan area. The Pearl, Portland's new high-density, transit-oriented neighbourhood, has 7 200 new dwelling units and 4.6 million ft^2 of new commercial space along the streetcar line in the existing urban areas.

Source: OECD (2012), *Compact City Policies: A Comparative Assessment*, OECD Publishing, Paris, http://dx.doi.org/10.1787/9789264167865-en.

Redevelop urban centres

Cebu city is featured by a vibrant city centre with a high concentration of people and activities. A striking fact is that, often as a result of high inflows of people and commercial activities, road traffic circulation is considerably affected, exacerbating traffic congestion and posing a threat to pedestrian safety. In addition, the streets are not well maintained and existing drainage system is poor. A point often overlooked is that the city has evolved with population outnumbering the threshold for which the centre was planned to accommodate. Moreover, the absence of "idle land" has prevented any significant improvements to these areas. As a result, private investors have often focused on developing on reclaimed parcels of land and the urban suburbs which further accelerates sprawl. The redevelopment of the major city centres in Metro Cebu is important taking into consideration the growing need for a vibrant, safe and properly managed city core. It will also be essential in helping breathe new life and placing emphasis on an attractive people centred, economically and environmentally competitive area. This links up with the strategy on developing polycentric growth centres as it offers the opportunity to ensure provision of services that makes each jurisdiction and its catchment area independent and less reliant on a single city core.

Co-ordinated investment towards urban centres should be targeted to improve their effective functioning. In order to ensure co-ordinated development, it would be essential to put in place a comprehensive redevelopment plan which provides a strategic long term vision and guiding principles for the development of the city centres. The plan should ensure co-ordinated development in light of the economic, cultural and sustainable aspirations of the city. The city centres are of strategic importance especially due to their political, economic and historic value to the province and the region. In addition, redevelopment of downtown Cebu requires a multi stakeholder approach so as to generate positive outcomes in the public interest. Observations point out that for ongoing projects consultation of stakeholders can be broadened further and made more inclusive. Applying this to the context of the city centre redevelopment, a Task Force can be established to bring together user interest, identify principles for design, management and operation thereby helping to achieve a win-win for all parties as seen in the case of Brisbane (Box 2.3). The Urban Renewal Taskforce of Brisbane now known as Urban Renewal Brisbane (URB) initiated innovative approaches and championed diverse ways of re-imaging the city centre.

Box 2.3. **Brisbane CBD Redevelopment**

From the late 1980s, Brisbane, Australia was suffering from economic stagnation, population decline and ageing infrastructure as suburbanisation gained acceleration. Abandoned industrial sites littered the city centre. As a response, the Urban Renewal Taskforce (now known as Urban Renewal Brisbane, URB) was established in 1991, under a tri-government partnership. The taskforce was in charge of revitalising the city through thinking of the city in new ways. Reporting directly to the Brisbane City Council's City Planning Committee and Lord Mayor Graham Quirk, URB has achieved great success in breathing new life into the city of Brisbane.

Four key elements contributed to Brisbane's urban renewal success: a flexible planning approach, community involvement, catalyst projects and developer innovation. The 2006 City Centre Master Plan met with tremendous success, leading to an improved 2014 City Centre Master Plan that has been designed as a co-ordinated strategy to guide the future of Brisbane's development, transport and public space investment over the following 20 years. More than 16 000 residents and stakeholders contributed ideas to this new master plan. The 2014 Master Plan aims to achieve its sole vision of Brisbane as an "open" city – a city that is open for business, has an open outdoor lifestyle and open for both locals and foreigners to enjoy.

According to the Brisbane City Council, Brisbane's CBD, encompassing an area of just 2.2 km^2, is responsible for about 5% of Queensland's economic activity. Brisbane's economy in 2014 was valued at an estimated AUD 146 billion, with the CBD contributing 18.5%. There are 150 000 employees within the CBD, with some 20 000 night time workers and visitors and close to 9 000 residents. As part of the revitalisation plans for the city centre, upgrades have been made to, amongst others, enhance pedestrian space expansion and improvement, increase street planting and landscaping as well as addressing place-making issues. Property and business owners and interest groups have been included in the concept planning and design processes. Successful examples include the Mooney Fountain Plaza revitalisation, Fish Lane upgrade and Gardens Point Road upgrade. In addition, the Brisbane City Council now offers free Wi-Fi services in the CBD, thereby enhancing visitor experiences. Many other initiatives have been successfully developed in and around Brisbane's CBD, making it a vibrant city centre for both work and play.

Source: Brisbane City Council (2016), "Brisbane City Centre: An Open City", CBD Revitalisation initiatives, www.brisbane.qld.gov.au/planning-building/planning-guidelines-tools/brisbane-city-centre-master-plan-2014

Use reclaimed land and coastal zones more strategically

In need of land for expanding urban development, Cebu has been relying on coastal reclamation to increase its land area (Table 2.2). The high cost of land contributes to local governments joining private investors to pursue the policy of coastal reclamation because it appears a less expensive means to acquire land for additional industrial and commercial use (Montenegro et al, 2005). The proposed and already reclaimed land currently forms nearly 3% of Metro Cebu's land area.

Table 2.2. **Land reclamation projects in Metro Cebu**

Project	Size	Status
North Reclamation Area	160 hectares	First major reclamation work, 1964
Cebu South Reclamation Project (South Road Properties)	300 hectares	Project began in 1998, completed in May 2004
North Mandaue Reclamation Project	295 hectares	Approved in 2001
Cebu International Container Port	60 hectares	Reclamation idea proposed in 2002, revisited in 2011
Mandaue reclamation project	131 hectares	Approved in 2013
Cordova reclamation project	1 500 hectares	Selection of private sector proponent undertaken in 2015; ongoing studies for final approval by the PRA (Philippines Reclamation Authority) and the NEDA (National Economic Development Authority) Board
Minglanilla-Ming-mori Reclamation and Industrial Park Development (MMRIPD) project	100 hectares	Approved in 2015
Mactan North Reclamation Development Project	400 hectares	Work was expected to start in 2016, current status unclear

Source: Metro Cebu Development and Coordinating Board (2016), "Answers to the OECD case study questionnaire", internal document, unpublished.

Analysis of land reclamation in Metro Cebu indicates that many reclaimed land remains not fully utilised. Two reasons could be considered. The first is related to project management. Bureaucratic red-tapes, poor co-ordination across relevant authorities, and financial conditions may lead to project delays and thus keep reclaimed land vacant. Such issues have in the past created problems for LGUs, investors and designated government agencies that had financed the reclamation project through loans and were liable for repayment (Dacayo, 2005). The second is related to the quality of urban development. It is observed that some reclamation project sites are yet to be fully integrated into existing urban systems. While strategic location of reclaimed land demonstrates potential, isolated reclaimed areas with monotonous land use and poor public transport accessibility may significantly lose the attractiveness of the areas for investors. In addition, the use of individual private vehicles has negative impacts on the environment.

An important step for sustainable urban development, including urban reclamation, is to critically assess future land needs at the metropolitan scale, and to integrate these areas into existing urban systems. An option to help identify unused land to be developed is through a land registry and buildable land inventory. Portland's land inventory system provides a good example for assessing future development needs and capacity of available land (Box 2.4). Adopting such a system in Metro Cebu would assist in the setting of targets to promote redevelopment of areas or underused land in the urban cores. The JICA roadmap has identified available land supply for urbanisation (a total of 11 948 ha). Such efforts should be continued and the results should be incorporated into the CLUP processes.

Box 2.4. Portland's Buildable Lands Inventory and "refill rate" as monitoring tools for brownfield development

Portland Metro is required by state law to review the capacity of the Urban Growth Boundary (UGB) every five years to ensure a 20-year land supply. The metropolitan government has developed the Buildable Lands Inventory, a detailed and sophisticated land-monitoring process to inventory vacant land and track the "refill rate". This is defined as the rate at which new development occurs through "infill" (when more units are constructed on an already developed lot) or "redevelopment" (when a structure is removed and another built in its place).

In 2009, Metro found that the refill rate for new industrial development was 20%. For non-industrial use, 52% of new capacity was built on developed land (Metro, 2009). The residential refill rate has climbed steadily, from 30.4% in the period 1997-2001 to 33% in 2001-06 (Metro, 2009). Metro predicts the rate will rise to 38% from 2010 to 2030 (Metro, 2010). If it does, the urban growth boundary will be able to accommodate 11 300 additional dwellings without expanding. Refill rates are highest in the central city and lowest in suburban residential neighbourhoods. Most residential refill is multifamily housing, often as part of transit-oriented development (TOD). Portland prioritises transport projects that support refill and investment in TODs to achieve higher density and a greater mix of uses than prevailing market conditions would support in terms of developers' construction costs and income from rent or sale (Metro, 2011).

Source: OECD (2012), *Compact City Policies: A Comparative Assessment*, OECD Green Growth Studies, OECD Publishing, Paris, http://dx.doi.org/10.1787/9789264167865-en.

Besides, reclamation projects need extra care for long-term environmental sustainability. Reclamation may come at a high environmental cost, for example in the form of the loss of mangroves and coral reef, which may affect flood risks and economic benefits of tourism. Some researchers even argue that Cebu could pursue an alternative development strategy through sustainable ecotourism, instead of urban development through reclamation (Montenegro, 2016). In addressing such environmental concerns, the potential impacts of reclamation projects on the coastal eco-systems of Cebu and Central Visayas as a whole should be taken into account when making development decisions. In addition, its social impacts should be carefully assessed. In Barcelona, Spain, the Moll de Fusta is a platform that was designed on the waterfront and extended to the seafront in between the districts of Barceloneta and the southern foothills of Montjuic. The port is regarded as one of the most influential developments throughout the country of Spain; it gives a total of 300 hectares of land for social gathering space for the public (Marshall, 2004). The Moll de Fusta port continues to serve as a walkway that attracts a huge amount of visitors each year. Given the importance of waterfront for Metro Cebu, its coastal zones must be used more strategically to enhance local tourism and boost local economy and social interaction with greater care for environment, such as bird viewing centres, maritime museum, and recreational courts for games or heritage walkways with complimentary services. Terminals for sea ferries for local commuters as well as tourist attraction could also be considered. Ensuring flexibility in design fosters adaptive reuse, helping to cater for diverse audiences and functions in different seasons. Metro Cebu can centre such developments on showcasing its local identity in addition to protection of bio diversity.

Diversify transport modes in Metro Cebu

In the Philippines, road transport is dominant, accounting for 98% of passenger and 58 % of cargo traffic (ADB, 2012). Metro Cebu, likewise has witnessed an overwhelming reliance on road transport. It is particularly prone to high levels of traffic congestion due to multiple factors such as increasing vehicle ownership, insufficient investment in road infrastructure, non-compliance with traffic regulation, inadequate connectivity of road networks and congested intersections. While the total vehicle registration increased by 107% in the Cebu Province between 2003 and 2012 (Figure 1.16), the road length only increased by about 9% (NSCB, 2016). Traffic congestions are observed especially at the north-south corridor as well as between Cebu City and Mactan Island. To address issues of connectivity between the two islands, a third bridge (the Cebu-Cordova Bridge) is planned to relieve the traffic on the two existing bridges whilst providing connectivity for traffic from the south of Metro Cebu. However, the absence of diverse transport modes, including public transport system as well as non-motorised transport plays a crucial role in the persistent challenge or road traffic.

Developing rail transport

One of the first large public investments in clean transport infrastructure in Cebu will be the Cebu Bus Rapid Transit (BRT) project, which is now under construction. The project is expected to cost USD 228.5 million (World Bank, 2014). The objective of the BRT project is to improve the performance of the urban transport system in the areas of quality of service, safety and environmental efficiency. The BRT will run between Barangay Talamban in the north and Barangay Bulacao in the south. The project is a bold step to address the urban transport challenges in Metro Cebu especially concerning congestion in the central Cebu city and reduction of carbon in the transport sector.

On a broader metropolitan scale, combining the BRT with a high-capacity, regional scale rail transport can effectively address the complex transport needs of Metro Cebu. In view of the increasing population and the need for wider spatial transportation coverage of all the LGUs in Metro Cebu, faster and high occupancy modes of transport such as trains would be needed. This is confirmed by the JICA report which points out that the design capacity of Cebu's BRT may not be able to respond to demand along the planned route. For example, it is estimated that along the planned service routes an aggregated capacity of 5 400 passenger seats per hour in a single direction is required (JICA and MCDCB, 2015). Given that on average the capacity of BRT is about 3000 passengers per hour in a single direction and granting exclusive priority to BRT through the removal and relocation of public utility vehicles (PUV) along the service lanes, a backlog of about 2400 passengers will need to be catered for. Similarly, in terms of the route length, the BRT has a system length of 16km and does not cover the whole Metro Cebu which from the City of Danao to Carcar is about 72 km. In the short to medium term, expansion of the bus routes would need to be considered if the BRT is to have a tremendous impact on changing transport behaviour. Integration with existing as well as planned modes would also need to be considered which can be made possible through the integrated transport master plan.

Developing a high capacity rail transport appears a feasible option to address traffic concerns and provide a sustainable means of transport capable of meeting travel needs in the long term. Cities such as Paris, London, Hong Kong, Seoul and Tokyo have demonstrated the long term benefits that can be derived from urban rail transport, such as seamless connectivity of adjoining areas and decongestion on roads. Rail development will be a means to futureproof Metro Cebu's urban development for long term growth. Studies have already been undertaken in Metro Cebu recommending the introduction of a rail transit to increase accessibility of the metropolitan area. Yet, it has not received the needed commitment for implementation. The unsustainability of road width expansion projects in Metro Cebu lends more credence to the urgent need to develop alternate means of transport especially either a Mass Rail Transit (MRT) or Light Rail Transit (LRT) based on a feasibility study. Rail systems can be instrumental in the development of the growth poles envisaged in the metropolitan plan proposed for the metro areas and serve as a catalyst for social and economic development. Light rail becomes a preferable means of transport due to the ability to easily adjust timing or capacity to respond to ridership and its low emissions. Their exclusive right of way and separation from road transport increases its reliability and efficiency which could attract high ridership. Moreover, the economic and industrial development of Metro Cebu from a competitive perspective could best be served through a modern rail transport. MCDCB and NEDA should prioritise the implementation of a rail system thorough national government support and supplementary financing mechanisms such as public private partnership scheme. Singapore is a good example demonstrating how the country has benefited from urban rail transport through a strong commitment (Box. 2.5).

Box 2.5. **Urban rail transport: The case of Singapore**

With the highest private car ownership prices in the world and a growing population, providing an adequate public transport system is of utmost importance in the city-state of Singapore. Singapore's urban rail network began with 2 lines in operation in 1987: the North-South line and the East-West line. Known as the Mass Rapid Transit (MRT), this 150 km rail network is the backbone of Singapore's public transport network with more than 2.5 million people riding the MRT daily (Land Transport Authority, 2017). It has since expanded to 5 lines that spread throughout the island. Plans have been drafted to extend this network to 8 lines by 2030. The evolution of the MRT system in Singapore has not only been carefully thought through, but also extremely efficient. By the end of 2015, the number of MRT stations in Singapore was slightly under 120 and plans are underway to increase this to more than 140 by 2020. By 2030, Singapore's rail network is slated to become as dense as in cities such as London, New York and Tokyo. However, Singapore achieved this well-connected public rail network in just over 40 years, while other cities built their respective networks in about 100 years (Ministry of Transport, 2017).

Currently, six in every ten households live within a ten-minute walk to an MRT station; by 2030, this will increase to eight in every ten households, due to an MRT extension or a new line opening almost every year between 2015 and 2020 (Ministry of Transport, 2017). New trains have also been added to the system, increasing the number of weekly train trips from 15 000 in 2011 to 19 000 in 2015 (Ministry of Transport, 2017). The maximum wait time is 5 minutes and trains serve passengers at an average of every 2 minutes during peak hours. MRT reliability has also increased due to regular checks and thorough investigations when necessary. Delays lasting more than 5 minutes have been reduced by more than 30% since 2011. The relevant authorities have achieved such successes by investing more resources, adopting new technologies and innovative maintenance approaches while also upgrading equipment (Ministry of Transport, 2017).

Recognising that a better travelling experience is a multi-faceted endeavour, the Land Transport Authority (LTA) has several initiatives in place such as free MRT rides before the morning peak hours, free WIFI at MRT stations and convenient payment systems such as using existing credit and debit cards, hence eliminating the need for a separate transit card and fare top-ups (LTA, 2015). Singapore plans to double the current rail network to 360 km with the opening of 2 new rail lines. Other improvements include extending existing lines, expanding train fleets (such that train trips will eventually increase by 8%) and further decrease wait times. The New Rail Financing Framework (NRRF) is also being implemented. This would transfer ownership of operating assets such as trains and signalling systems from the rail operators to the LTA to ensure timely investments in the urban rail system (Land Transport Authority, 2015).

Source: Ministry of Transport (2017), "Fact Sheet – Public Transport Improvements and Future Plans"; Land Transport Authority (2015), "Walk. Cycle. Ride. Singapore: Land Transport Authority Annual Report 2015/2016", www.lta.gov.sg/content/dam/ltaweb/corp/publicationsresearch/files/annualreports/1516/lta_ar_1516.pdf; Land Transport Authority (2017), "Riding a Train", https://www.lta.gov.sg/content/ltaweb/en/public-transport/mrt-and-lrt-trains/riding-a-train.html.

In furtherance of the above, there is a need to ensure good connectivity between the core transport corridors and surrounding areas with an effective feeder transport. Urban transport systems must be integrated holistically in what is referred to as "last half-kilometre" or "last mile" connectivity. This ideally means that a passenger should be able to leave home and walk less than 500 metres to reach a bus stop or train station connecting to a larger public transport network. Connectivity is the single most important characteristic of any fully functional and profitable urban public transport system.

Jeepneys in this regard have a unique role to play. Jeepneys do not only have a cultural and historic value but also provide frequent services and access to neighbourhoods that larger vehicles may not be able to service. However, to unleash such potential, there is a need to improve their reliability and safety, which calls for better regulations. Moreover, regulatory measures such as a ban on highly polluting Jeepneys would be needed for better urban environment and to reduce GHG emissions. Financial incentives could assist owners to replace their vehicles with low emission vehicles or even electronic Jeepneys (e-jeepneys). Metro Cebu could set a target and support such transition. Globally, under the Urban Electric Mobility Initiative, city governments have pledged that electrical vehicles will account for 30% of light duty vehicles plying their cities by 2030 (UEMI, 2017).

Encouraging non-motorised transport

Non-motorised transport use in Metro Cebu remains relatively low but can be encouraged to support low-carbon mobility. These means such as bicycles offer a healthy choice of mobility for urban residents and the environment. The absences of infrastructure such as segregated cycle lanes and bicycle parking spots, as well as road indiscipline discourage the use of such modes. Increasingly, many urban governments have embraced bicycle sharing schemes as means to promote a modal shift from automobiles to cycling. This has been complemented with the development of the infrastructure and safety mechanisms for pedestrians and cyclist.

Bike sharing infrastructure could further complement the green loop project and should be part of the transport agenda of Metro Cebu. In Paris, the bike sharing scheme, *Velib* has over 23 600 bikes in 1 800 bike stations within a five minutes-walk across the city (*Velib*, 2017). In China, Hangzhou has successfully demonstrated the feasibility of a sustainable bike sharing scheme. Launched in 2008, the initiative was the first bike sharing scheme in China and started with 2 800 bicycles (Shaheen et al, 2011). The public bike sharing scheme which has a high patronage among residents had risen to about 78 000 bicycles in 2013 and is aiming for 175 000 by 2020 (Thorpe, 2014). Another remarkable scheme was also developed by Guangzhou, China which integrated its bike sharing scheme with its BRT to address the "hub to home" connection challenge.

Bike sharing scheme is not new to the Philippines. The *Tutubi* bike sharing scheme was the first in the Philippines to be launched in Pasig City (Clean Air Asia, 2013). It was a demonstration project supported by the Asian Development Bank intended to demonstrate the feasibility of green transport. Due to the success of the project, plans are underway to expand the system to other cities and set up 250 stations with approximately 22 500 bicycles. Subsequent phases of the project are planned to target Metro Manila. In Metro Cebu the demand for cycling is growing and the metro area learning from cases such as that of the Tutubi bike-sharing scheme and Hangzhou could achieve tremendous impact in ensuring a significant modal shift to shared bicycles by developing such schemes at the same time as it develops its high capacity mass transport. This is crucial as the use of mass public transport and non-motorised transport are mutually linked.

Create co-ordination mechanisms for metropolitan transport in Metro Cebu

The increasing multiplicity of transport policy actors both at horizontal and vertical levels reinforces the need for alignment of priorities and investments (OECD, 2015a). At the horizontal level, the lack of prior co-ordination among municipal authorities in the functional metropolitan area generates inconsistencies in the design of routes and complexity in the ticketing system. At the vertical level, the allocation of responsibilities across national, regional and municipal levels requires coherent multi-modal, multi-year strategic planning that is sometimes particularly challenging to implement in metropolitan areas (OECD, 2015a).

Metropolitan-wide, comprehensive transport strategy

In Metro Cebu, the lack of an integrated metropolitan transport system contributes to significant urban and environmental problems, by reinforcing car dependence and congestion. Thus the most urgent task for Metro Cebu is to develop a comprehensive transport strategy at the metropolitan scale. It should integrate diverse modes of transport such as trains, buses, ferries, cycling or walking to produce a connectivity that promotes the most optimum use of land and effective freight and passenger movement across Metro Cebu. This might mean to revisit the Metro Cebu Land Use and Transportation Study (MCLUTS) in 1979, in a sense that it attempted to remedy critical transport and traffic problems at the metropolitan scale. The MCLUTS was a strategic plan specifying particular projects for implementation across different time scales between 1979 and 2000 (Villarete and Cal, 2007). Although the MCLUTS focused mainly on road transport, this time Metro Cebu will need to look beyond roads and integrate diverse transport options.

Metropolitan-wide transport authority

In terms of governance structure, a metropolitan-wide transport authority is essential in harmonising the situation of dispersed responsibility for transport and urban development among different players thereby allowing for effective long-term co-ordinated investment. Such institutional arrangement is becoming increasingly common in many OECD metropolitan areas, and different types of metropolitan authorities are co-ordinating transport planning decisions (Table 2.3). The OECD Metropolitan Governance Survey has found that the share of residents who are satisfied with the public transport provision in their cities is 14 percentage points higher if a transport authority exists (Figure 2.2). It appears likely that this is at least partly due to the better integration of public transport in these cities.

There are a variety of institutional settings for metropolitan transport authorities, which provides different implications on how they operate. For example, a metropolitan transport authority could be autonomous exclusively in charge of transport issue, or part of a metropolitan authority in charge of wider policy issues at the metropolitan level. While autonomous authorities have clear mandates on transport, allowing efficient decision making and more transparent and accountable organisational management, they may find it more difficult to co-ordinate with other policy issues such as land use. In contrast, co-ordination challenges are expectedly minimised when a single authority is in charge of planning both transport and land use (OECD, 2015a).

Table 2.3. **Governance of transport in selected OECD metropolitan areas**

	Metropolitan areas	Governance of transport
Informal/soft co-ordination	Athens-Attica (Greece)	The Athens Urban Transport Organisation (OASA) is the single co-ordinating authority for public transport planning.
Inter-municipal authorities	Marseille (France)	Around ten transport authorities in the metropolitan area, including six inter-municipal transport authorities (*autorités organisatrices des transports*, AOT), one departmental public transport syndicate (*Syndicat Mixte des Transports en Commun*, SMTC), regional authorities in charge of regional railways.
	Frankfurt (Germany)	• The Rhein-Main Verkehrsverbund (RMV, created in 1995) is the single authority over public transport in the larger area of Frankfurt that covers around 5 million inhabitants. • The RMV brings together 3 levels of government: 11 municipalities, 15 districts (Kreise, the next upper level) and the State of Hesse.
	Chicago (United States)	• The Chicago Metropolitan Agency for Planning (CMAP) develops a comprehensive regional plan integrating transport and land use for seven counties. The Regional Transportation Authority (RTA) co-ordinates the three public transport service boards (Chicago Transit Authority [CTA], Metra and Pace).
Supra-municipal authorities	Puebla-Tlaxcala(Mexico)	• The Chicago Metropolitan Agency for Planning (CMAP) develops a comprehensive regional plan integrating transport and land use for seven counties. The Regional Transportation Authority (RTA) co-ordinates the three public transport service boards (Chicago Transit Authority [CTA], Metra and Pace). • The Metropolitan Council is in charge of distributing funds from the federal Metropolitan Fund to strategic metropolitan projects, including transport but the main criterion of eligibility is population size and the modest funds are distributed to small individual projects in municipalities in each of the two states. • The two states (Puebla and Tlaxcala) are in charge of roads and railways. • Public transport is provided by private operators which apply for a concession to the state government and operate low-capacity vehicles.
"Metropolitan cities"	Daejeon (Korea)	The Daejeon metropolitan government (transport department) is in charge of transport planning for the entire metropolitan area.

Source: OCDE (2015a), *Governing the City*, OECD Publishing, Paris, http://dx.doi.org/10.1787/9789264226500-en.

Figure 2.2. **Share of population satisfied with public transport provision**

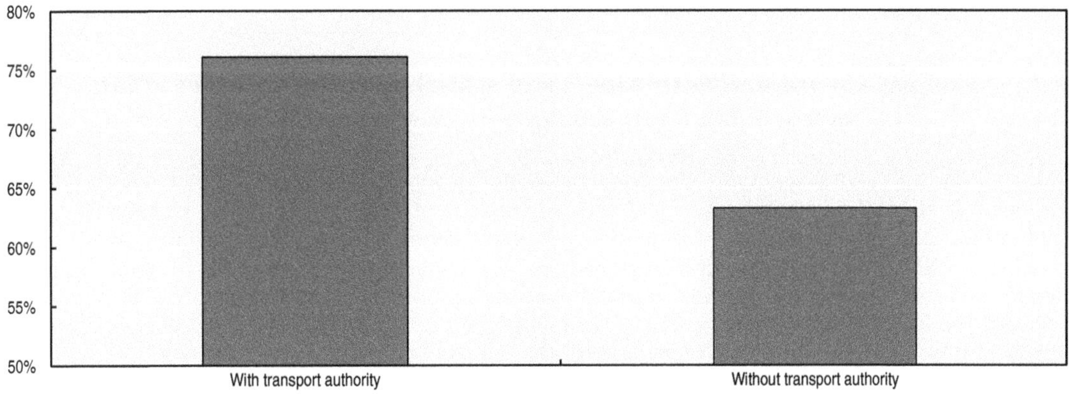

Notes: Estimates are based on the share of respondents from 37 cities in the Urban Audit Perception Survey who state that they are either "satisfied" or "very satisfied" with the public transport provision in their city. The difference between the two groups is statistically significant at the 95% confidence level.

Source: Ahrend, R., C. Gamper and A. Schumann (2014), "The OECD Metropolitan Governance Survey: A quantitative description of governance structures in large urban agglomerations", *OECD Regional Development Working Papers*, No. 2014/04, OECD Publishing, Paris, http://dx.doi.org/10.1787/5jz43zldh08p-en.

In Metro Cebu, the proposed bill on Mega Cebu Development Authority (MCDA) provides an immediate opportunity to form a metropolitan transport authority. If the bill is enacted, a commission will be created to render services regarding metropolitan-wide transport and traffic management. Although the exact roles and responsibilities of this commission need to be determined at a later stage, it envisions unifying fare collection (single ticketing system). Such a system allows users to ride most public transport systems with a single pass and benefit from discounts when they transfer from one mode to another, thereby encouraging public transport use and multimodality. As the transport modes in Metro Cebu are diversified, the commission's role will be further extended to a wide range of services. In London, United Kingdom, the Transport for London (TfL) is the integrated transport authority which performs functions ranging from operational responsibilities over rails, buses, trams, taxi regulation, private hire trade, congestion charging scheme, operation of all of the 6 300 traffic signals in the London area and works to ensure the safety of all road users (TfL, 2016).

A possible concern is how to ensure co-ordination between the MCDA and relevant LGUs. For example, the process of developing a metropolitan transport strategy should be a backbone for co-ordination. More specifically, an extensive consultation must be ensured to align priorities and goals between the metropolitan and municipal transport strategies. Ideally, such a strategy would be expected to draw directly from municipal input, or at a minimum, include mechanisms to allow adequate dialogue and co-ordination between the metropolitan authority and the LGUs (OECD, 2015a). Furthermore, the transport commission within the MCDA will need to co-ordinate across transport planning and spatial planning decisions. As previously discussed, the MCDA is in a good position to minimise such co-ordination challenges, as it will be in charge of both transport and overall sustainable development plans for Metro Cebu. However, the fact that LGUs remain to be responsible for their land use plans (CLUPs) underscores the need for effective co-ordination on spatial development. In Vancouver (Canada), the regional planning authority Metro Vancouver aligns the spatial plans of its member municipalities and influences the strategic plan of the separate regional transport authority TransLink (Box 2.6).

Box 2.6. Co-ordinating transport and spatial planning decisions at the metropolitan level: Example in Vancouver, Canada

In Vancouver (Canada), the Greater Vancouver Regional District (GVRD), renamed Metro Vancouver in 2007, is a supra-municipal authority created in 1967, which brings together 24 local authorities (22 municipalities, 1 "Electoral Area" and 1 aboriginal community called "Treaty First Nation"). Metro Vancouver provides regional services, including three core utilities (water, liquid waste, solid waste), and co-ordinates regional planning by producing the Regional Growth Strategy (RGS). The RGS calls for the alignment of the spatial plans of member local authorities as it requires each member local authority to provide a Regional Context Statement to "demonstrate to the Metro Vancouver Board how its Official Community Plan Supports the RGS".

There is a separate metropolitan public transport authority called TransLink, which was created in 1998 and is responsible for setting and administrating fares for regional public transport services. TransLink is governed by the Mayors' Council on Regional Transportation (where all 24 member local governments of Metro Vancouver are represented) and the TransLink Board of Directors. Metro Vancouver is responsible for formulating the RGS and regional air quality objectives that TransLink must consider when developing long-term transport strategies. Metro Vancouver also provides input to TransLink on its long-term transport strategies and ten-year transport investment plans. Finally, it provides input to the Mayors' Council on proposed borrowing limit increases in ten-year transport investment plans.

Source: OECD (2015a), *Governing the City*, OECD Publishing, Paris, http://dx.doi.org/10.1787/9789264226500-en.

Moving towards "zero-waste" Metro Cebu

This section examines how Metro Cebu has been managing municipal solid waste towards "zero-waste" from the following three dimensions: i) an overall policy framework to ensure a comprehensive approach to the issue; ii) policies to influence households' and industries' behaviour to minimise waste and create conditions for resource recovery; and iii) policies to effectively manage landfills and material recovery facilities.

Policy frameworks for effective "zero-waste" policy

Need for an ambitious "zero-waste" policy

In the Philippines, the Republic Act 9003 (RA9003) or the Philippines Ecological Solid Waste Management Act of 2000 provides frameworks for LGUs to adopt a comprehensive solid waste management programme. It aims for solid waste volume reduction, better resource conservation and recovery, prohibits certain actions and products, provides penalties and appropriates funds. LGUs are primarily responsible for the implementation and enforcement of the provisions of the Act. Despite the comprehensive policy framework, LGUs are struggling to implement the policy. The challenges observed include poor enforcement mechanism, lack of resources, low capacity and citizens' awareness.

As part of the implementation of the RA 9003, each city or municipality is expected to form a Solid Waste Management Board (SWMB) and prepare a management programme in line with the city's objective. However, this has not been fully complied with in Metro Cebu as some SWM plans have expired (Table 2.4).

Table 2.4. **Status of SWM by LGU in Metro Cebu**

City or Municipality	Type of disposal facilities	Location of landfill sites	SWM Plan	SWM Ordinance	Type of collection
City of Cebu	SLF	Inayawan	-	-	-
City of Carcar	FDRCON / RDF	City of Naga	2016-2026	CO # 3-05	mixed
Minglanilla	FDRCON / RDF	City of Naga	2015-2025	MO # 010	mixed
City of Naga	FDRCON / RDF	Pangdan	2007-2017		mixed
San Fernando	Open Dumpsite		2011-2021	MO # 01-2007	mixed
City of Talisay	SLF	Tapul	2005-2014	CO # 2007-03	mixed
Compostela	Open Dumpsite	Cambayog	2005-2014	MO # 9	segregated
City of Danao	Open Dumpsite	Tak-an	2005-2014	CO # 27-05	mixed
Liloan	Controlled Dumpsite	Sta. Cruz	2006-2016	MO # 2007-03	segregated
Consolacion	SLF (Asian Energy)	Polog		MO # 2 s 2006	mixed
Cordova	RCF	Mohon	2015-2024	MO # 002-2008	segregated
Mandaue City	SLF	Umapad	2010-2019	CO # 2001/02	mixed

Notes: SLF: sanitary landfill; FDRCON / RDF: waste-to-energy facility.

Source: Provincial Environment and Natural Resource Office, Province of Cebu (2015).

Given the current rapid urbanisation and emerging policy opportunities for better SMW management, it is timely for each LGU in Cebu to review the current SMW policy framework. In addressing the land-filling challenges the metropolitan area is facing, an ambitious "zero-waste" target could be considered for all the LGUs, so that the metropolitan area could demonstrate its commitment to drastically divert waste being sent to landfills. San Francisco (Box 2.7) is a good example of a city that has managed to divert waste to landfills by 80% in efforts to reach zero waste by the year 2020 (SF environment, 2016). Sweden is similarly a good example as only 1% of waste goes to landfill sites. Several jurisdictions in OECD countries such as New York City, Kamikatsu, Japan; Toronto, Canada; Seattle, Washington and New South Wales have all adopted a long-term zero waste goal. For Metro Cebu, this would entail intensifying education and awareness programmes, extensive recycling and composting measures as well as effectively implementing the "no segregation, no collection policy" among others. The zero waste policy would need to provide targets and mechanisms for monitoring compliance with targets as well as the incentives for industries and households. A zero waste target is essential for a drastic shift from a linear consumption model to a circular model which charts a path focusing on sustainable material use over the long run.

It is also of importance for Cebu to realise the policy synergies and complementarities that waste management could have with other sectors such as air and water pollution, electricity generation, transport, industrial development and agriculture. The close links between these policy areas calls for a policy mix of instrument which would meet multiple objectives for example some waste facilities could generate energy and at the same time cut down on final residue to be landfilled. Promoting a circular consumption model and encouraging material recycling could as well cut down on resource overexploitation and associated pollution.

Box 2.7. **San Francisco's zero-waste policy**

In 2002, San Francisco set a goal of 75% diversion by 2010 and Zero Waste by 2020. The city's comprehensive Environment Code Exit, created in 2003, is based on the Precautionary Principle Exit. The city's Mandatory Recycling and Composting Ordinance Exit, passed in 2009, requires all of San Francisco to separate recyclable materials, compostable materials and landfilled trash.

San Francisco implemented an innovative "Fantastic Three" residential curb side collection programme that includes separate collection of commingled recyclables; compostable materials, including all food scraps, food-soiled paper and yard trimmings; and any remaining trash in three separate bins with various size and rate options. Zero Waste is sending nothing to landfill, incineration or high temperature technologies. We create policies and programmes that reduce waste, and increase access to recycling and composting. SF Environment is doing everything we can to make it happen.

The city implemented the first and largest urban food scraps composting collection programme in the United States, covering both commercial and residential sectors. San Francisco has collected more than a million tons of food scraps, yard trimmings, and other compostable materials and turned it into compost that is used by local farmers and wineries in Napa and Sonoma counties. San Francisco diverted nearly 80% diversion in 2012 – the highest rate of any major U.S. city

Source: EPA (2016), "Zero Waste Case Study: San Francisco, CA", www.epa.gov/transforming-waste-tool/less-waste-case-study-san-francisco-ca.

Need for SMW policy frameworks and data collection at the metropolitan scale

A critical issue which Metro Cebu should urgently address is a lack of effective policy co-ordination across 13 LGUs. As identified by the JICA Roadmap study, a comprehensive study and formulation of a masterplan for solid waste management at the metropolitan scale needs to be prioritised. The proposed MCDA bill makes provision for the establishment of public commissions of which Solid Waste Management is included. Facilitating trans-boundary solid waste management issues and waste management planning to ensure efficiency and cost reductions can be best assigned to such an entity. One of the most urgent actions to be taken is to develop a mechanism to collect data on municipal solid waste (waste generated, composted, recycled, disposed at landfill sites, etc.) and make reliable forecast to inform policymakers.

Changing households' and industries' behaviour

The rising population along with the increasing material consumption in Cebu has and will further increase municipal waste generation due to the linear consumption pattern currently observed in the metro area. The waste generated per capita in Metro Cebu as pointed out in chapter one is estimated to rise from 0.436 in 2010 to 0.8 kg/day in 2050 (JICA and MCDCB, 2015). Since urban lifestyle, resource consumption and income status are factors contributing to the rising household waste generation, targeted efforts at controlling household behaviour needs to be considered to minimise waste in this regard.

A broad range of policy instruments has been identified to influence household behaviour (Table 2.5). These policy instruments offer varied incentives to promote environmentally responsive consumer choices among households whether through economic instruments, direct regulation or information based measures.

Table 2.5. **Instruments targeting household behaviour to reduce MSW**

Economic instruments	
Charges	Unit-based waste charges on volume or weight
Subsidies/grants	Refund for recyclable bottles
Direct Regulation	
Performance technology standards	Minimum recycled content standard
Bans/Mandates	Bans on presence of certain products. Take back requirements
Information-based measures	
Labels	Label indicating recyclable items and products manufactured from recycled materials
Information campaigns and education programmes	Tips on how to recycle and dispose waste (3 R's)
Supply measures	Provision of waste collection and recycling services

Source: OECD, (2014a).

Promoting waste separation at source

Promoting waste separation at source is the most important policy target to effectively implement the "3Rs" (OECD, 2016). Cebu City has a policy of "no segregation, no collection", which compels waste sorting at source with penalties for non-compliance. The following categories have been used for waste separation: biodegradable, recyclable, residual, special waste and plastics. The Cebu City ordinance 2031, introduced in 2010, provides the legislative backing for the policy. The benefit for sorting at source should enable a drastic reduction in the final quantity of residue needed to be permanently landfilled. The policy is expected to influence residents' behaviour to achieve impact in the waste sector to advance sustainable use of scant environmental resources. Optimism of this nascent policy lends to a favourable prognosis that Cebu would better be able to achieve sustainable resource and solid waste management. However, progress to date has been slow, partly due to low public awareness and understanding of the need to separate garbage at the household level into different containers and pay for services. While compliance among commercial establishments is observed to be higher, the implementation of the policy has had its setbacks especially among households (Semilla, 2016). The enforcement strategy seems problematic; in Cebu City, the Environmental Sanitation Enforcement Team (CESET) has been established to supervise the Barangay Environmental Officers (BEO), who fine residents who fail to segregate and adhere to proper sanitation. However, CESET is under-resourced to deliver on its mandate.

Advancing the "no segregation, no collection" agenda requires concerted efforts. A variety of instruments could be combined to influence residents' behaviour, including awareness campaign, technical and financial support. For example, a potentially effective approach is to provide households with colour coded disposal bins/receptacles and temporary storage facilities. Currently, institutions and centres have such colour-coded receptacles and strongly encourage using them on their premises. Such a practice would be also effective for households, as they would have visual cues to direct waste discard through colour coded bins.

Ensuring proper waste pricing

The analysis undertaken indicates that, waste collection is heavily subsidised in Metro Cebu. For example in 2000, revenue from garbage fees accounted for only 6.3% of total expenditure spent on waste management (IGES, 2012). In the past years, subsidies on waste management had reached a tune of PHP 47 million (Premakumara et al, 2014). This deprives the LGUs of the needed funds that could have been invested on other social interventions or infrastructural developments. In Cebu City for instance, according to the city ordinance 1361 which is currently under review, garbage fees are paid quarterly and fixed for majority of businesses while some business and all residential houses are charged based on floor area.

Metro Cebu should consider an effective waste pricing in line with the polluter pays principle which makes the environmental cost of waste more visible to the consumer, thereby creating the economic incentives for households and businesses to reform waste disposal. Such a measure can provide the financial resources needed for service improvement and shift the financial burden away from municipalities. Metro Cebu would need to reform its waste pricing mechanism to be better resourced to improve and expand upon its waste collection service. Simultaneously, a stronger enforcement of the anti-littering regulation must be enforced to accompany pricing reforms and deter indiscriminate disposal and illegal dumping across the metro area.

In OECD metropolitan areas, different waste pricing systems are used centred on a flat rate or a variable fee based on either unit pricing (pay as you throw [PAYT]) or on municipal waste management cost. In Japan, Korea and Switzerland where a number of households are subject to the PAYT, significant positive impacts have been seen as waste generated has decreased. An OECD study indicates that PAYT reduces waste generation between 16% and 20% (OECD, 2014a). Likewise, volume charging for mixed waste also saw increases in rate of household composting. PAYT is more suitable for a door to door collection service and achieves its objective of waste reduction best if combined with an effective recycling programme. PAYT is an effective approach for which Metro Cebu would need to experiment with and based on evaluation of outcomes upscale to cover the whole jurisdiction. It can be an appropriate strategy to nudge residents to recycle more.

There appears to be great potential for further privatisation of SWM services in Mega Cebu, but several key impediments/obstacles remain, such as creating more government incentives, public awareness about the benefits and costs associated with providing proper SWM services and limited financing available for SWM privatisation.

Enhancing awareness and community involvement

Individuals often are unaware of how their consumption produces waste and generates external cost. Hence, they are inclined to generate more than is socially optimal. Awareness and educational campaigns would need to be strengthened in Metro Cebu to enlighten and constantly remind residents of their responsibilities and the environmental impact of their consumption patterns. Civil Society Organisations (CSOs) should be seen as key partners in this, as they can complement local government action to support sustainable consumption objectives. The educational campaign through innovative yet impactful messages should aim to target each demographic group and ensure effective household waste practices. Furthermore, residents can be encouraged through information outreaches to reconsider lifestyles and consumption patterns by buying eco–products or reusable items such as shopping bags. To this effect, LGUs should support community groups or associations which promote such environmentally friendly lifestyles. At the same time industries and manufacturers should be actively brought on board to provide ample information through proper labelling of products to guide consumers on best disposal methods.

Community involvement in waste management can be broadened in other areas than composting and improved in Cebu. This ranges from collecting feedback on service satisfaction to involvement in waste separation at source, involvement in recycling and opportunities for employment of low income households in giving new life to waste materials. Practical experiences involve vocational training in use of recycled items such as plastics in making new useful items. Already in a few barangays this is being done but would need to be encouraged more.

Creative industries in Metro Cebu could support efforts aimed at developing a market for recycled items. Encouraging a stronger market for both supply and demand of recycled products, for example products from the Trash initiatives could offer employment and raise revenue for low income households engaged in these activities. Furthermore, encouraging online classifieds or marketplaces offering opportunities for residents to sell or exchange items they do not need on the internet could be a useful approach towards awareness creation on using material over their life-cycle.

Encouraging producers to take responsibility

An interesting option to minimising waste is to introduce the concept of Extended Producer Responsibility (EPR) which encourages materials to be looked at from the wider perspective of life-cycle analysis rather than the preoccupation with "end of use" disposal. In this case, manufacturers and retailers also have a role to play, as Extended Producer Responsibility (EPR) could be a useful mechanism to help minimise waste to be landfilled (Box 2.8). EPR would work best when there is a national policy that provides the legislative framework for the EPR programme as done in many countries such as Germany, Korea, Japan and France and that which makes EPR mandatory rather than voluntary. EPR could benefit Cebu and the Philippines as a whole in their waste minimisation effort through the product-take back scheme and by stimulating eco-design activities that ensures minimum packaging content for consumer products. At the same time, EPR could help to shift some of the financial burden for waste management from municipalities and taxpayers to producers, as well as to reduce the public costs of waste management (ibid).

Box 2.8. **Extended Producer Responsibility (EPR)**

The OECD defines Extended Producer Responsibility as a policy approach under which producers are given a significant responsibility – financial and/or physical – for the treatment or disposal of post-consumer product (OECD, 2016). This responsibility could provide incentives to promote product design for the environment and support the achievement of public recycling and materials management goals. In order to realise EPR, policy makers have a four broad categories of EPR instruments to consider. These typically address specific aspects of waste management, and can be implemented concurrently:

Product take-back requirements. Take-back policies require the producer or retailer to collect the product at the post-consumer stage. This objective can be achieved through recycling and collection targets of the product or materials and through incentives for consumers to bring the used product back to the selling point.

Economic and market-based instruments. These include measures such as deposit-refund schemes, Advanced Disposal Fees (ADF), material taxes, and upstream combination tax/subsidy (UCTS) that incentivise the producer to comply with EPR. In South Korea for example, ADFs are imposed on importers and producers of products that are hazardous and more difficult to recycle.

Regulations and performance standards such as minimum recycled content. Standards can be mandatory or applied by industries themselves through voluntary programmes.

Accompanying information-based instruments. These policies aim to indirectly support EPR

Box 2.8. **Extended Producer Responsibility (EPR)** *(continued)*

programmes by raising public awareness. Measures can include imposing information requirements on producers such as reporting requirements, labelling of products and components, communicating to consumers about producer responsibility and waste separation, and informing recyclers about the materials used in products.

Source: OECD (2014b), "The State of Play on Extended Producer Responsibility (EPR): Opportunities and Challenges", www.oecd.org/environment/waste/global%20forum%20tokyo%20issues%20paper%2030-5-2014.pdf.

Managing waste collections and disposal systems

Despite the growing policy practices to minimise waste, the amount of waste generated in Metro Cebu is expected to increase for the time being. This underscores the most pressing need to address issues of efficient management of landfill sites and other waste collection processes.

Effective management of landfills

The land scarcity of Metro Cebu points to a need to strategically ensure judicious land use especially in terms of waste treatment and disposal. Currently among 13 LGUs in Metro Cebu, only four cities (Cebu, Consolacion, Talisay and Mandaue) have sanitary landfill sites. There are at least three open dumpsites which are not complying with the law RA9003. The poor compliance at the local level with regards to their solid waste mandate is evident not only in Metro Cebu but at the national level as well where only 14% of the more than 1 500 local government units (EMB-7, 2015) have proper disposal facilities. Coincidentally, the Central Visayas Region has the highest number of open dumpsites in the Philippines. The lack of pro-active planning, insufficient investment in landfill and resource recovery facilities and ineffective management of illegal open dumpsite, combined with the rapid increase of waste generation, has led to the Inayawan landfill site in Cebu City operating beyond capacity (Box 2.9). Moreover, considerable proportion of waste generated in Metro Cebu may remain at interim disposal facilities or end up in illegal dumpsites, leading to health and environmental complications. According to the JICA study, out of 1113 tonnes of waste generated in Metro Cebu, only 486 tonnes (44%) is disposed in sanitary landfills. While 350 tonnes (34%) goes to MRFs for material recovery, considerable amounts are not utilised and disposed either in sanitary landfills or other locations. Besides, 122 tonnes (11%) is estimated to be disposed at illegal dumpsites (JICA and MCDCB, 2015).

Box 2.9. **Inayawan landfill site, Cebu City**

Funded and constructed by the Japan International Corporation Agency in 1998 at a cost of P312 million, the Inayawan Sanitary Landfill had a planned lifespan of 7 years (JICA, 2001). This landfill was meant to properly dispose of the collected waste in Cebu City, taking into account the increasing population. The construction of this landfill also brought secondary benefits such as the creation of a union of scavengers that would be allowed to operate on the landfill (thereby extending the lifespan of the site). However, 6 years after its supposed closure, the site was only partially closed in 2011 and up till 2016, continued to be operational.

Box 2.9. **Inayawan landfill site, Cebu City** *(continued)*

In 2016, the Court of Appeals ordered the City to permanently shut the landfill down due to the excessive amounts of waste being dumped there, as well as the related environmental and health concerns. In June 2016, the landfill received an average of 456 tonnes of garbage daily but by August the same year, this amount had increased to 600 tonnes. Health concerns are abound; the site has ceased operations as a sanitary landfill a long time ago and has since become a dumpsite, and complaints from nearby residents of the stench are commonplace. The landfill has also experienced several fires, most notably in April 2009 when the Cebu City Council declared a state of calamity in order to allocate funds to those affected by the smoke. In 2016, the Department of Environment and Natural resources (DENR) cited issued notice of violation stating Cebu City had violated 36 conditions of DENRs Environmental Compliance Certificate. The city was taking measures to address the violations such as enzyme spraying and covering with top material.

The JICA roadmap study for sustainable solid waste management recommends that Cebu undertakes and implements an environmentally sustainable closure of the Inayawan Sanitary Landfill. The recommendation is important to reduce the potential hazard the site could pose to society.

Source: JICA (2001), "Metro Cebu Development Project (II)", www.jica.go.jp/english/our_work/evaluation/oda_loan/post/2001/pdf/e_project_57_all.pdf.

For effective management of landfills, in a short term, it is critically important to avoid potential hazard any landfill sites could pose to society. In particular, with threat to climate change and natural disasters, it is crucial for Cebu to reduce the susceptibility of its waste disposal facilities to suffering large-scale health epidemic outbreaks following floods or storms from the accidental, uncontrolled release of untreated sewage, solid and liquid wastes, and toxic substances mixing with flood waters in their immediate environment. In a longer term, Metro Cebu needs to address the issue of illegal landfill sites (e.g. open dumpsites); either close them or make them comply with regulations to keep operation. In the case of Inayawan landfill site, it is essential to start developing a strategy on the use of the site after closure. The Hiriya landfill site in Tel Aviv offers a good example (Box 2.10). Finally, pro-active planning for future sanitary landfills is essential for Metro Cebu's long-term waste management strategy. Such planning needs to be included in comprehensive solid waste management policies at the metropolitan scale. As already discussed, the metropolitan governance arrangement plays a pivotal role in determining the success of such planning.

Box 2.10. **Ariel Sharon Park: from a landfill site to an eco-park**

The Hiriya landfill site in Tel Aviv received waste from 1952 to 1999. During its operations, the landfill grew to a height of 70m and contained 17 million cubic metres of waste (Park Sharon, n.d.). By its final year of operation in 1998, the landfill was receiving 3 000 tons of household waste per day before the Ministry of Environmental Protection made the decision to transform the landfill site into a transfer station in 1999. The immense amount of garbage in the landfill site also attracted flocks of birds such that at one point, the birds were a hindrance to the safe landing of airplanes landing and taking off from the nearby Ben-Gurion airport. The Dan Municipal Sanitation Association began rehabilitation works in 2001, intending to convert the landfill site into a green park. An international architectural competition was thus held in 2004, citing importance that designs should not try to flatten the original dumpsite mountain. Instead, the mountain should act as a focal point, encouraging visitors to the park to learn more about waste management. Finally, renowned landscape architect Peter Latz was awarded the challenging task of redesigning the landfill site.

Officially inaugurated in 2014 and named after then-Prime Minister, Ariel Sharon, the Ariel

Box 2.10. **Ariel Sharon Park: from a landfill site to an eco-park** *(continued)*

Sharon Park is slated to be larger than New York's Central Park when fully completed in 2020. There are currently walking and cycling trails, a recreational pond, a tiny zoo and picnic areas in the western section of the park known as Menachem Begin Park. In addition, there is an agricultural school, a farm, and a recycling centre that offers tours for groups. By 2020, the 2 000 acre park will offer a 50 000 seat amphitheatre, making the transformed dumpsite a venue for concerts (Tourist Israel, 2017). The park is the largest new urban park built in the last century in the world, and will act as a green lung of Israel's densely populated coastal plain (Tourist Israel, 2017), serving inhabitants of Tel Aviv and other neighbouring cities (Tourist Israel, 2017). Offering free entry to visitors, Ariel Sharon Park is an ecological masterpiece offering 360-degree views of Tel Aviv and central Israel.

Source: Park, S. (n.d.), www.parksharon.co.il/html5/?_id=9543&did=10116&g=9054&sm=9543 (accessed 24 February 2017); Tourist Israel (2017), "Ariel Sharon Park", www.touristisrael.com/ariel-sharon-park/702/ (accessed 24 February 2017).

Effective management of material recovery facilities and other waste treatment facilities

LGUs should aim to improve the conditions of their material recovery facilities (MRF). According to Section 32 of RA 9003, each Barangay should have a MRF for final sorting, segregation composting and recycling. Yet as at 2011, out of 349 barangays only 101 (29%) had operational MRFs. This is mainly due to lack of financial resources as well as inadequate capacities of barangays to plan and operate such facilities.

An option is to allow for shared MRFs for several barangays. Instead of small-sized facilities, investments would need to be directed into an environmentally friendly large scale MRF which has a higher capacity to process waste for a given number of barangays. Consolidating the MRFs produces value for money and helps introduce technological innovation and efficiency which is not viable on small scales. Though this could temporarily create job losses for some workers in this area, these people can be shifted to other associated areas where opportunities would be created in material collection, processing and manufacturing. These opportunities created will arise from waste diversion that is from material per ton recycled. For example it is estimated that while landfilling creates one job per 1 000 tons of waste, recycling creates between six to thirteen jobs per 1 000 tons with plastic having the highest job potential followed by paper and lumber (Goldstein, 2014).

Furthermore, given the capacity challenges in developing and operating an LGU-specific waste management facility, it may be useful for Metro Cebu to consider a shared facility for several LGUs. For example, two such facilities could be planned, one for the LGUs in the north, the other for the LGUs in the southern part of Metro Cebu. Such inter-LGU co-operation is a central concern of the proposed MCDA and the public commissions on solid waste management, and thus should be further discussed in a comprehensive solid waste management plan for Metro Cebu.

Improving access to waste collection services

Data analysis in Chapter one indicates that only 65% of households have access to waste collection service. Increasing access of households to waste collection services would be essential to avoid indiscriminate waste disposal, increase segregation, reduce pollution and avoid waste induced flood from blocked drainages in the metro area. An OECD study found that the collection system in a given community plays an important role in determining separation rates (OECD, 2014c). Hence improving quality of service and making collection regular, as well as reaching out to hitherto out of service areas in waste collection would contribute to a responsive attitude from households. Bicarts, a bicycle with a large waste container situated in the middle, may be convenient to reach out to neighbourhoods in mountainous areas or areas with insufficient road networks. Such method in waste collection is already being used in Metro Cebu (Ancog et al, 2012). A dual system of waste collection involving door-to-door and drop-off-systems should be combined in the barangays to allow for efficient collection of segregated waste based on convenience and practicality.

Given the limited administrative and technical capacity of barangays in Metro Cebu, an option is to explore more public-private co-operation in providing higher-quality household and commercial collection, separation and recycling, and final disposal services. To date, there have been a number of contracts signed among LGUs such as cities of Naga, Carcar, Lapu-Lapu, and Minglanilla with a private firm (FDR-IRRMI) to manage their solid waste collection, recycling and composting, and final disposition systems. It now runs the first integrated resource recovery facility in the City of Naga, which handles over 130 tons of solid waste a day.

Recovering energy from waste

Waste-to-Energy systems offer a cost effective role in marrying waste reduction efforts with energy generation in Metro Cebu. Increasing potential exists especially through harnessing biogas from landfills or other special wastes as well as generating electricity from residue. While some municipal solid waste is considered renewable others are not. Municipal waste can be categorised as either renewable or non-renewable depending on whether the waste is biodegradable or not (IEA, 2016a). These options could offer additional revenue streams for the LGUs while diverting waste from landfills.

Waste-to-energy (WTE) can drastically reduce the amount of residue to be landfilled by 95% and even with that the bottom ash (residue) could be used as construction material (WMR 2009; Cheng and Hu 2010). However, WTE from incineration remains a contested issue in Cebu due to opposition and protest from some local organisations and residents. A critical prerequisite to this is the employment of environmentally friendly technology which should significantly cut down on emissions to acceptable standards. Central and local governments working together can enforce emission standards and allow WTE facilities with improved pollution control technologies to operate. This should be well backed by extensive consultations and educational campaigns. Furthermore, the national Clean Air Act needs to be revisited and accurate information disseminated.

In OECD, between 2000 and 2015 the energy generation from biofuels and waste increased by 62% and accounted for 55.1% of renewable energy supply in 2015 (IEA, 2016a). Renewable municipal waste alone accounted for 2.9% of OECD renewable energy supply. In Sweden, 50% of household waste is incinerated to produce energy, with pollutants being filtered through a robust process involving dry filters and water (Freden, 2015). Comparing the Philippines to a select number of contemporaries in Southeast Asia in terms of energy production from biofuels and waste, it can be seen that there is huge potential for the country to catch up with its peers by increasing energy generation from waste (Figure 2.3). In Metro Cebu, considering the capacity and economic feasibility of such waste-to-energy facilities it might be necessary for waste volumes to be combined from different LGUs to make up for sufficient volume input. Further studies are also needed to establish that the calorific value of the waste generated for all seasons is not below 7mj/kg, beyond which waste is not suitable for incineration (Rand et al., 2000).

Figure 2.3. **Energy production from biofuels and waste (*ktoe*)**

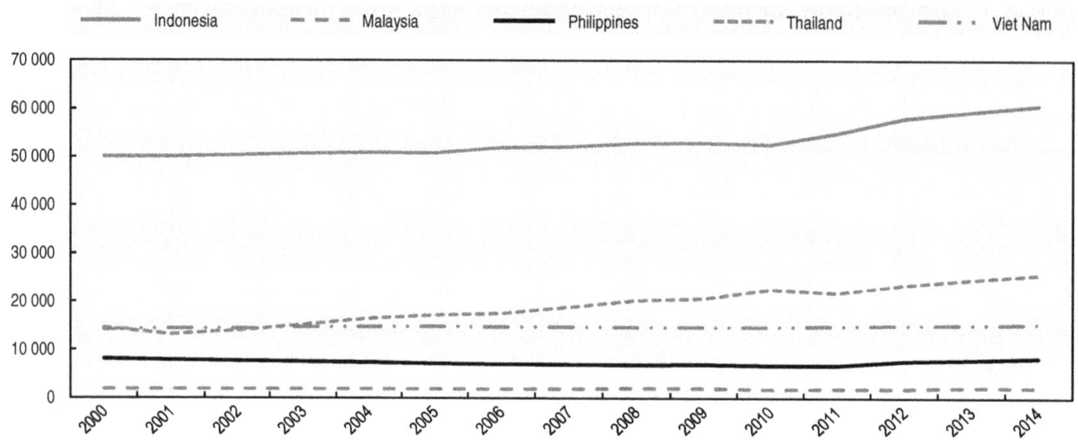

Source: IEA (2017).

Promoting circular economy in manufacturing industries

This section assesses Metro Cebu's policies for greening industries, in particular manufacturing industries. Cebu has witnessed strong growth in the secondary sector which is driven by manufacturing and construction (Chapter 1). The current challenge remains with attracting more industries and reducing the negative environmental externalities arising from the operation of the industries. As seen in Chapter 1, industry accounts for 36% of energy consumption and 38% of GHG emissions in Cebu City (Ostojic et al., 2013). Air and water pollution from industries is an immediate threat and will have a strong impact on liveability and quality of life of the people in Metro Cebu.

Promoting greener micro, small and medium enterprises

In the Philippines, 99.5% of establishments by enterprise size are MSMEs (89.9% micro, 9.2% small and 0.4% medium) while only 0.5% can be classified as large (PSA, 2015). MSMEs contribute to about 70% of employment. Therefore, the activities of MSMEs have been identified to negatively impact the environment and could erode their long term economic development. Though progress has been made, there is still a need for more sensitisation and support mechanisms to ensure compliance and commitment to environmental standards.

To promote greening measures and strategies among MSMEs, a number of initiatives have already been undertaken at the national level. The German Federal Ministry for Economic Cooperation and Development (BMZ) together with the Department of Trade and Industry (DTI) as lead executing agency implemented the Promotion of Green Economic Development (ProGED) project. The three year project, which commenced in 2013 aimed to improve the competiveness of micro, small and medium enterprises (MSMEs) to enable an adoption of climate-smart and environmental friendly approaches in their value chain coupled with market system development (DTI, u.d). The approach of the project was through policy advice, the facilitation of multilevel political and economic framework conditions to mainstream green initiatives and business promotion and matchmaking. Cebu Province was one of the selected pilot regions and lessons learnt are intended to be scaled up on a national scale. Though the focus of the pilot was on helping the tourism sector adopt climate-smart and environmental friendly strategies it was expanded to include other sectors. A major success of the project has been the adoption of greening practices in operations of enterprises, enjoyments of lower production costs and increased sales (GIZ, 2016). Another project launched in Cebu was the SMART Cebu which was implemented by a consortium of European and Philippine organisation with the purpose of encouraging cleaner production and eco-products and assisting MSME gain access to green markets in Europe and Asia (Switch-Asia, 2014).

Metro Cebu, together with the Province, has an important role to scale up or extend such knowledge and practices to MSMEs in other sectors which could not benefit from such initiatives. It would also be important for sustainability mechanisms to be put in place for LGUs or even business associations to continue on with such programmes after donor support has ended. Furthermore, regular engagements with associations of MSMEs would be necessary to better develop mechanisms for adoption of less polluting and environmentally friendly approaches in their work since such technologies and approached keep evolving. This could help mobilise the needed support to ensure Cebu in all its spheres remain on an environmentally sustainable path. Greening industries is not only beneficial to residents but for the business as well, since cost reductions increases the economic returns to the business whilst at the same time conserves the environment to mitigate effects of climate change.

Promoting greener economic clusters/zones

The national government has established the Philippines Economic Zone Authority (PEZA) which is tasked to promote investments, offer assistance, register, incentivise and facilitate the commercial operations of investors in export-oriented manufacturing and service facilities inside designated areas (PEZA, 2016a). The fiscal and non-fiscal incentives given to registered economic zones are highlighted in Table 2.6. Out of the 358 registered PEZA Economic Zones (EZ) nationwide, 39 (11%) are located in the Province of Cebu (PEZA, 2016b)

Some Economic Zones in Metro Cebu such as the Cebu Business Park have shown a greater green potential through its solid waste management practices, green gas emission management and lighting system. Policy makers in Metro Cebu can through incentives encourage industries to undertake resource and energy assessments and audits to identify areas of the production process that can be enhanced to reduce carbon emissions and energy intensity. Industrial assessments provide a picture of the current situation with regards to resource use and indicate areas to be improved with a clear understanding of the return on investment. Businesses aiming to reduce cost and maximise revenue could harness this opportunity to achieve above-mentioned objective while contributing to an environmentally worthy goal. UNIDO working with manufacturing industries through this assessment has yielded tremendous cuts in production related cost and reduction in adverse environmental impacts. UNIDO (2016) showcases an example where an initial assessment identified the need for the Lao Agro Industry Company to replace rather than retrofit an old boiler. The new boiler installed generated five tons of steam per hour compared to the old which generated two to three tons per hour. Taking advantage of savings, improved efficiency and increased capacity allowed the company to invest in new products for export, thereby allowing it to employ more people in the locality and increase its revenue (ibid).

In addition, a green industrial grading system can also be developed as a comprehensive mechanism to assess the environmental performance of industries in Metro Cebu. Different parameters such as energy intensity, solid waste, water and resource use among other could be scored with points awarded to companies. A comprehensive consultative process should be employed in the development of this scheme, as well as leadership and partnership opportunities offered to allow lagging industries to benefit from the knowledge and experiences of successful ones.

Also, considering that the manufacturing process of industries is sometimes inefficient leading to waste, industries would need to consider embracing an ecological perspective to manage the sector's excesses and by-products which would normally go waste. An approach policy makers in Cebu could adopt as part of safeguarding the environment is through eco-industrial parks and industrial symbiosis. Policies towards industrial symbiosis (IS) can be an effective means to reduce waste and promote reuse among industries in Metro Cebu especially when applied to Economic Zones. Industrial symbiosis, a value chain approach for eco-innovation, helps create a cyclical manufacturing loop for industries in close geographical proximity to exchange by-products (Gibbs, 2008; Chertow and Park 2016). Industrial symbiosis deems the by-product/waste of one industry as resources/inputs for the other allowing for innovation, cost reductions, increased revenues and above all, additional economic prospects in an environmentally conscientious manner. Symbiotic networks can develop spontaneously or be planned.

Kalundborg, Denmark is a pioneer of the industrial symbiosis concept and the approach has since spread globally with many cities facilitating its establishment among industries in its jurisdiction (Box 2.11). Kawerau, New Zealand is applying this concept to reduce its carbon footprint by closing the loop between its wood processing centres and its geothermal energy industries (Embracechange, 2014). Similarly, in Landskrona, Sweden, though an organic synergy existed among some operational industries, its full potential was realised in 2003 when the government assisted with an agreement to collaborate and catalyse IS development leading to the establishment of the Landskrona industrial symbiosis programme (Chertow and Park 2016). In this vein, an assessment for inter-industrial synergy needs to be undertaken and the result if positive fully pursued as an initiative under the MCDCB. Industrial symbiosis creates win-win outcomes among industries and the local governments involved. Some advantages emanating from this system aside reduced carbon emissions include:

- Reduced waste disposal cost for industries and waste diversion from landfill sites.
- Opening up new business opportunities, creating employment and offering economic growth for metropolitan areas (Desrochers, 2001).
- Welfare and social benefits as well as enhanced urban service delivery, e.g. electric energy generation (Albino et al, 2015).

Metro Cebu is well situated to implement an eco-industrial park based on symbiotic networks and should experiment with this. Various agents such as universities, associations, government institutions and industries are all important partners who have to be brought on board to accomplish specific roles towards the realisation of symbiotic networks. Metro Cebu would need to provide the enabling environment such as acting as facilitator/champion and the site allocation while universities engage in research and analysis needed for effective decision making (Table 2.6). Metro Cebu facilitating dialogue and collaboration among industries could serve as an opportunity for business leaders to discover synergistic possibilities and potential exchanges that could fuel the symbiotic networks.

The enabling environment created by cities in terms of the legal framework, green agenda and infrastructure provision will invariably contribute to the success or otherwise of the industries within it. It is therefore important that Metro Cebu continues the support to industries through policies aimed at skill development, green procurements, environmental technology diffusion, innovation hubs, and economic incentives.

Table 2.6. **Roles of agents in developing symbiotic network in eco-industrial parks**

Agents	Role
Government	• Local governments can implement planning ordinances for eco-industrial developments, involving the design, development and management of the site; • Economic incentives: tax cuts for adhering companies, funding brownfield/greenfield development, funding design teams; • Environmental regulation: water, air and waste (target/limits requirements; management process).
Government Institutions	• Economic incentives: financing and/or subsidies; • Part of design teams/management; • Material Flow Analysis/By-product or waste matching; • Informational and decision tools developer; • Intermediary to establish synergy; • Emission of permits.
Private associations (e.g. industry, business, environment)	• Intermediary to find "fitting" companies; • Network development and promotion; • Information exchange platform; • Mediation role; • Monitoring.
Universities	• Part of design teams; • Material Flow Analysis/By-product or waste matching; • Informational and decision tools developer; • Uncovering of linkages; • Economic/Environmental analysis of linkages; • Report of synergies.

Source: Costa, I. and P. Ferrão (2010), "A case study of industrial symbiosis development using a middle-out approach", *Journal of Cleaner Production*, Vol. 10/18, pp. 984-992.

Box 2.11. **Eco-industrial park**

One of the pioneers of eco-industrial parks is the Kalundborg Eco-industrial Park in Denmark. Rather than being the result of a carefully planned process, the eco-park developed gradually through co-operation by a number of neighbouring industrial companies. The main participating companies were a coal-fired power plant (Asnæsværket), a refinery (Statoil), a pharmaceutical and industrial enzyme plant (Novo Nordisk and Novozymes), a plasterboard factory (Gyproc), a soil remediation company (AS Bioteknisk Jordrens), and the municipality of Kalundborg through the town's heating facility.

The eco-park was initiated when Gyproc located its facility in Kalundborg to take advantage of the butane gas available from the Statoil refinery. This also enabled Statoil to stop flaring this gas.

Box 2.11. **Eco-industrial park** *(continued)*

Since then, the network has grown, and the participating companies are now highly integrated. For instance, surplus heat from the power plant is used to heat about 4 500 private homes and water for fish farming, and fly ash is supplied for cement production. Process sludge from fish farming is supplied to nearby farms as fertiliser. Novo Nordisk also supplies farms with surplus yeast from insulin production for pig food. The Statoil refinery supplies pure liquid sulphur from its de-sulphurisation operations to a sulphuric acid producer (Kemira). These exchanges are only part of the material flow of the Kalundborg eco-park, which has been estimated at a total of around 2.9 million tonnes a year including fuel gases, sludge, fly ash, steam, water, sulphur and gypsum (Gibbs, 2008). This industrial symbiosis has led to significant economic savings and has reduced environmental impacts.

After Kalundborg's experience, eco-industrial parks have emerged and multiplied across many OECD countries as a strategy for environmental sustainability. The case of Kitakyushu is similarly a good example. The Kitakyushu Eco-Town is an environmental industrial park that facilitates resource circulation and eco-industries. In 1997, the Japanese government recognised it as the first of its kind in Japan. The Eco-town is situated on 38.8 ha in the Hibikinada area of the Wakamatsu ward and comprises 29 industrial plants, 16 research facilities and a waste-to-energy (WTE) plant. Recycling ranges from plastic PET bottles, automobiles and electronic home appliances, to mixed construction waste, fluorescent tubes and office equipment, etc. All non-recyclable residuals are processed in the Kitakyushu Eco-Energy Co. Ltd.'s direct melting furnace situated in Eco-Town. This WTE plant recycles melted materials into slag and metals and provides 99 870 MWh of electricity to the adjacent recycling facilities, meeting all of Eco-Town's electricity demand. Eco-Town reduces 380 000 tonnes of CO2 per year through recycling and WTE. Since its launch in 1991, Eco-Town has created 1 418 jobs and aims to attract more companies and jobs to the area. In co-operation with businesses, government, academia and government, enclosed research facilities in Kitakyushu focus on practical research areas, in particular on higher value-added recycling activities.

The experience of Ulsan Eco-Industrial Park (UEIP), Korea which is a planned symbiosis network is a luminary case. To develop and implement the planned symbioses networks, a "research and development into business" (R&DB) framework was designed by the UEIP centre for the conversion of traditional industrial complexes into EIP. As a result of the framework in 2012, 13 symbiotic networks had been developed involving 41 companies (Behera et al., 2012). The diverse symbioses involves (ibid): i) Industrial waste incineration plant supplying steam to a paper mill ii) Municipal solid waste incineration plant supplying steam to a terephthalic acid manufacturing company iii) Steam swap network among four companies iv) Organic waste from 1.4-BDO process used as carbon source for denitrification in a municipal wastewater treatment plant (MWWTP) v) Conversion of high strength ammonia containing industrial wastewater to a nutrient for microorganisms vi) Steel plant supplying neutralising agent to a non-ferrous metal alloy industry vii) Reuse of waste aluminum chips as virgin raw material viii) Recycling of waste oil through a network employing an emulsified fuel oil (EFO) process ix) Recycling of waste oil through a network employing an emulsified fuel oil (EFO) process x) Production of value-added zinc flakes from zinc dust xi) Steam and carbon dioxide network between a zinc smelter and a paper mill xii) Recycling of waste activated sludge to be used as oil degradation material xiii) Steam network between a petrochemical company and a chemical manufacturing company. Aside from the financial gains industries derived, government policy instruments such as emission and waste reduction targets played a role in the success of the industrial symbiotic network.

Source: OECD (2010), *Eco-Innovation in Industry: Enabling Green Growth*, http://dx.doi.org/10.1787/9789264077225-en; Mengethetti and Nardin (2012), *Enabling industrial symbiosis by a facilities management optimization approach*, http://dx.doi.org/10.1016/j.jclepro.2012.06.002; OECD (2013), *Green Growth in Kitakyushu, Japan*, http://dx.doi.org/10.1787/9789264195134-en; Behera, S. K., Kim, J. H., Lee, S. Y., Suh, S., & Park, H. S. (2012), "Evolution of 'designed' industrial symbiosis networks in the Ulsan Eco-industrial Park:'research and development into business' as the enabling framework", *Journal of Cleaner Production*, Vol. 29, pp. 103-112.

Greening procurement

Public procurement can be a powerful tool to advance sustainable consumption and it has been recognised by the national government through its policy on green procurement (Executive Order No. 301). Local governments in Metro Cebu being huge consumers in terms of services and products can adopt green procurement targets and measures in their procurement action plan to increase the "market pull", and incentivise industries in the development of green solutions. DENR and the appropriate agencies should conduct regular or on demand training for LGUs, and consider instituting award schemes for good performances. Making procurement data openly available also reduces administrative burdens and encourages more uptakes. The private sector also has a similar role to play as well as ensuring the affordable and sufficient supply of eco-products and services.

Green/Eco labelling can support procurement because it sets the standards. The National Ecolabelling Programme – Green Choice Philippines (NELP-GCP) provides opportunities for Metro Cebu to ensure that its industries conform to environmentally friendly practices in their production process while consumers have access to varied healthy choices of products. The Seal of Approval to green products and services also offer increasing opportunities for MSMEs to assume competitiveness and penetrate international markets as the global demand for eco-labelled products have risen over the past years (Nielson, 2015). Metro Cebu would not necessarily have to develop its own system but rather encourage a closer partnership with Green Choice Philippines and increase public information campaigns for eco-labelling which would invariably encourage industries to green their production. Bangkok, Malaysia and Singapore are successful case studies that have witnessed tremendous improvements in local economy through eco-labelling (Azizan et al., 2014; SEC, 2017). Similarly Germany's environmental label "Blue Angel" has resulted in positive effects for firms and the localities within which they operate (Gertz, 2005).

Improving energy efficiency and promote renewable energy

This section examines Metro Cebu's policies for energy efficiency in buildings and renewable energy. Since residential consumption of electricity in Cebu is rising (DOE, 2016), urgent efforts are called for. In addition, there are some untapped opportunities to increase renewable energy generation in urban areas of Metro Cebu.

Improving energy efficiency

There have already been efforts to improve energy efficiency of electric appliances in Cebu by private and public institutions, including promotion of Compact Fluorescent Lamps (CFLs) and energy efficient appliances by the Visayan Electric Company. Cebu City government has demonstrated commitment to improving energy efficiency by retrofitting its city hall building with a central air conditioning system (Ostojic et al., 2013).

In addition to such existing efforts, more opportunities remain that can be tapped to further enhance energy efficiency. One option is to introduce energy classification for buildings. Since buildings have different energy consumption and performance intensities, conducting detailed analysis to identify specific building stock for energy classification and policy interventions would be necessary (IEA, 2016a). Most local governments demonstrate commitment and exemplary leadership by using public buildings as demonstration cases. LGU's could build their capacity or work with the private sector to deliver such energy assessments for classifying buildings within their jurisdictions. Such assessments could further help the LGUs take concrete actions to enhance energy efficiency. In Turin, Italy, when such an assessment was undertaken it came to light that one building segment, multifamily, high-rise buildings constructed before 1980 accounted for more than 70% of total residential floor area and about 70% of total energy consumption for heating (IEA, 2016a). This information allowed for better targeted energy saving measures. Also, In Paris, an energy information advisor has been providing support to building permit applicants for energy saving projects since 2008 covering issues on sustainable building renovation (Mairie de Paris, 2012).

Promoting public awareness for energy efficiency should be seen as vital for successful energy use reductions especially in encouraging energy-saving behaviour. Currently, across the Philippines and in Cebu many efforts are being made such as the Cebu Unplugged Campaign of the Visayan Electric Company (VECO, 2015). This awareness drive does not only focus on teaching practical energy conservation measures but also touches on water conservation as well, which is a prudent policy complementarity approach. Areas that can be strengthened include provision of information on labelling of appliance's energy efficiency to consumers. Furthermore, installation of smart meters that give households access to real-time information on their energy consumption could guide energy use. Moreover, integrating energy efficiency into classroom curricula could also help shape the behaviour of the youth to be more environmentally conscious of their actions. Much attention has been paid to this for which some OECD countries have collaborated to develop comprehensive educational programmes (OECD, 2016).

Lastly, energy efficiency reporting can provide an evidence-based approach to assess progress and inform decision making. Following the Department of Energy's Memorandum Circular Number 93-03-05 on Energy Consumption Monitoring, all industrial, commercial and transport establishments consuming more than one million fuel oil equivalent litres of energy annually are to submit Quarterly Energy Consumption Reports (QECR). Similarly, establishments consuming 2 million litres of energy, in addition to the QECR, are required to submit an Annual Energy Conservation Program Report (AECPR). Such efforts could be further expanded to a wider range of actors across different sectors, including both private and public sectors. Furthermore, the reported information should be used strategically for policy making.

Promoting green buildings

The Philippines has a national green building code that provides guidelines to improve the performance of buildings through efficient environmental and resource management. The code applies to new constructions and/or alterations with a specified minimum total gross floor area and it also adopts six performance standards (Table 2.7). The performance standards refer to areas where efficient practices are to be adopted. Enforcement of the national green building code is left to local governments; therefore LGU's in Metro Cebu should strongly enforce the green code not only through local ordinances but allocating the needed resources and effectively monitoring its implementation for improvement. Furthermore, in addition to regulation, green building ratings are also necessary to provide indication of energy and resource performance of the actual building.

In 2015, Mandaue City introduced a Green Building Ordinance (Box 2.12). This is a bold and remarkable step indicating a great commitment to realising sustainable objectives to which other LGUs are strongly encouraged to follow suit. MCDCB could co-ordinate with the various LGU's to develop incentives (financial, marketing and technical) for establishments to adhere to these guidelines. Metro Cebu has the benefit of tapping from the knowledge of the Philippines Green Building Council as well as learning from the experiences of the Quezon City government that has had an early start with implementation of green buildings since 2009. An important factor that this report would like to stress is that, in efforts to green buildings, Cebu should not only limit itself to new constructions but could also develop green standards for existing buildings to promote retrofitting to ensure an all-round resource and energy efficient metro area. The metro area could take advantage of this opportunity to develop the skill base of workers needed for the green building industries.

Table 2.7. **Green Building Code Standards in the Philippines**

Performance standards	Occupancy classification	Total gross floor areas
Energy efficiency	Residential dwelling: Condominium	20 000 sqm
Water efficiency	Hotel / resort educational:	10 000 sqm
Material sustainability	Institutional: hospital	10 000 sqm
Solid waste management	Business: office	10 000 sqm
Site sustainability	Mercantile: mall	15 000 sqm
Indoor environmental quality	Mixed occupancy 210 000 sqm	10 000 sqm

Source: Department of public Works and Highways (2015), "The Philippines Green Building Code", www.dpwh.gov.ph/dpwh/sites/default/files/laws_codes_orders/pgbcbooklet23march.pdf (accessed 4 December 2016).

Box 2.12. **Mandaue Green Building Ordinance**

As cities consume large amounts of electricity and therefore contribute to high carbon emissions, it is imperative to adopt green building measures. As of 2013, the Philippines did not have an energy law that mandated building owners to adopt green building measures (UNEP, 2013). However, it was also in 2013 when discussions surrounding the passage of an ordinance promoting greener building construction, operation and maintenance in Mandaue City, took place. Six months after the National Building Code of the Philippines was passed in June 2015, Mandaue City was exemplary in following the course of greener building construction, and passed the Green Building Ordinance. All public and private projects located in PUD areas within Mandaue City are obliged to comply with this ordinance (with heritage or cultural buildings and post-disaster infrastructure exempted), while other projects have the choice to comply with the ordinance, or not (IIEE, 2015). The city has also employed the use of the Building for Ecologically Responsive Design Excellence (BERDE) Green Building Rating System as a tool to measure, assess, verify and monitor the environmental performance of building projects in terms of management, use of resources and mitigation of emissions. The Green Building Ordinance requires building owners to use environmentally-friendly construction methods and resources that would have less damaging effects on the environment. For instance, the use of sunlight as a natural source of energy and ambient air for natural ventilation is encouraged. Expected benefits include more economic savings and a healthier environment. On the other hand, those who do not comply with this ordinance will be fined P5 000. To incentivise the construction of green buildings, building owners are provided Real Property tax (RPT) rebates, instalment payment of permit fees, Green Building Tax Credits and higher Floor Area Ration (FAR), all of which are dependent on the BERDE Certification of the buildings. In addition, the Asia-Pacific Economic Cooperation adjudged Mandaue City in 2015 as a low carbon model town for its programmes promoting low-carbon technologies that were well aligned to reduce growing energy consumption as well as carbon emissions.

Source: IIEE (Institute of Integrated Electrical Engineers of the Philippines, Inc.) (2015), "Smart Buildings and Green Standards", http://iiee.org.ph/wp-content/uploads/2015/12/fr4_sec-prs-2015-1127-iiee.pdf (accessed 21 February 2017); UNEP (2013), "Ozone2Climate Industry Roundtable", presentation by Amado P. de Jesus, Jr, www.unep.org/ozonaction/Portals/105/documents/network/PHILGBI.pdf (accessed 21 February 2017); APEC (2017), Policy Review for APEC Low-Carbon Model Town Phase 6: Mandaue City, Cebu Province, Philippines.

Furthermore, constant evaluations are needed to ensure compliance with the procedures as mainly stipulating them is not enough for developers to comply. Additionally, post occupancy evaluation of building is important as well since the feedback helps to design better infrastructure and behaviour solutions responsive to stakeholders' needs and environmental sustainability.

Greening informal settlements

The quality of housing stock sheltering all residents in Cebu need to be of high quality to contribute to a stronger urban resilience taking into consideration the frequency of natural hazards such as earthquakes, typhoons and storms in the Philippines. Though high quality buildings can be seen in various communities of the metro area, informal settlements with clusters of housing which do not meet minimum standards can be seen to house poor households often on government land and in areas along riverbanks and under the bridge. Although there is no official statistics on informal settlements or informal settlers, the National Statistics Office gathers data on households occupying lot rent-free without consent of the property owners, which is used as a proxy of informal settlers. In 2010, it was estimated that the incidence of such informal settlers in Cebu city was 6.24%, 6.98% in Mandaue and 3.20% in Lapu-Lapu (Philippine Statistics Authority, 2014). The poor layout and construction materials used render structures in these areas easily vulnerable to fires and floods yearly. The urban informal housing in Cebu is due to an inadequacy of affordable housing as well as high numbers of poor rural-urban migrants.

In the Philippines, there are two major laws that promote the settlement programme for informal settlers. These are the Local Government Code (1991) and the Urban Development and Housing Act (1992). It is the primary responsibility of LGUs to include the land intended for social housing in their land use plans and subsequent zoning regulations. Consequently, LGUs shall likewise identify areas for social housing programmes especially for the informal settlers from the urban poor sector to enable resettlement processes. Though some LGUS have sites reserved for relocation they have not been fully developed. The inability of LGUs to house the urban poor and the rising informal settlement necessitated a new approach. The Informal Settlements Upgrading Strategy for the Philippines was conceived as a policy framework to institute corrections and has the vision to transform such settlements across the country into formal residents in resilient, vibrant, and connected communities (HUDCC, 2014).

In Metro Cebu different approaches have been taken with mixed results by the various LGUs to address the issues of informal settlements including forced evictions, relocation and slum upgrading. Mandaue City and Talisay have benefitted from the Urban Partnerships for Sustainable Upliftment, Renewal, Governance, and Empowerment (UPSURGE) project in the past. The project sought to provide means through which strategies could be refined and incorporated as regular features of urban slum upgrading initiatives at all levels of government (Veneracion, 2010). The project had a strong community involvement and appears to have incorporated lessons from earlier slum upgrading projects (HUDCC, 2014).

The experiences of other cities could offer inspiration to Metro Cebu in its bid to improve housing conditions of slum dwellers. The Baan Mankong slum upgrading in Bangkok, Thailand, allows for the integration of slum dwellers into society through a demand-side approach (Archer, 2012). Baan Mankong is implemented by the Community Organisations Development Institute (CODI) and allows for community organisations established by informal settlement residents to be the managers in developing and planning solutions to their housing problems. CODI, aside offering technical assistance and support to the community organisations, also supports through infrastructure subsidies and direct loans to the communities to enable them negotiate and upgrade the infrastructure stock (CODI, 2011). Morocco's experience in managing to reduce its slum urban population from 9.2% in 1994 to 5.6 in 2014 (Morocco High Commission for Planning, 2015) through the slum upgrading project remains an example for emulation in the Philippines (Box 2.13). Partly due to the intervention of the project known as "cities without slums", the number of urban households owning houses shot up from 48.5% to 62.7% 2014 within that same period.

In addressing the housing challenges of Metro Cebu, the MCDCB should co-ordinate and ensure an adequate supply of social housing. Estate developers need to abide by the Urban Development and Housing Act of 1992 (RA7279) that states that developers of proposed subdivision shall develop socialised housing equivalent to 20% of total subdivision. While this law exists, the 20% allocation for socialised housing does not necessarily require the developer to build the units within the LGU. Mandaue City is the only exception, requiring the 20% allocation to be built within the LGU. This statutory provision has not been given the due recognition and should be fully adhered to. In Catalonia, Spain, it is mandatory that residential developments keep 30% of total amount of dwellings for both social housing (20%) and price-controlled housing (10%). These regulations are minimum percentages. For example, in 2010, due to the lack of social housing in Catalonia, several general plans were promoted which established much higher standards. The general plans called "*Àrees Residencials Estratègiques*" fixed a minimum standard of 50% of the residential dwellings for social housing, and also 50% of the land for public spaces (green spaces, roads and public facilities).

Addressing urban poverty through sustainable housing provision becomes an important avenue to green the lifestyle of marginalised groups and goes a long way towards allowing otherwise vulnerable groups to actively contribute productively to society. Pursing this ambition is in furtherance of the Sustainable Development Goals which metropolitan areas have been identified as key players.

Box 2.13. **Morocco Slum Upgrading Project**

Since the 1960s, Morocco has experienced a strong rural exodus. The share of the urban population increased sharply from 29% in 1960 to 60.3% in 2014 (HCP, 2015). Indecent housing and shantytowns flourished in large cities. In 2011, 2 million people resided in informal settlements without access to basic services (AFD, 2011). The very precarious buildings, barracks in sheet metal and other materials of recovery, multiplied in conditions of extreme insalubrity. While the slum population appeared to be declining in the first half of the 1990s, the severe droughts that hit Morocco repeatedly before 1990 and 2000 resulted in a new rural exodus, draining thousands of the most vulnerable families to the cities. Slums swelled at the same time as new settlements appeared.

In 1994, the Agence Nationale de Lutte contre l'Habitat Insalubre (ANHI) was created to fight against unhealthy housing which indicated a real political will to tackle the issue of insalubrious housing. Since 1998, the sector has been revitalised through the introduction of a tax linked to sales of cement, which will provide financial resources to the Fonds Social de l'Habitat (FSH), which provides a levy of 15 centimes/kg (Fawzi Zniber, 2015).

The "Cities without slums" programme ("*Ville Sans Bidonville*") was initiated in 2005 with the aim to eliminate informal settlements permanently. It involved 324 000 households (1.6 million inhabitants) in more than a thousand districts in 85 cities, of which nearly a third concentrated in the Casablanca agglomeration alone (AFD, 2011). The implementation and monitoring of the programme was entrusted to the Ministry of Housing and Urban Policy (MHUAE) and the public planner Al Omrane (AFD, 2013). The goal of the PVSB is to eliminate urban slums as a whole in reference to the Millennium Declaration and with the support of numerous donors and co-operation actors. The

Box 2.13. **Morocco Slum Upgrading Project** *(continued)*

funding of this programme was mainly provided by the contribution of households from the shantytowns (with the use of own funds and/or loans) and by various subsidies such as funds from the state budget, 41% of the resources of the FSH and the AFD (a EUR 15 million loan).

Half of the projects operations carried out by ANHI are aimed at the resettlement of slum dwellers. The serviced plots are handed over to the "shantytowns" for a very modest price, representing one third of the cost price and with highly staggered regulations. Only one condition is fixed: land previously occupied in an irregular area must be returned. In its second part, the project anticipates and prevents the creation of new slums by making new land viable and constructible. Some of the lots are then reserved for modest families, to offer them an affordable alternative to unsafe housing. Finally, the project aims at financial equilibrium in order to be reproducible and to have as great an impact as possible on the lives of the populations concerned. To compensate for the shortfall on lots sold at very low prices, the best-placed lots (for example, a business) are sold at market prices (Toutain, 2014). In 2016, the programme's assessment indicated the following success (MHPV, 2015):

- 56 towns had been declared without slums with more than 1 300 000 inhabitants now living in improved conditions;
- The majority of households are satisfied with their housing and are not ready to leave in the short term;
- Improved access to cooking and toilet facilities for households with a satisfaction rate of about 90%;
- Relative to the location of resettlement project a satisfaction rate of 61% was expressed.

Source: Toutain, O. (2014), "Financer le relogement des bidonvilles au Maroc", www.proparco.fr/jahia/webdav/site/proparco/shared/portails/secteur_prive_developpement/PDF/spd19/spd19_olivier_toutain_fr.pdf; AFD (2013), "Quartiers informels d'un monde arabe en transition: réflexions et perspectives pour l'action urbaine"; AFD (2011), "Villes sans bidonvilles au Maroc", www.afd.fr/home/projets_afd/villes/projets-cld/lutte-contre-exclusion/maroc-sans-bidonvilles; MHPV (2016), "Presentation and Advancement of the VSB Programme", www.mhpv.gov.ma/?page_id=956; Fawzi Zniber, M. (2015), "L'enjeu des bidonvilles au Maroc: conditions de développement et évolution actuelle", http://ecolearchicasa.com/wp-content/uploads/2015/11/Pr%c3%a9sentation2.pdf; HCP (2015), "Results of the 2014 Census", www.hcp.ma/downloads/rgph-2014_t17441.html.

Increasing renewable energy uptake in Metro Cebu

In the Philippines, energy prices are relatively higher than other countries in the region due to a successful removal of consumer energy subsidies. This is a remarkable step despite the numerous challenges faced in the subsidy reform process (IMF, 2013; ADB, 2016a). Nonetheless, ensuring access to reliable and affordable energy remain crucial issues for the national government to address. In this direction, the national policy on energy, Philippine Energy Plan (2012-2030) aims at providing "energy access for more". The plan has three major thrust under the Energy Reform Agenda (ERA) namely i) ensuring energy security through the development of indigenous energy ii) achieving optimal energy pricing and iii) developing sustainable energy system (DOE, 2011). The plan intends to aggressively pursue fossil fuel exploration in the country while also doubling installed renewable energy capacity by 2030 using 2011 as base year under a low carbon scenario. The strong pursuit of fossil fuel could hinder the achievements of the Philippines commitment to reduce carbon emissions to about 70% by 2030 relative to its BAU scenario (2000-30) as spelt out in the country's commitment to the COP21 agreement. That notwithstanding, the country also plans to strongly pursue a renewable energy drive which in 2015 accounted for 25% of gross power generation. Between 1990 and 2015 renewable energy uptake has increased by 75% from 11 959 Gwh to 20 963 Gwh (DOE, 2015). In terms of percentage of renewable energy as percentage share of total primary energy supply, the Philippines has the highest rate (38%) compared to other Southeast Asian countries such as Malaysia (3%), Thailand (20%), Viet Nam (31%) and even the OECD average of (10%) (Figure 2.4).

Figure 2.4. **Renewable energy percentage of TPES**

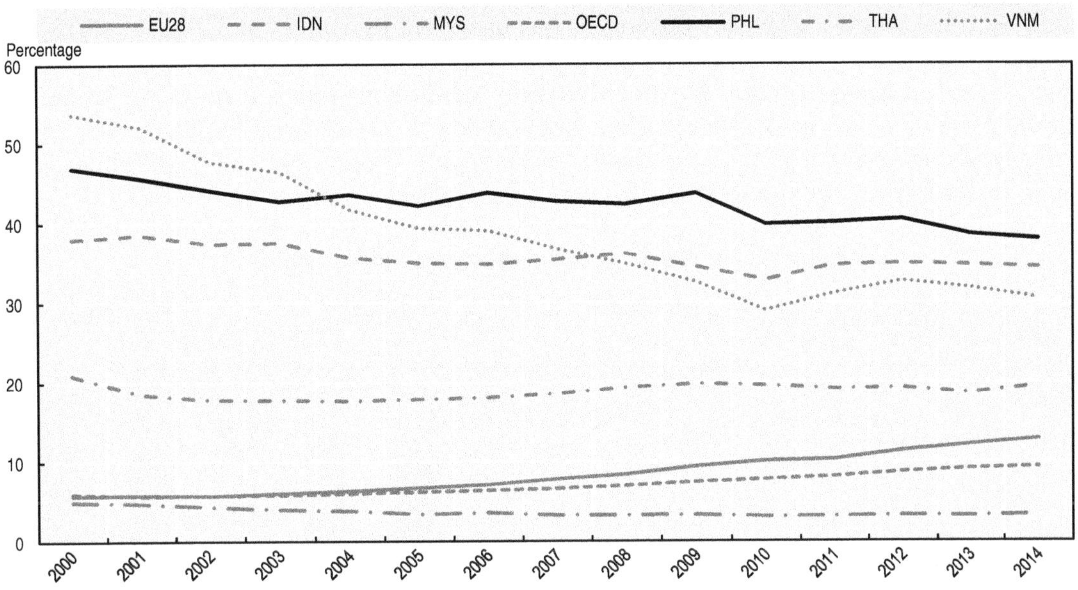

Source: OECD (2014d), Renewable Energy (indicator), http://dx.doi.org/10.1787/aac7c3f1-en

The National Renewable Energy Act of 2008 (Republic Act No. 9513) sets a strategic direction for clean energy in the Philippines with the aim of accelerating the development of the country's renewable energy resources to achieve energy self-reliance. The law envisages reductions in GHG emission while promoting economic growth, protecting health and safeguarding the environment. The act has received commendation for its forward looking and comprehensive approach (Maniego, 2012) which takes into accounts both on-grid and off grid systems such as Renewable Portfolio Standard (RPS), Feed-in Tariff (FIT), Net metering, Green Energy Option Program and Waste to Energy technologies (Aquino and Abeleda, 2014). Fiscal and non-fiscal incentives including tax exemptions, tax holidays, and financial assistance and charge exemptions are stipulated which indicate a stronger commitment for Renewable Energy (RE) at the national level. The Green Energy Option program is a mechanism to be established by the Department of Energy (DOE) which shall provide end-users the option to choose RE Resources as their source of energy. The DOE through the National Renewable Energy Program is charged with implementation based on outcomes derived from local and national RE planning. The Act stipulates financial support for RE through the Renewable Energy Trust Fund which is to fund research and development, however this is yet to materialise. The role of LGUs has been limited to the approval of construction permits for energy facilities, facilitating investments in energy and promoting energy efficiency (PPEI, 2013).

The well-articulated policy notwithstanding, implementation has been beset with the following challenges; high capital intensity, low competitiveness among market players, inaccessible financial packages and low social acceptability (Richmund, 2015). Regulation of the RE Sector has been beset with difficulties pertaining to the implementation of the Feed-in Tariff rules; the setting up of the Renewable Portfolio Standards; and the formulation of guidelines on net metering as well as the green energy option programme (ibid).

Per the breakdown of Visayas sub-grid generation by plant, Cebu province has witnessed increasing power generation from coal power plants (Figure 2.5). The data indicates that while coal power generation has increased by 540% from 2005 to 2015 the share of oil–based power generation in the province has drastically decreased (decreased by 75%). The share of hydro has however been dwindling- rising from 6 242 MHW in 2008 to 6 858 WMH in 2012 and falling to 4 476 MHW in 2015 (DOE, 2016). The share of renewable energy in the generation mix remains relatively low highlighting the importance of the Province to scale up its renewable energy production.

Figure 2.5. **Cebu Province power generation by plant**

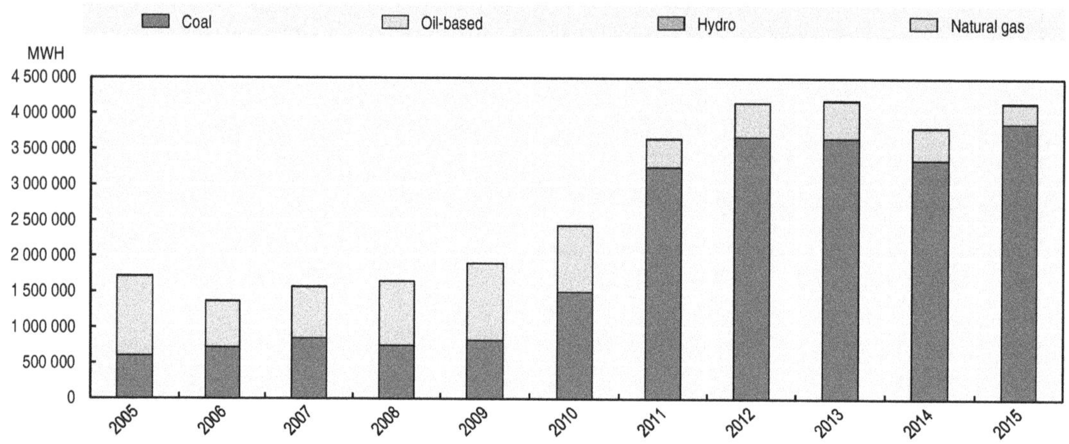

Note: The data includes natural gas and hydro however it is invisible due to the low generation.

Source: DOE (2016), "Philippines statistics 2015 gross generation by sub-grid", www.doe.gov.ph/sites/default/files/pdf/energy_statistics/power_statistics_2015_gross_generation_subgrid.pdf.

The Visayas power grid of which Cebu belongs relies on geothermal as the largest source of energy for electrification followed by coal fired power plants and diesel generating plants (Chapter 1). The geothermal energy is sourced from outside the Cebu province and is supplied by the Tongonan Geothermal power plant, in Leyte through submarines cables. Thanks to that, geothermal accounts for 46.40% of power supply. Hydro power for Cebu is sourced from three facilities located in the western side of Cebu Island (0.50MW Mantayupan Hydroelectric Power Plant in Barili, 0.50 MW Basak 1 Hydroelectric Power Plant and 0.750 MW Matutinao Hydroelectric Power Plant in Badian). Together, all the above sources boost the share of RE to about 54.73% of the energy mix for electrification. This share is higher than the OECD national average of 23% (IEA, 2016b).

Metro Cebu's energy assessment from the first chapter indicates a potential capacity for increased renewable energy supply. More renewable energy uptake is essential to help Cebu to confine to the past resource price shocks, energy poverty and high air pollution (UNEP, 2015). Moreover, development of decentralised energy power generation less reliant on the national grid offers Cebu the flexibility for greater adaptability considering the exposure to hazards such as storms. With diverse cleaner energy options such as solar, wind, geothermal, hydro and sea, the dependence on coal for electricity could be reduced. In Metro Cebu, three energy projects are in the pipeline:

- 0.62 MW FDR-Integrated Resource Recovery Management, Inc., Biogas Power Project in Naga City
- Amihan Energy Corp., Cebu City Wind Power Project
- 60 MW Menlo Renewable Energy Corp., Naga City Solar Power Project

Solar energy represents a major untapped RE opportunity in the urban areas of Metro Cebu. Average exposure to sunshine in Metro Cebu is about 5kwh/m2/per day which is one of the highest in the Philippines (The National Renewable Energy Laboratory, 2000). The continuous drop in the global price of PV systems by nearly 67% and the increased generating capacity of cells due to advances in technology make solar an attractive option either for utility-scale systems or rooftop systems (IEA, 2014).

In-situ installations on roof tops of building's and other surfaces are suitable options for the city to consider especially considering the scarce land resources. Roof top surfaces of public buildings such as schools, city halls and malls could serve as models for later up-scaling. Futureproofing Cebu for solar development would also require regulatory provisions such as stipulating all future constructions to have at least a minimum roof structural integrity suitable for solar installations. Furthermore, enforcement of the net metering policies in the renewable energy law (RA 9513), that enable consumers to sell to the grid excess energy generated could also serve as strong economic incentives for household investment in on-site solar energy generation while meeting renewable energy targets. An important direction for Metro Cebu would also be to craft a renewable energy vison and define strategies complaint with the national energy policy for itself. The DoE could support this pioneering initiative with technical capacity to enable the local government to contribute to the overall renewable energy programme of the country.

In some OECD cities, the passing of solar ordinances mandating installation of rooftop solar panels or solar water heaters have led to increases in the area of collectors. This has been combined with regulation, financial and information instruments. Solar obligations have been useful in providing a minimum share of solar powered energy in new constructions as well as renovated buildings. Increasingly municipalities and metro governments are playing a leading role through their regulatory and planning powers. For instance Barcelona is seen as the pioneer of solar regulation in Europe (Estif, 2017). As at 2008, solar thermal energy associated with the solar ordinance had seen drastic improvements. Solar collectors to heat water had risen from 2 500m2 in 1999 to 65 506 m2 (OECD, 2016c). In Los Angeles, USA, the city by the end of 2014 had the highest total solar PV installed in the United States with a capacity of 215MW direct current (ECRPC, 2016). Realising that residential rooftop solar systems could help meet renewable energy goals, the Los Angeles County has streamlined the permit process for small residential rooftop solar energy systems (CSE, 2016). Furthermore, a programme in the city called the CLEAN LA Solar has also been instrumental in allowing businesses and property owners to generate power for the city's grid by taking advantage of the vast unutilised rooftop spaces to install rooftop solar panels (Cleanlasolar, u.d). The programme has led to the production of energy within as opposed to generation and transmission from outside the city, thereby helping to create jobs and encourage private investment in clean energy. What has made Clean La Solar successful is the strong support from the Los Angeles City Council, the mayor, businesses, civic community as well as knowledge/academic partners such as the UCLA Luskin School of Public Policy.

LGUs in Metro Cebu should likewise, based on consideration of local factors, implement a solar ordinance to encourage solar installations in residential and commercial rooftops as well as policies aimed at zero-net energy home. Financial support packages (government support schemes) to install packages could be a useful incentive to encourage more households in the uptake of renewable energy.

Metro Cebu has implemented solar utility scale systems which created some controversy in the past. In 2015, about 1 000 trees were cut down in attempts by a private company to construct a solar farm, leading to the loss of premium and native tree species (Mangubat, 2015). This challenge is made more pressing due to the competing needs for scarce land resources and the environmental cost of developing in green areas. These trade-offs have to be carefully evaluated by policy makers for optimum outcomes. One pertinent issue to be taken into consideration is site selection. Utility scale site selection should have least impact on forest resources. Alternatively, compensation mechanisms could be factored as prerequisite for permits, such as afforestation and reforestation responsibilities.

The potential for wind energy generation has been indicated to be commercially viable in some locations of Metro Cebu's. The wind speed at 80 m ranges between 4m/s to 7m/s (NREL, 2014). Although Cebu's exposure to tropical storms challenges wind-energy generating facilities along the coast, leaving them vulnerable to the effects of regular shutdown and exposure to breakdowns as well as possible prolonged repairs which might be costly in the long term. Nonetheless, technological advancement is making it possible for robust wind turbines resistant to strong storms, and also able to operate at low wind speeds which might be conducive for installation in Metro Cebu. Metro Cebu can capitalise on in-country experiences for expertise and technology transfer. The Chicago Tri-State acts as a good example for wind-energy case study. Investment incentives encouraging greener wind-turbine manufacturing and component suppliers helped the region to shift from car manufacturing to the green wind-energy industry. In addition to investment incentives, the governance environment helped to attract the headquarters of a large number of global wind-energy companies (OECD, 2012, 2015).

The rising energy demand would call for a sustainable mix of energy for the metro area. What this is pointing out is that, though energy security is important for Metro Cebu, the energy mix must be based on an environmentally cost effective solution. It is also worth indicating that the economic development of the Metro Area hinges on a reliable source of power that adequately and consistently meets residential and industrial needs. At the same time, Metro Cebu's grid needs to be able to balance between internally generated energy and external sources to make up for shortfalls during peak periods at the right time.

To make effective decisions, policy makers have to continually invest in the compilation of robust energy statistics. Such data which has not always been present for metro Cebu is vital to understand sources of energy demand and supply as well as the expected benefits from deployment of efficient technology. In this regard it will be important for all LGUs in Metro Cebu with the help of experts to conduct an energy consumption baseline scenario to influence decision of policymakers to identify sectors (transport fuel, residential electricity etc.) which show the greatest need for energy efficiency.

Main policy recommendations

- Develop a work plan to harmonise the comprehensive land-use plans of the LGUs in the metro area based on the joint spatial plan developed with JICA as part of the Roadmap for Sustainable Urban Development.
- Update LGUs' Comprehensive Land Use plans (CLUP) and zoning ordinances to sustainably direct growth and avoid lock-ins which would be costly to reverse in the future through a compact city model.
- Produce a comprehensive redevelopment plan for urban centres, placing priority on developing unused land and promoting mixed land-use with high density housing.
- Develop high-capacity public transport such as rail transit (MRT or LRT) and promote low emission transport (bicycle, walking, ferries) through development of needed infrastructure and awareness campaigns. Develop an integrated transport master plan and establish a transport authority to mobilise needed resources for investment and ensure its implementation.
- Encourage waste minimisation and segregation of waste at source by supporting households with colour coded waste receptacles.
- Review waste pricing to reflect actual cost of municipal waste service delivery and update LGUs Solid waste management plan based on a zero-waste policy approach. Encourage energy recovery from waste to divert waste from landfill.
- Promote metropolitan-wide co-ordination and shared services of waste management
- Engage and support MSMEs to mainstream environmentally friendly techniques in their work while encouraging large industries to undertake energy and resource. assessments to improve efficiency of production systems and avoid wastage. Facilitate symbiotic networks among industrial clusters to promote material and energy exchange as a key driver of green growth in the manufacturing sector.
- Promote energy-saving behaviour among households and the use of certified energy efficiency appliances. Adopt regulatory ordinances and building ratings to encourage resource and energy efficiency in buildings as exemplified by Mandaue.
- Promote renewable energy in residential and commercial establishments by mandating large-scale buildings to install rooftop solar PVs. Support skill training of labour force, building administrative capacity and encouraging innovation.

References

Abadiai, J. (2016), "Mandaue City Presentation", Presentation made at the Bridging the EE Perception Gap session during the Asia Clean Energy Forum 2016, https://d2oc0ihd6a5bt.cloudfront.net/wp-content/uploads/sites/837/2016/04/3rd-james-abadia-mandaueacef2016_abadiaj_script_v30may2016_final_storyboard.pdf (accessed 4 December 2016).

ADB (2016a), "Fossil Fuel Subsidies in Asia; Trends, Impacts, and Reforms, Integrative Report", www.adb.org/sites/default/files/publication/182255/fossil-fuel-subsidies-asia.pdf.

ADB (Asian Development Bank) (2016b), "Sector Assessment (Summary): Energy", www.adb.org/sites/default/files/linked-documents/cobp-phi-2014-2016-ssa-02.pdf (accessed 21 November, 2016).

ADB (2016c), "Philippines: Mactan-Cebu International Passenger Terminal Project", www.adb.org/projects/48271-001/main (accessed 13 June 2016).

ADB (2014), "Philippines National Urban Assessment", www.adb.org/publications/republic-philippines-national-urban-assessment (accessed 19 January 2017).

ADB (2012), "Philippines Transport Sector Assessment, Strategy and Road Map", www.adb.org/sites/default/files/institutional-document/33700/files/philippines-transport-assessment.pdf.

AFD (Agence Française de Développement) (2013), "Quartiers informels d'un monde arabe en transition: réflexions et perspectives pour l'action urbaine", www.afd.fr/webdav/site/afd/shared/publications/recherche/scientifiques/conferences-seminaires/07-conferences-seminaires.pdf.

AFD (Agence Française de Développement) (2011), "Villes sans bidonvilles au Maroc", www.afd.fr/home/projets_afd/villes/projets-cld/lutte-contre-exclusion/maroc-sans-bidonvilles.

Ahrend, R., C. Gamper and A. Schumann (2014), "The OECD Metropolitan Governance Survey: A quantitative description of governance structures in large urban agglomerations", *OECD Regional Development Working Papers*, No. 2014/04, OECD Publishing, Paris, http://dx.doi.org/10.1787/5jz43zldh08p-en.

Albino, V., L. Fraccascia and T. Savino (2015), "Industrial symbiosis for a sustainable city: Technical, economical and organizational issues", Procedia Engineering, Vol. 118, pp. 950-957, http://dx.doi.org/10.1016/j.proeng.2015.08.536.

AMB (Area Metropolitana de Barcelona) (2014), "Presentation of the new PDU", www.amb.cat/web/territori/urbanisme/pdu/presentacio.

Ancog, R.C., N.D. Archival and C.M. Rebancos (2012), "Institutional arrangements for solid waste management in Cebu City, the Philippines", *Journal of Environmental Science and Management*, Vol. 2/5.

Asia-Pacific Economic Cooperation (APEC) (2017), Policy Review for APEC Low-Carbon Model Town Phase 6: Mandaue City, Cebu Province, Philippines.

Aquino, A.P. and C.L. Abeleda (2014), "Renewable Energy Act for Energy Self-Sufficiency and Harmful Emission Reduction", http://ap.fftc.agnet.org/ap_db.php?id=287.

Archer, D. (2012), "Baan Mankong participatory slum upgrading in Bangkok, Thailand: Community perceptions of outcomes and security of tenure", *Habitat International*, Vol. 1/36, pp. 78-84.

Azizan, S.A.M. and N.M. Suki (2014), "The potential for greener consumption: Some insights from Malaysia", *Mediterranean Journal of Social Sciences*, Vol. 16/5, pp. 11.

Behera, S. K., Kim, J. H., Lee, S. Y., Suh, S., & Park, H. S. (2012), "Evolution of 'designed' industrial symbiosis networks in the Ulsan Eco-industrial Park:'research and development into business' as the enabling framework", *Journal of Cleaner Production*, Vol. 29, pp. 103-112.

Brisbane City Council (2016), "Brisbane City Centre: An Open City", *CBD Revitalisation initiatives*, www.brisbane.qld.gov.au/planning-building/planning-guidelines-tools/brisbane-city-centre-master-plan-2014.

Cebu City Government (2015), "Cebu City Waste Action Plan", www.waste.ccacoalition.org/sites/default/files/files/Cebu%20City%201%20Philippines_0.pdf (accessed 25 November 2016).

CSE (Center for Sustainable Energy) (2016), "Los Angeles County Solar PV Permitting Case Study", https://energycenter.org/permitting/guidebook/los-angeles-county-solar-pv-permitting-case-study#_edn1 (accessed 23 November 2016).

Cervero, R. and C.D. Kang (2011), "Bus rapid transit impacts on land uses and land values in Seoul, Korea", *Transport Policy*, Vol. 1/8, pp. 102-116.

Cheng, H. and Y. Hu (2010), "Municipal solid waste (MSW) as a renewable source of energy: Current and future practices in China", *Bioresource technology*, Vol. 11/101, pp. 3816-3824.

Chertow, M.R. (2000), "Industrial symbiosis: literature and taxonomy", *Annual review of energy and the environment*, Vol. 1/25, pp. 313-337.

Chertow, M. and J. Park (2016), "Scholarship and Practice in Industrial Symbiosis: 1989-2014" in *Taking Stock of Industrial Ecology*, Springer International Publishing, pp. 87-116.

Clean Air Asia (2013) "Bicycle Sharing Launched in Pasig City" http://cleanairasia.org/node12100/ (accessed 22 June 2017).

Clean La Solar (n.d), http://cleanlasolar.com/The-First-Project (accessed 13 February 2017).

Costa, I. and P. Ferrão (2010), "A case study of industrial symbiosis development using a middle-out approach", *Journal of Cleaner Production*, Vol. 10/18, pp. 984-992.

Dacayo, J. (2005), "Final Report on Land Reclamation", Technical Report submitted for review to USAID/Philippines OEDG, http://pdf.usaid.gov/pdf_docs/Pnadh576.pdf (accessed 23 January 2014).

Department of Energy (2015) "2015 Philippines power situation", https://www.doe.gov.ph/electric-power/2015-philippine-power-situation (accessed 22 June 2017).

Department of Public Works and Highways (2015), "The Philippines Green Building Code, A Referral Code of the National Building Code of the Philippines", www.dpwh.gov.ph/dpwh/sites/default/files/laws_codes_orders/PgbcBooklet23March.pdf (accessed 4 December 2016).

Department of Trade & Industry, Philippines (n.d), "Promotion of Green Economic Development (PROGED)", www.dti.gov.ph/programs-projects/faps/proged (accessed 17 June 2016).

Desrochers, P. (2001), "Cities and industrial symbiosis: Some historical perspectives and policy implications", Journal of Industrial Ecology, Vol. 5(4), pp. 29-44, http://dx.doi.org/10.1162/10881980160084024.

DOE (Department of Energy) (2016), "Philippines statistics 2015 gross generation by sub-grid", www.doe.gov.ph/sites/default/files/pdf/energy_statistics/power_statistics_2015_gross_generation_subgrid.pdf.

DOE (2014), "Energy Efficiency and Conservation Roadmap: Milestones and Challenges", www.switch-asia.eu/fileadmin/user_upload/Events/Bali/2._Philippines_energy_efficiency_conservation_roadmap_.pdf.

DOE (2011), "Philippine Energy Plan 2012-2030, Energy access for more", www.doe.gov.ph/sites/default/files/pdf/pep/2012-2030_pep.pdf.

ECRPC (2016), "Shining Cities 2016, How Smart Local Policies Are Expanding Solar Power in America", http://www.environmentamerica.org/sites/environment/files/reports/EA_shiningcities2016_scrn.pdf (accessed 27 June 2017).

Elmido, L.G. (2016), "Convergence: Lantawan 2016 Magazine", http://todayscarolinian.net/2016/01/26/convergence-lantawan-2016-magazine/ (accessed 27 May 2016).

EMB-7 (2015), " National Solid Waste Management Status Report (2008 – 2014)", http://119.92.161.2/portal/Portals/38/Solid%20Wastefinaldraft%2012.29.15.pdf (accessed 22 June 2017).

EPA (Environmental Protection Agency) (2016), "Zero Waste Case Study: San Francisco, CA", www.epa.gov/transforming-waste-tool/less-waste-case-study-san-francisco-ca.

EPA (2015), "Energy and Environment Guide to Action: State Policies and Best Practices for Advancing Energy Efficiency, Renewable Energy, and Combined Heat and Power", www.epa.gov/sites/production/files/2015-08/documents/guide_action_full.pdf.

ESTIF (European Solar Thermal Industry Federation) (2017), "Solar Ordinances", www.estif.org/policies/solar_ordinances/ (accessed 13 February 2017).

Fawzi Zniber, M. (2015), "L'enjeu des bidonvilles au Maroc: conditions de développement et évolution actuelle", http://ecolearchicasa.com/wp-content/uploads/2015/11/Pr%c3%a9sentation2.pdf.

Freden, J. (2015), "The Swedish recycling revolution", https://sweden.se/nature/the-swedish-recycling-revolution/ (accessed 28 November 2016).

Gertz, R. (2005), "Eco-labelling—a case for deregulation?", *Law, Probability and Risk*, Vol. 3/4, pp. 127-141.

Gibbs, D., (2008), "Industrial Symbiosis and Eco-Industrial Development: An Introduction", *Geography Compass*, *2*(4), 1138-1154.

GIZ (Deutsche Gesellschaft für Internationale Zusammenarbeit) (2016), "Green Economic Development. Programme description", www.giz.de/en/worldwide/18237.html#header (accessed 15 February 2017).

Goldstein, J. (2014), "From Waste to Jobs: What Achieving 75 Percent Recycling Means for California", www.tellus.org/pub/from%20waste%20to%20jobs-%20what%20achieving%2075%20percent%20recycling%20means%20for%20california.pdf.

HCP (Haut Commissariat du Plan) (2015), "Results of the 2014 Census", www.hcp.ma/downloads/rgph-2014_t17441.html.

HUDCC (Housing and Urban Development Coordinating Council) (2014), "Developing a National Informal Settlements Upgrading Strategy for the Philippines", www.hudcc.gov.ph/sites/default/files/styles/large/public/document/nisus%20final%20report_july2014.pdf (accessed 5 December 2016).

ICT (Indianapolis Cultural Trail) (2015), "Economic Impact Figures Released: Indianapolis Cultural Trail has Positive Economic Impact", http://indyculturaltrail.org/2015/07/23/economic-impact-figures-released/ (accessed 20 January 2017).

IEA (International Energy Agency) (2016a), *Renewables Information 2016*, International Energy Agency, Paris, http://dx.doi.org/10.1787/renew-2016-en.

IEA (2016b), "Philippines: Balances for 2014", www.iea.org/statistics/statisticssearch/report/?year=2014&country=philippine&product=bal.ances (accessed 22 November 2016).

IEA (2014), *Technology Roadmap, Solar Photovoltaic Energy*, 2014 edition, www.iea.org/publications/freepublications/publication/TechnologyRoadmapSolarPhotovoltaicEnergy_2014edition.pdf.

IGES (Institute for Global Environmental Strategies) (2012), "Solid Waste Management in Cebu City", Kitakyushu Initiative for a Clean Environment, http://kitakyushu.iges.or.jp/docs/sp/swm/3%20Cebu%20(Paper).pdf (accessed 26 November 2016).

IIEE (Institute of Integrated Electrical Engineers of the Philippines, Inc.) (2015), "Smart Buildings and Green Standards", http://iiee.org.ph/wp-content/uploads/2015/12/fr4_sec-prs-2015-1127-iiee.pdf (accessed 21 February 2017).

ITF (International Transport Forum) (2014), *Valuing Convenience in Public Transport*, OECD Publishing, Paris, http://dx.doi.org/10.1787/9789282107683-en.

Inquirer Business (2013), "Are we ready for mandatory green building measures?", http://business.inquirer.net/116583/are-we-ready-for-mandatory-green-building-measures (accessed 23 June 2017).

JICA (Japan International Cooperation Agency) (2001), "Metro Cebu Development Project (II)", www.jica.go.jp/english/our_work/evaluation/oda_loan/post/2001/pdf/e_project_57_all.pdf (accessed 24 February 2017).

JICA (Japan International Cooperation Agency) and MCDCB (Metro Cebu Development and Coordination Board) (2015), "The Roadmap for Sustainable Urban Development in Metro Cebu", http://open_jicareport.jica.go.jp/pdf/12235529.pdf.

Kingdom of Morocco High Commission for Planning (2015), "Morocco between Millennium Development Goals and Sustainable Development Goals, Achievements and Challenges", *National Report 2015*.

Kumar, A. and O.P. Agarwal (2013), *Institutional labyrinth: designing a way out for improving urban transport services – lessons from current practice*, Washington DC, World Bank Group, http://documents.worldbank.org/curated/en/903181468346145008/Institutional-labyrinth-designing-a-way-out-for-improving-urban-transport-services-lessons-from-current-practice.

Land Transport Authority (2017), "Riding a Train", https://www.lta.gov.sg/content/ltaweb/en/public-transport/mrt-and-lrt-trains/riding-a-train.html.

Land Transport Authority (2015), "Walk. Cycle. Ride. Singapore: Land Transport Authority Annual Report 2015/2016", www.lta.gov.sg/content/dam/ltaweb/corp/publicationsresearch/files/annualreports/1516/lta_ar_1516.pdf.

Lorenciana, C.S. (2016), "Region's power consumption continue to rise", www.philstar.com/cebu-business/2015/11/28/1526815/regions-power-consumption-continue-rise (accessed 21 June 2016).

Mairie de Paris (2012), "Paris Climate and Energy Action Plan", http://api-site-cdn.paris.fr/images/70923.

Mangubat, E.G. (2015), "982 Trees Cut", *Cebu Daily News*, http://cebudailynews.inquirer.net/73683/982-trees-cut-2 (accessed 20 June 2016).

Maniego, P.H. (2012), "Country Perspectives Philippines", Fair FIT workshop, http://pdf.wri.org/wri_fair_fit_workshop_presentation_philippines_nreb.pdf (accessed 21 June 2016).

Mengethetti, A. and G. Nardin (2012), "Enabling industrial symbiosis by a facilities management optimization approach", *Journal of Cleaner Production*, Vol. 35, November, pp. 263-273, http://dx.doi.org/10.1016/j.jclepro.2012.06.002.

Metro Cebu Development and Coordinating Board (2016), "Answers to the OECD case study questionnaire", internal document, unpublished.

MHPV (Ministère de l'Habitat et de la Politique de la Ville) (2016), "Presentation and Advancement of the VSB Programme", www.mhpv.gov.ma/?page_id=956.

Montenegro, L.O. (2016), "Environmental Trade-Offs from Coastal Reclamation: The Case of Cebu, the Philippines", in *Marine and Coastal Ecosystem Valuation, Institutions and Policy in Southeast Asia*, Springer Singapore, pp. 225-238.

Montenegro, L.O., E.M. Remedio and A.G Diola (2005), "The environmental costs of coastal reclamation in Metro Cebu, the Philippines", *Economy and Environment Program for Southeast Asia*.

National Competiveness Council (2015), *Cities and Municipalities Competiveness Index*, www.competitive.org.ph/cmcindex/ (accessed 17 June 2016).

National Renewable Energy Laboratory (2000), Assessment of solar, micro-hydro and wind energy resources in the Philippines, Final draft report of tasks, Philippine Renewable Energy Project, USAID, three volumes.

Nielsen (2015), "Green Generation: Millennials Say Sustainability is a Shopping Priority", www.nielsen.com/us/en/insights/news/2015/green-generation-millennials-say-sustainability-is-a-shopping-priority.html (accessed 22 June 2016).

NREL (2014), "Wind Prospector", https://maps.nrel.gov/wind-prospector/#/?al=uvfk3h%255bv%255d%3dt&bl=groad&ce=0&lr=0&mc=10.319648088037958%2c124.27322387695312&zl=10.

OECD (2017), *The Governance of Land Use in OECD Countries: Policy Analysis and Recommendations*, OECD Publishing, Paris, http://dx.doi.org/10.1787/9789264268609-en.

OECD (2016a), *Extended Producer Responsibility: Updated Guidance for Efficient Waste Management*, OECD Publishing, Paris, http://dx.doi.org/10.1787/9789264256385-en.

OECD (2016b), *OECD Investment Policy reviews: Philippines 2016*, OECD Publishing, Paris, http://dx.doi.org/10.1787/9789264254510-en.

OECD (2016c), *Urban Green Growth in Dynamic Asia*, OECD Publishing, Paris, http://dx.doi.org/10.1787/9789264266360-en.

OCDE (2015a), *Governing the City*, OECD Publishing, Paris, http://dx.doi.org/10.1787/9789264226500-en.

OECD (2015b), *Report of the 5th OECD Knowledge Sharing Workshop on Urban Green Growth in Dynamic Asia*, unpublished internal report.

OECD (2014a), *Greening Household Behaviour: Overview from the 2011 Survey – Revised edition*, OECD Publishing, Paris, http://dx.doi.org/10.1787/9789264214651-en.

OECD (2014b), "The State of Play on Extended Producer Responsibility (EPR): Opportunities and Challenges", www.oecd.org/environment/waste/global%20forum%20tokyo%20issues%20paper%2030-5-2014.pdf.

OECD (2014c), "Greening Household Behaviour: Overview of Results from Econometric Analysis and Policy Implications", *Environment Working Paper*, No. 79 www.oecd.org/officialdocuments/publicdisplaydocumentpdf/?cote=env/wkp(2014)17&doclanguage=en (accessed 27 November 2016).

OECD (2014d), *Renewable energy (indicator),* OECD Publishing, Paris, http://dx.doi.org/10.1787/aac7c3f1-en (accessed 05 July 2017).

OECD (2013), *Green Growth in Kitakyushu, Japan*, OECD Publishing, Paris, http://dx.doi.org/10.1787/9789264195134-en.

OECD (2012), *Compact City Policies: A Comparative Assessment*, OECD Publishing, Paris, http://dx.doi.org/10.1787/9789264167865-en.

OECD (2010), *Eco-Innovation in Industry: Enabling Green Growth*, OECD Publishing, Paris, http://dx.doi.org/10.1787/9789264077225-en.

Ostojic, D.R. et al. (2013), *Energizing Green Cities in Southeast Asia: Applying Sustainable Urban Energy and Emissions Planning*, World Bank Publications.

Park, S. (n.d.), www.parksharon.co.il/html5/?_id=9543&did=10116&g=9054&sm=9543 (accessed 24 February 2017).

PEZA (Philippine Economic Zone Authority) (2016a), "Implementing Rules and Regulations", www.peza.gov.ph/index.php/about-peza/implementing-rules-and-regulations.

PEZA (2016b), "Operating Economic Zone Map", www.peza.gov.ph/index.php/economic-zones/list-of-economic-zones/operating-economic-zones.

Philippine Statistics Authority (2015), "Number of Establishments and Total Employment Report 2015".

Philippine Statistics Authority (2014), "2010 Census of Population and Housing", www.psa.gov.ph/statistics/census/population-and-housing.

PPEI (Philippine Poverty Environment Initiative) (2013), "Improving access of local communities to quality, secured and sustainable energy in the Philippines", http://ppei.dilg.gov.ph/improving-access-of-local-communities-to-quality-secured-and-sustainable-energy-in-the-Philippines.

Premakumara, D.G.J. (2012), "Establishment of the Community-Based Solid Waste Management System in Metro Cebu, the Philippines", https://pub.iges.or.jp/pub_file/cebunoteenglishfinalpdf/download (accessed 8 February 2017).

Premakumara, D.G.J. (2011), "Survey of Household Solid Waste generation and Public Awareness on Waste Separation and Composting Practices in Cebu City", http://pub.iges.or.jp/modules/envirolib/upload/3585/attach/Cebu.Survey.Report[final].pdf (accessed 10 June 2016).

Premakumara, D.G.J. et al. (2014), "Policy implementation of the Republic Act (RA) No. 9003 in the Philippines: a case study of Cebu City", *Waste management*, Vol. 6/34, pp. 971-979.

Provincial Environment and Natural Resource Office, Province of Cebu (2015), "Status of SWM Compliance of LGUs in Province of Cebu".

Rand, T., J. Haukohl and U. Marxen (2000), "Municipal solid waste incineration: requirements for a successful project", *World Bank technical paper*, No. WTP 462, The World Bank, Washington, D.C., http://documents.worldbank.org/curated/en/886281468740211060/pdf/multi-page.pdf.

Richmund C. (2015), "The law on renewable energy, Amicus curiae", www.accralaw.com/publications/law-renewable-energy (accessed 21 June 2016).

Semilla, N.L. (2016), "No Segregation, No Collection", *Cebu Daily News*, http://cebudailynews.inquirer.net/96796/no-segregation-no-collection (accessed 2 December 2016).

Shaheen, S. et al. (2011), "China's Hangzhou public bicycle: Understanding early adoption and behavioral response to bikesharing", *Journal of the Transportation Research Board*, No. 2247, pp. 33-41.

Singapore Department of Statistics (SDS) (2016), *Population Trends, 2016*, Department of Statistics, Singapore, www.singstat.gov.sg/docs/default-source/default-document-library/publications/publications_and_papers/population_and_population_structure/population2016.pdf (accessed 29 November 2016).

Singapore Environmental Council (SEC) (2017), "About Singapore Green Label Scheme", https://sgls.sec.org.sg/cms.php?cms_id=3 (accessed 27 June 2017).

Singapore Green Labelling Scheme (SGLS) (2017), "About Singapore Green Label Scheme", https://sgls.sec.org.sg/cms.php?cms_id=3.

Smolka, M.O. (2013), "Implementing Value Capture in Latin America", Policy Focus Report.

Suzuki, H. et al. (2015), *Financing transit-oriented development with land values: Adapting land value capture in developing countries*, World Bank Publications.

Switch-Asia (2014), "Impact sheet: Building sustainable and competitive industry in Cebu, Philippines", www.switch-asia.eu/fileadmin/user_upload/publications/2014/impact_sheets/switch_asia_impact_sheet_-_2014_-_smart_cebu.pdf (accessed 17 June 2017).

The Economist (2015), "Such quantities of sand: Asia's mania for 'reclaiming' land from the sea spawns mounting problems", www.economist.com/news/asia/21645221-asias-mania-reclaiming-land-sea-spawns-mounting-problems-such-quantities-sand (accessed 8 June 2016).

Thorpe D. (2014), "China Has Almost Half the World's Bike-Share Bicycles", www.sustainablecitiescollective.com/david-thorpe/328996/china-has-almost-half-worlds-bike-share-bicycles.

Tourist Israel (2017), "Ariel Sharon Park", www.touristisrael.com/ariel-sharon-park/702/ (accessed 24 February 2017).

Toutain, O. (2014), "Financer le relogement des bidonvilles au Maroc", www.proparco.fr/jahia/webdav/site/proparco/shared/portails/secteur_prive_developpement/pdf/spd19/spd19_olivier_toutain_fr.pdf.

Transport for London (TfL) (2016), "Transport for London Business Plan", http://content.tfl.gov.uk/tfl-business-plan-december-2016.pdf (accessed 22 June 2017).

UEMI (Urban Electric Mobility Initiative) (2017), "Urban Electric Mobility Initiative", www.uemi.net/ (accessed 1 February 2016).

United Nations (2016), "The new urban agenda", https://habitat3.org/the-new-urban-agenda/ (accessed 1 February 2016).

UNEP (United Nations Environment Programme) (2015), "District Energy in Cities: Unlocking the Potential of Energy Efficiency and Renewable Energy", http://wedocs.unep.org/handle/20.500.11822/9317.

UNIDO (United Nations Industrial Development Organization) (2016), "Making it Green", Department of Environment, www.unido.org/fileadmin/user_media/services/environmental_management/unido-makingitgreen-onepage.pdf.

Velib' (2017), Mairie de Paris, http://en.velib.paris.fr/index.php (accessed 1 February 2017).

Veneracion, C.C. (2010), Partnerships for Scaling up Slum Improvement in Philippine Cities, http://media.wix.com/ugd/4d76b7_c4102ba2cffe46f18bc3129e5d05e892.pdf (accessed 5 December 2016).

Villarete, P.C. and C. Cal (2007), "The Metro Cebu Land Use and Transport Study (MCLUTS)", Revisited, http://ncts.upd.edu.ph/old/estnow/pdf/CBSMEST-20070830-31/CBSMEST-cebu-villarete.pdf.

Visayan Electric Company (VECO) (2015), "VECO's 'Cebu Unplugged' campaign aims to save power", www.veco.com.ph/newsroom/cebu-unplugged-campaign/ (accessed 5 December 2015).

Waste Management Resources (WMR) (2009), "Incineration", www.wrfound.org.uk/articles/incineration.html.

World Bank (2017), "Cebu Bus Rapid Trasnsit (BRT) Project", http://projects.worldbank.org/P119343/cebu-bus-rapid-transit-brt-demonstration-project?lang=en&tab=overview (accessed 6 February 2016).

Chapter 3

Water security and green growth in Cebu, Philippines

Chapter 3 examines water security and its potential benefits for green growth in the Province of Cebu. This chapter is structured into the following four sections: 1) Water security issues in Metro Cebu; 2) Water supply and sanitation; 3) Urban resilience to floods; and 4) Water governance. This chapter benefited from discussions at the 5th OECD Knowledge-Sharing Workshop on Urban Green Growth in Dynamic Asia, held in Cebu on 9-10 December 2015 and supported by the OECD Knowledge Sharing Alliance.

Key findings

- **Water security is a cornerstone of urban green growth strategies for Cebu.** The entire Province and in particular Metro Cebu area face great water challenges, including increasing water demand in a context of diminishing resources, relative inefficiency of the water distribution network, and suboptimal coverage of the water supply and sanitation infrastructure, leading to quality issues in surface and ground water. Floods also periodically occur in some areas of Metro Cebu. These are accentuated by rapid urbanisation, economic growth and climate change, which increase the pressure on water resources and infrastructure.
- **Strategies need to be diversified to effectively address water supply and sanitation challenges.** Non-revenue water is at 25%; and 80% of grey water (i.e. wastewater without human wastes) receives no treatment. Water demand is also expected to triple by 2040. These issues put greater strain on the current infrastructure and these need to be addressed urgently. While investing in "grey" infrastructure (i.e. dams, reservoirs) and diversifying sources of water supply in the long-term are critical, exploring complementary or alternative policy strategies, in particular green infrastructure, demand-side management tools, and smart technologies can provide greater flexibility and alleviate the demand for "grey" infrastructure.
- **Comprehensive strategies to address water-related risks need to be urgently developed.** Climate change impacts and socio-economic changes are likely to increase the exposure of the Province to such risks. 43% of households in Metro Cebu do not benefit from a drainage system and rainfall can be intense during the monsoon season. In addition, existing drainage infrastructure tends to be both insufficient and inefficient. The Local Government Units (LGUs) most affected by floods are Mandaue, Talisay, Danao and Cebu City. Most LGUs first need to design robust Disaster Risk Reduction and Management strategies informed by a thorough assessment of vulnerability to floods under different scenarios, in particular critical infrastructure such as power utilities, landfills and water treatment stations. Strategies to ensure resilient land-use and mechanisms to enhance the resilience of businesses and industries should also be explored at the local level.
- **Water governance** in Cebu is complex and at the heart of challenges that LGUs need to address in this sector. Municipal fragmentation, lack of relevant scale for investment, lack of incentives for co-operation, lack of staff, difficulties in raising tariffs, and limited information sharing are issues observed in Cebu, as in many OECD cities. While the creation of the Mega Cebu Development Authority and the Provincial Water Resources Authority is an opportunity to address the territorial and sectoral fragmentation of water responsibilities, the proper means and power to harmonise regulations, reform tariffs and charges, and technical capacities – including data collection – should be further secured. The responsibilities and use of financial resources between the national government and LGUs should also be further aligned to achieve common goals: the national government for instance could financially support metropolitan-wide water projects with high fixed costs.

Introduction: Water security issues in Metro Cebu

Water supply, sanitation and disaster risk reduction are critical strategic development sectors in the Philippines, in both urban and rural areas. The World Health Organisation (WHO) – United Nations Children's Fund (UNICEF) Joint Monitoring Programme (JMP) reported that 93% of urban population and 92% of rural populations have access to drinking water (JMP, 2012). However, the quality of water supply has not kept pace with the growing population in the last few decades (ADB, 2013a). According to the JMP March 2012 Report, only 43% of the country's population has access to water piped into private houses (Level III) (61% in urban areas and 25% in rural areas) while others are served by stand-alone water points (Level I) or piped water with a communal water points (Level II). In addition, the country faces severe water scarcity issues, adding to the pressure put on water resources and systems. ADB (2013) identifies the following persistent problems in water supply: i) institutional fragmentation; ii) weak sector planning and monitoring due to lack of sector information; iii) poor performance of many water utilities; iv) low public and private sector investment and limited access to financing for service expansion; and v) inadequate support for poor urban communities and rural water utilities.

Water sanitation also presents major challenges. The Clean Water Act of 2004 requires LGUs and water districts to create septage management programmes in areas without sewerage systems. However, most LGUs and water districts have lacked the capacity, technical knowledge, or funds to take action since the passage of the Act. Existing industrial waste and wastewater treatment systems, and private septic tank desludging services often do not meet environmental standards in the Philippines (ADB, 2013a). The JMP March 2012 Report indicates that while 74% of the country's population had access to sanitation facilities in 2010 (79% in urban areas and 69% in rural areas), the quality of sanitation is suboptimal. Few households in the Philippines are connected to a sewerage network, and the majority of households with toilets are connected to septic tanks that are poorly designed or maintained, therefore most effluent is likely to be discharged without treatment. This contributes to the pollution of surface and ground water. Problems include i) lack of policies and effective governance and regulation, ii) low levels of awareness and political will for improving sanitation; iii) inadequate funds for financing infrastructure; and iv) lack of sanitation capacity (ADB, 2013a).

Water-related disasters (e.g. typhoons, floods) are recurrent and severe in the Philippines. The country has one of the lowest water-related disaster resilience of the Asia-Pacific region and one of the highest ratios of fatalities per 1 000 inhabitants (ADB, 2013b). In November 2013, Super Typhoon Haiyan became a Category 5 typhoon, the strongest ever recorded at the time, with wind gusts in excess of 300 kilometres per hour and an associated storm surge that reached a high of 3.5 metres along some coastlines with more vulnerable bathometric profiles. More than6 300 people were killed, over two million were left homeless, and over 13 million people were affected in the Philippines. It caused about USD 15 billion in damages, equivalent to 5% of the Philippines' total GDP in 2013. An equivalent level of damage to the United States of America's economy would amount to USD 850-900 billion in damages, an amount four times greater than that caused by Hurricane Katrina in 2011.

This chapter demonstrates that Cebu Province is affected by water-related risks for which there is an urgent need for Metro Cebu to enhance its water security. Water security is defined as "the availability of an acceptable quantity and quality of water for health, livelihoods, ecosystems and production, coupled with an acceptable level of water-related risks to people, environments and economies" (Grey and Sadoff, 2007). It is also understood as the management of four water risks: scarcity, floods, pollution and freshwater ecosystem resilience (OECD, 2013). Because of its significant long-term economic, environmental and social dimensions, addressing challenges related to access to water, water sanitation and water-related disasters is of utmost importance and is a critical lever for green growth. This chapter reports on specific water security issues faced in Cebu and proposes policy recommendations for a more sustainable management of water.

Developing diverse policy instruments for water supply and sanitation in Cebu

The water supply and sanitation (WSS) issues faced by the Province of Cebu illustrate the country-level trends introduced above. These include increasing water demand in a context of diminishing resources, relative inefficiency of the water distribution network, and suboptimal coverage of the water supply and sanitation infrastructure, leading to quality issues in surface and ground water. These trends are particularly acute in the Metro Cebu area, and are accentuated by the rapid urbanisation and economic development patterns of the metropolitan region. These water challenges contain both environmental (e.g. depletion of local water resources, untreated wastewater) and economic dimensions, (e.g. cost of inaction to catch up with expanding infrastructure needs, water losses, lack of resilience to floods) and in this regard, are critical green growth obstacles. While there is increasing recognition, in particular by the Metro Cebu Development Co-ordinating Board (MCDCB), of the urgent need to tackle these problems in order to ensure the sustainable long-term development of the Province, this section proposes alternative or complementary policy recommendations to the existing WSS strategies, following OECD and non-OECD countries and cities' experience in this sector.

Some of the data presented in this chapter refer to the Metro Cebu Water District (MCWD). MCWD is a corporatised entity delivering water supply and sanitation services to the following jurisdictions of Metro Cebu: four cities – Cebu City, Talisay, Mandaue and Lapu-Lapu – and four municipalities – Consolacion, Liloan, Compostela and Cordova – covering in total eight LGUs among the 13 LGUs of Metro Cebu. However, MCWD only serves 57% of the population (1.2 million residents) in its franchise area, the remaining population being served by Community Water Associations or private suppliers (JICA and MCDCB, 2015). Water supply and sanitation in the five other LGUs of the metropolitan areas is either undertaken by LGUs or by private suppliers. MCWD is not unique in the Philippines. The existence of water districts originated in the Provincial Water Utilities Act of 1973, which created the Local Water Utilities Association (LWUA) – Water District concept, encouraging LGUs to transfer their water supply systems to water districts, on a similar model as MCWD (ADB, 2013a). The data presented below will often reflect the fragmentation of water suppliers and the lack of harmonised and available information across all areas of Metro Cebu (see section 4 for a discussion on data in the water sector).

Water supply and sanitation challenges in Cebu

Cebu faces increasing water demand in a context of diminishing resources. In Metro Cebu, there is a shortage of supply of over 153 000 cubic metres per day (m3/day) of potable water for residents, businesses, and farmers. In addition, projected total water demand in the Metro Cebu area is expected to almost triple from 227 225 m3/day in 2013 to 651 825 m3/day in 2040, requiring water authorities and suppliers to fulfil a potential gap of 437 000 m3/day by then (Figure 3.1). MCWD area accounts for most of the water demand of Metro Cebu. Residential consumption exerts most pressure on local water demand, as commercial and industrial activities only account for 12.7% of water supply in MCWD area. Per capita domestic water consumption is at 161 litres per day in 2013 among the population served by MCWD, 119 litres per day in non-MCWD areas in northern Metro Cebu (Danao City) and 147 litres per day in non-MCWD areas in southern Metro Cebu (Carcar, Minglanilla, Naga and San Fernando). The increasing pressure on local water resources is mostly put on ground water, which account for 98% of water supply in MCWD service area, against 2% from surface water (e.g. dams, reservoirs).

Figure 3.1. **Projected water demand in Metro Cebu (2013-2050)**

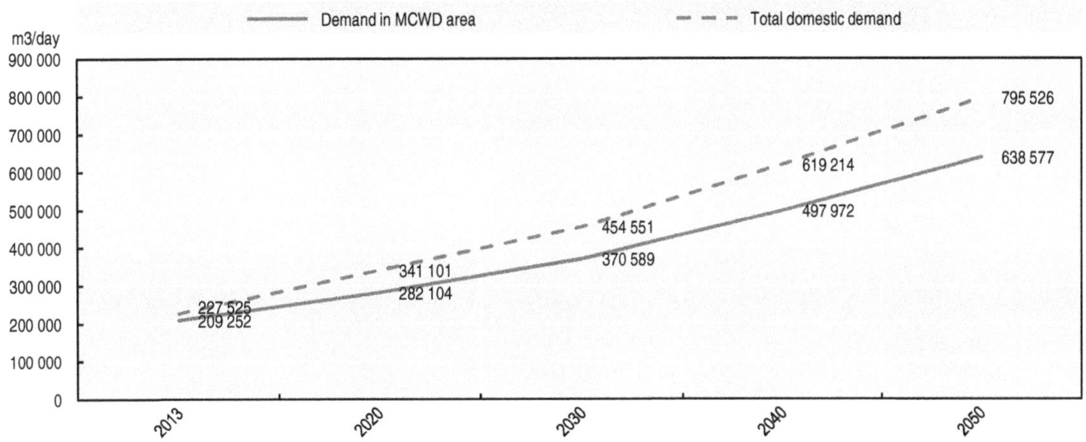

Source: JICA and MCDCB (2015), "Roadmap Study for Sustainable Urban Development in Metro Cebu", Cebu, the Philippines.

Water distribution networks are relatively inefficient. Unaccounted-for-water (UFW) accounted for 23% of total water supply in MCWD service area in 2016. This figure falls in line with trends observed in other cities, in comparison to the GDP per capita of MCWD compared to OECD cities (Figure 3.2). In addition, local authorities are making good progress in reducing UFW: in 2010, the share was at 30.8% (JICA and MCDCB, 2015). There is no data for LGUs outside MCWD service area, and considering that LGUs often perform lower than water districts (ADB, 2013a), unaccounted-for-water in the whole Metro Cebu may be higher. In addition, the figure for MCWD should not hide the fact that MCWD only serves 56% of the population in its franchise area, and that the water systems in place for the remaining population may be less efficient. The poor coverage of MCWD's services can be partly explained by the cost of extending pipe infrastructure and the difficulty to build new infrastructure in already urbanised areas, which complicates procedures such as obtaining excavation permits from the Department of Public Works and Highway (DPWH).

Figure 3.2. **Water losses and GDP per capita in MCWD and selected OECD cities**

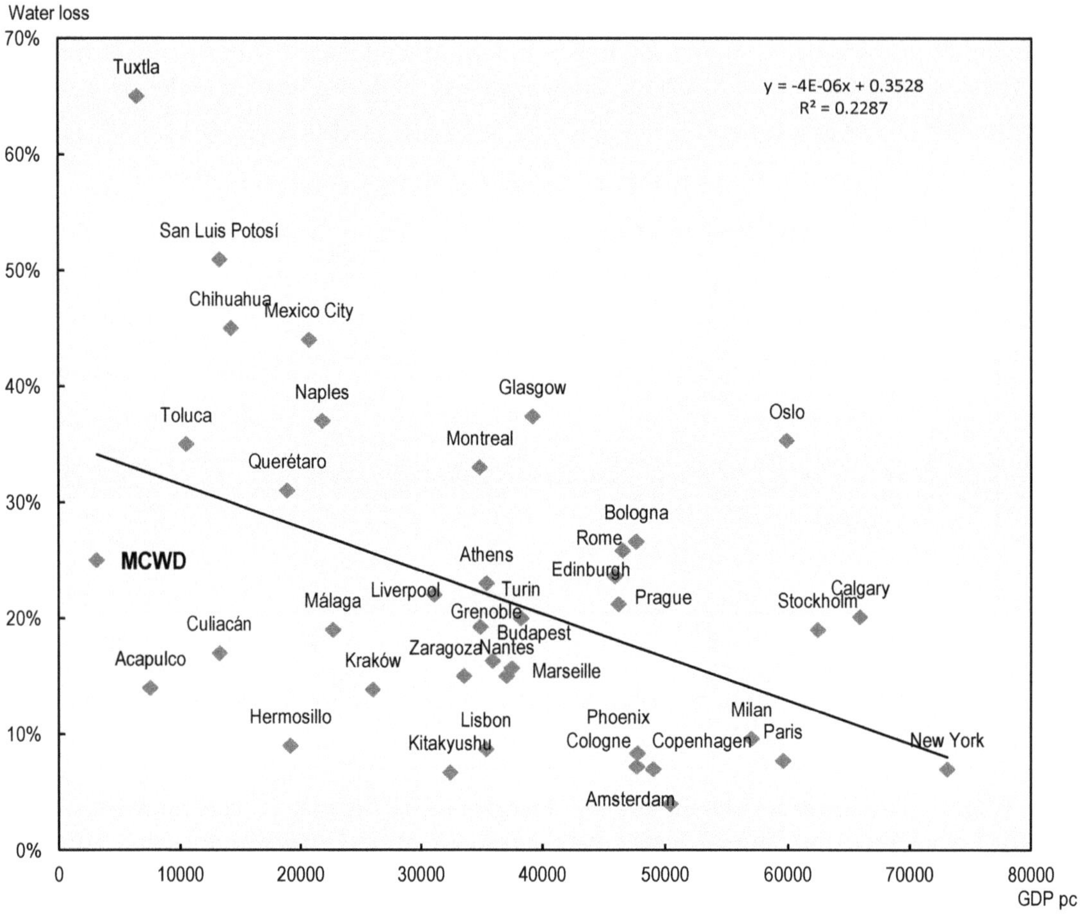

Source: Adapted from OECD (2016), *Water Governance in Cities*, OECD Publishing, Paris, http://dx.doi.org/10.1787/9789264251090-en.

Water is supplied through a diversity of means, and only a fraction of the total population is served through a private piped connection (Level III). Only 12.5% of drinking water is supplied through pipe connections in Metro Cebu, while 68.9% is supplied through water refilling stations. 49.9% of water used for purposes other than drinking is supplied through pipe connections. Public taps, wells (public, households', neighbours'), bottled water, rain and freshwater are the other sources of water supply in Metro Cebu. These figures reflect a general preference for commercially purchased water over pipe water, due to the poor quality and coverage of the piped system, as mentioned previously. This is slightly lower than national average, as 61% of urban areas in the Philippines are served through a Level III connection (ADB, 2013a). In Danao City and Carcar City, only 40% and 39% of the total population is served by piped water, respectively. There is no data in other non-MCWD service areas (JICA and MCDCB, 2013). Although the water in MCWD's piped connections is potable, its quality seems suboptimal: a survey indicated that most households' satisfaction regarding water quantity, quality, pressure, and continuity (i.e. hours of supply) are only "average" (JICA and MCDCB, 2015). In addition, a growing number of private wells are being built, for residential (88% of households in Metro Cebu own a well), commercial and industrial activities (many commercial and industrial establishments indeed possess their own well to supply their needs). The number of private wells in the MCWD service area is estimated at around 25 000, of which only around 1 000 are registered (JICA and MCDCB, 2015). This can be partly explained by the fact that registration to the National Water Resources Board (NWRB) is mandatory for wells used for domestic purposes and for business and industrial purposes (according to the Water Code of the Philippines). NWRB, located in Manila, also faces difficulties in fulfilling its oversight duties across entire country.

Cebu suffers from salinity intrusion of the freshwater aquifer, due to over-exploitation of groundwater. Salinity was measured at 250 mg/TDS (total dissolved solids) near Fuente Osmena Circle, 2 kilometres inland from the Cebu Strait. Lapu-Lapu City, Mandaue and Talisay are the most affected LGUs (JICA and MCDCB, 2015). Salinity intrusion into groundwater aquifers makes it difficult to use for drinking purposes. Desalination is a possible response, but desalination processes are hardly financially achievable, but have been experimented in Cebu. The manufacturer of water treatment equipment Mactan Rock supplies MCWD with desalinated water in Mactan Island. Their subsidiary, Pilipinas Water Resources Inc, also provides desalinated water for establishments in the SRP (South Road Properties) (Citi di Mare, SM Seaside City) and produces an excess as the developments in SRP are limited. Additionally, some major resorts, such as Shangri-la, use desalination technology for their own water supply. Continued saltwater intrusion of lower-lying areas near the coast due to sea level rise (and over-extraction of groundwater), is expected to result in the contamination of up to 25% of all abstraction wells by 2025 (JICA and MCDCB, 2015). In general, saltwater intrusion is one of the major challenges facing the country's water resources and also affects Davao City and certain areas of Metro Manila (ADB, 2013a).

Finally, surface and groundwater are also polluted by human waste, due to a lack of proper sanitation system. Currently, there is no centralised sewerage system but MCWD opened its first septage treatment plant in Cordova which serves Cordova and Lapulapu City. The plant has been operational since August 2016. MCWD has plans of opening up to three additional septage treatment plants with the assistance of JICA as recommended in the Roadmap Study. Region VII is one of the regions with the lowest percentage of households with sanitary toilets (79.9%), according to the Annual Poverty Indicator Survey (ADB, 2013a). The majority of Metro Cebu population (80.4%) owns pour-flush toilets, the remaining population uses flush toilets (4.4%), pit latrines (8.7%) or do not have any toilet at all (6.5%). Only 3.4% of households evacuate black water (i.e. wastewater with human wastes) through sewers, while 86% is evacuated into septic tanks and 10% through drainage and therefore have no treatment. In addition, only 7% of grey water (i.e. wastewater without human wastes) is evacuated through sewerage, most being evacuated through drainage with no treatment (80%) or into septic tanks (13%) (Figure 3.3). In preparation for MCWD's expanding septage programme, all but one LGUs within MCWD's franchise area have passed resolutions requiring residents to desludge (or empty) septic tanks. However in practice around half of the households in Metro Cebu have never removed sludge from the tanks, resulting in pipe clogging and further sanitation issues. Domestic wastewater therefore largely goes untreated into groundwater or public canals and drainage systems, and eventually into rivers and other water bodies, creating not only public health risks but also further issues to use local water resources for water supply. High levels of Escherichia coli, nitrate (NO_3) and phosphate have been measured in ground water. Butuanon River's biochemical oxygen demand (BOD) was recently measured at 70 mg/L, while the international standard is set at 10 mg/L (JICA and MCDCB, 2015).

Figure 3.3. **Treatment of black and grey water in Metro Cebu**

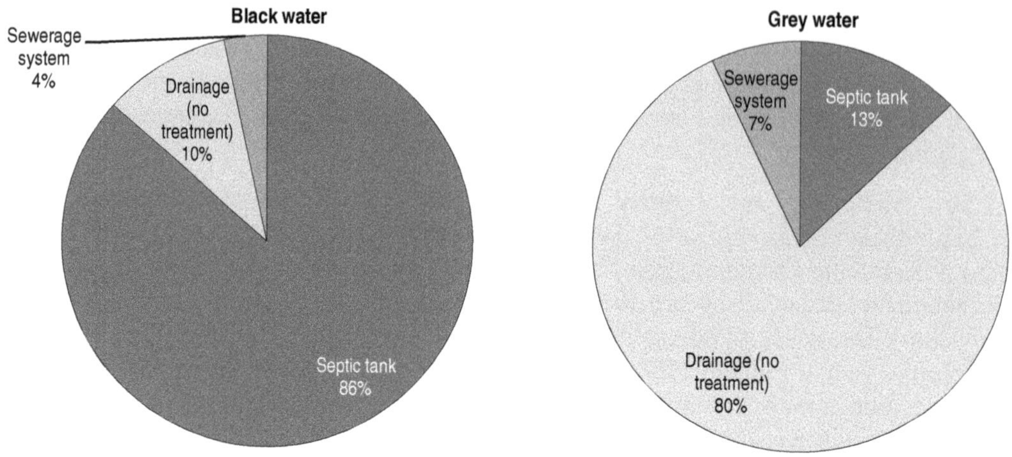

Source: JICA and MCDCB (2015), "Roadmap Study for Sustainable Urban Development in Metro Cebu", Cebu, the Philippines.

Current roadmap for water supply and sanitation in Metro Cebu

Authorities in Cebu have long been aware of a 'quiet' crisis affecting its limited freshwater resources. In 1999, the Water Resources Centre at the University of San Carlos in Cebu requested assistance from the Royal Netherlands Embassy and this resulted in the Water Remind Project (2003-2008). One of the main policies that emerged from that partnership was the Water Resources Management Action Plan for Central Cebu (2005-2030) (WRMA Plan). In 2015, the MCDCB presented a study on the 'Impacts of Groundwater Extraction' and commissioned a further study to analyse the water tariff structure and existing institutional structures as the basis for policy recommendations moving forward.

In addition, the *Roadmap Study* prepared by JICA and MCDCB includes a study and action plan for water supply and sanitation for Metro Cebu, with a vision to 2050. The Roadmap underscores the need to improve and develop basic "grey" infrastructure (i.e. dams, reservoirs) and diversify sources of water supply in the long-term, in order to meet the challenges described above. The main elements of the Roadmap are listed in Table 3.1. A feasibility study for the construction of dams and the creation for a Green Loop were identified as priority projects by the MCDCB. In addition, a pilot septage treatment plant has been built in Cebu City by Amcon Inc. with funding from JICA. The LGU is considering turning over to MCWD as part of a plan to build a 'cluster' of seven decentralised septage treatment plants throughout all of Metro Cebu. In this plan however the MCWD would not be responsible for taking care of septage in the LGUs outside of their franchise area.

Table 3.1. **JICA-MCDCB roadmap for water supply and sanitation in Metro Cebu**

	Water supply	Sanitation
Short-term	• Developing projects to build new water supply facilities (e.g. reservoirs, pump stations, well development) • Construction of Mananga II dam	• Construction of septage treatment plant • Improvement of inappropriate septic tanks • Construction of wastewater treatment facility in development areas
Medium-term	• Construction of Kotkot and Lusaran dams • Study for groundwater exploitation • Reduction of non-revenue water	• Construction of a centralised sewerage system • Promotion of ecological sanitation technologies
Long-term	• Development of surface water and groundwater in the northern and southern areas of Cebu • Construction of a desalination plant • Reduction of non-revenue water • Groundwater recharge • Use of recycled water	• Expansion of current sewerage systems

Source: JICA and MCDCB (2015), "Roadmap Study for Sustainable Urban Development in Metro Cebu", Cebu, the Philippines.

While investing in "grey" infrastructure (i.e. dams, reservoirs) and diversifying sources of water supply in the long-term are critical given the great infrastructure gap in the Province, exploring complementary – or alternative –options will be useful to optimise the investment. Indeed, the cost of dams, reservoirs and new pipelines can be high compared to other solutions. A study on Australia's water supply options has shown that long distance pipelines are very costly, while stormwater reuse, catchment thinning and demand management are amongst the least expensive alternatives (Figure 3.4). In addition, grey infrastructures are less flexible, an aspect which is non negligible in the context of such a fast-changing metropolitan area as Metro Cebu. The geological conditions of Cebu (soft land) also create risks of landslides and make the construction of large-scale infrastructure such as dams more difficult. LGUs in Cebu should therefore explore cost-efficient options to alleviate the demand for "grey" infrastructure, in particular:

- Green infrastructure can ensure water conservation and purification, reducing the need for surface water infrastructure and treatment facilities;
- Economic instruments can also be used to manage demand, reduce consumption and generate revenues to expand the quantity and quality of piped infrastructure and sanitation systems, and thereby support the infrastructure projects of the JICA-MCDCB Roadmap Study; and
- Innovative technologies, in particular smart city tools, can progressively help to enhance the performance of water infrastructure.

Figure 3.4. **Direct cost of alternative water supply options**

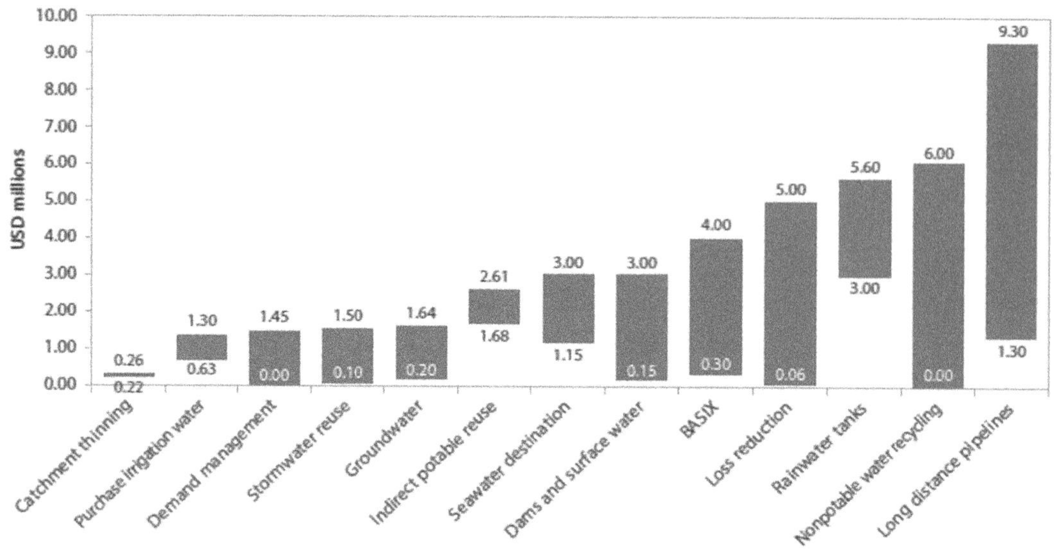

Source: Marsden Jacob Associates (2006), "Securing Australia's Urban Water Supplies: Opportunities and Impediments. A discussion paper prepared for the Department of the Prime Minister and Cabinet", www.environment.gov.au.

Developing green infrastructure for water conservation and purification

The current strategy in Cebu – shifting from groundwater use to surface water resources – is a process that has also been followed in many OECD cities in the past. However, water and ecosystem conservation strategies are now getting more attention and benefitting from larger investments in the OECD areas (OECD, 2015a). This is also relevant in the case of developing cities, where the alteration of natural hydrological systems results in an increased run-off rate and volume; decreased infiltration and groundwater recharge base flow; deterioration of water quality in streams, rivers, and shallow groundwater; and loss of natural habitat and biodiversity (OECD, 2015a) – all of which are affecting Cebu. Climate change is also projected to cause adverse impacts on freshwater species diversity and water quality as a result of an increase in water temperature and changes in the physical, chemical and biological properties of lakes and rivers (Intergovernmental Panel on Climate Change, 2007).

"Green" infrastructure, in this regard, can also support water supply and sanitation strategies in Cebu. Green infrastructures are defined as "a strategically planned network of natural and semi-natural areas with other environmental features designed and managed to deliver a wide range of ecosystem services (OECD, 2015a). It incorporates green spaces (or blue if aquatic ecosystems are concerned) and other physical features in terrestrial (including coastal) and marine areas" (European Commission, 2013). The benefits of green infrastructures are increasingly well-documented. The Nature Conservancy (2014) has computed that if cities invested in watershed conservation, 700 million people could receive better-quality water and water utilities could save USD 890 million a year in water-treatment costs. Watershed conservation may be particularly relevant to low-income cities that cannot afford the capital, and operation and maintenance (O&M) costs of built infrastructures (OECD, 2015a), and is therefore something on which Cebu must concentrate efforts.

A watershed is an area of land that drains rainwater into one location such as stream, lake or wetland, supplying drinking water, water for agriculture and manufacturing, and providing habitat to numerous species of plants and animals. Thus these water bodies are crucial for Metro Cebu and must be properly managed and protected. The Central Cebu Protected Landscape (CCPL) was constituted in 2007 under Republic Act No. 9486, and covers a consolidated area of 28, 312 hectares consisting of Buhisan Watershed Forest Reserve, Mananga Watershed Forest Reserve, Sudlon National Park, Central Cebu National Park and the Kotkot-Lusaran Watershed Forest Reserve located in the cities of Cebu, Talisay, Toledo and Danao and in the municipalities of Minglanilla, Consolacion, Liloan, Compostela and Balamban (Metro Cebu, 2016). The regional office of the Department of Environment and Natural Resources of the Central Visayas (DENR-7) is responsible for the management and conservation of the watersheds. The CCPL Protected Area Management Board is directed by the regional director, and the conservation project is supervised by the chief of the Provincial Environment Natural Resource Office (PENRO, part of DENR). However the CCPL still lacks the adequate resources to administer such large natural areas. It has currently has five organic employees, three contractual workers and third party warm bodies or labourers, who are poorly equipped, and requires more funds to function properly (Granert, 2017).

Furthermore, protection, conservation and management of CCPL should be a joint effort through the co-operation of the DENR-7 with local government units (LGUs), non-government organisations (NGOs), business sectors, but especially civil society organisations (CSOs) and local communities. The DENR should continue raising public awareness, furthering and reinforcing the 'dalaw and turo' (visit and teach) programme, that aims to teach and promote environmental messages on nature conservation, especially in the communities living near the watersheds. The DENR could also formalise co-operation with local inhabitants, taking inspiration from the DENR in the Cordillera Administrative Region, north of Luzon. In order to protect a watershed, the DENR-CAR signed a Memorandum of Agreement (MOA) with a homeowners association of the watershed area's inhabitants (Baguio City, 2016). The MOA stipulates that the occupants will not expand into determined areas and mandates that the occupants will maintain their structures for residential purposes and will be prohibited from transferring their rights over the allocated lots. It also provides that a core group will be formed to monitor the strict compliance of the association to the terms and conditions of the MOA, submit annual report on the compliance of the individual members, report any intrusion by squatters in the watershed and in co-ordination with the city government and the DENR-CAR will undertake an annual tree-planting programme to reforest what remains of the watershed. Indeed, reforestation with the support of local communities should be promoted. Forests in the watershed areas are fragmented, but could help to protect these natural assets, as they constitute a natural barrier, and trees limit the erosion of the soil.

Green infrastructures can bring multiple benefits that can help to address not only water supply issues through conservation but also water sanitation issues, while increasing resilience to floods (see next section for this last point). For instance, wetland construction or restoration not only provides water supply but also helps to purify water, ensures biological control, water temperature control, flood resilience and protection of ecosystems. Dams, in comparison, provide water supply and water temperature control, but separate facilities are needed to purify water and ensure biological control (OECD, 2015a). In addition, green infrastructures are cost-effective options; they do not necessarily substitute the need for basic grey infrastructure, but can prevent to some extent or postpone the cost of building and extending grey infrastructures. They are also more flexible and can be put in place more quickly, which is non negligible considering that socio-economic trends and climate change impacts are subject to considerable uncertainty. The following examples from OECD cities are worth mentioning (OECD, 2015a):

- In Philadelphia, the proposed eco-friendly "sponge-like" water system involving new forms of drainage (green roofs, wetlands, repaving with porous materials) would cost USD 2 billion, less than half as much as a conventional upgrade of the current pipe and basin system (WEF, 2014); achieving a similar level of service through an additional wastewater treatment plant would be 4 or 5 times more expensive at USD 8-10 billion (Walton, 2012).
- In Australia, a pilot project funded by Queensland Urban Utilities in partnership with SEQ Catchments to repair 500 metres of eroded riparian corridors near the Beaudesert Sewage Treatment Plant in the Logan River catchment can achieve the same level of environmental performance as upgrading the treatment plant at a lower cost.

A first type of green infrastructure that should be developed in Cebu is **decentralised rainwater collection and drainage systems in residences, public buildings and industrial areas.** Local authorities can more aggressively promote the installation of rainwater tanks (e.g. roof run-off collectors) and pervious surfaces, in particular. In addition to the obvious benefits they bring in terms of flood resilience, decentralised rainwater collection and drainage systems help to minimise pollution, as rainwater gets more heavily polluted when it flows over long distances on dry streets, pavements, or parking lots. In Cebu, significant amounts of garbage are discharged in the streets, and this aggravates the problem. Such infrastructure also improves the quality of water returned to the environment; pervious surfaces in particular allow rainwater to trickle through the ground and recharge aquifers, which should help to tackle the issue of aquifer depletion in the Province. They can also alleviate the need to build and extend sewerage and treatment infrastructure, and this is also a means to harness private capital: local authorities should indeed design mechanisms to incite property and land developers to participate directly in the construction of such infrastructure (OECD, 2015a) and therefore alleviate MCWD's and LGU's pressure to extend pipe infrastructure. Finally, such infrastructure would be even more useful in low-income communities with no access to water distribution and treatment networks; rainwater collection systems provide opportunities for direct use (e.g. toilet flushing) and decrease the need or at least the cost of transporting water (OECD, 2015a). In India, for instance, the State of Tamil Nadu has made eco-efficient approaches compulsory for new buildings to reduce depletion of its groundwater. Not only do households use the rainwater as an alternative source of supply, but it is also used to replenish groundwater. In Chennai, the groundwater table has risen 3 to 6 metres since households began to use rainwater and reduced groundwater extraction (UN ESCAP and UN HABITAT, 2015).

Generally speaking, **large green spaces and retention ponds** also offer similar benefits as decentralised rainwater collection and drainage systems: by catching rainwater and run-off, they help to recharge local aquifers and also, ensure natural water purification, decreasing the need for water treatment if such water is to be re-used for supply. In Cebu, such green spaces need to be preserved outside and inside urban areas, and more should be created over vacant land. In addition, they provide opportunities to create recreational areas and preserve biodiversity, if well managed.

Decentralised rainwater collection and drainage systems, and green spaces should be, in particular, developed on vacant land and green field projects where this is easier to undertake. Considering the expansion of the metropolitan area and the lack of space that has already started to contain urban development, it is urgent for local authorities to start implementing such solutions. In higher density areas, installing green infrastructure is more difficult, but nonetheless achievable. The examples of Malmo, Philadelphia and Portland have shown that it is possible to increase the quantity of permeable surfaces in urban centres (OECD, 2015a). In Cebu, considering that numerous constructions are taking place at the moment, there are opportunities for such infrastructure even in urban areas, in and on buildings. Urban areas of Metro Cebu also possess 10.9% of vacant land considered not hazardous and suitable for development, mostly concentrated in Lapu-Lapu, Danao and Carcar. There is also a certain area of undeveloped land which is considered hazardous (76% of total undeveloped land of Metro Cebu). Such sites could be ideal candidates for the development of green spaces and retention ponds serving water supply, sanitation and flood resilience purposes, and connected to existing infrastructures and settlements in safe urban areas. The proper regulations and incentives must, however, be put in place to ensure implementation of such measures (see section below on pricing instruments).

Finally, integrating grey and green infrastructure needs to be ensured to maximise the benefit of green infrastructure, noting that the demand/supply gap for water in Cebu is forecasted to reach 437, 000 m3 per day in 2050 (JICA and MCDCB, 2015) and non-grey infrastructures alone therefore cannot meet this increasing water demand. In short, non-grey infrastructures need to be developed in complementarity. This should also be reflected in the role of the upcoming Commission for Water Resources and Water Supply Management under the MCDA.

Managing demand, behaviours and water revenues through pricing mechanisms

An important set of instruments to manage water supply and sanitation is pricing mechanisms. Pricing mechanisms can be effective means to rationalise consumption and manage demand, therefore easing pressure on water resources use and treatment facilities, while saving costs and raising revenues that can be used for building new water infrastructure and local capacities. OECD cities tend to use a range of economic instruments for urban water management, in particular retail water tariffs, user charges, fines and penalties, water pollution charges and levies (Figure 3.5). MCWD and other local authorities on water supply and sanitation in Metro Cebu make some use of such instruments but should however expand them. They would come as great complement of the large infrastructure projects recommended in the JICA-MCDCB *Roadmap Study*.

Figure 3.5. **Use of economic instruments for urban water management in OECD countries**

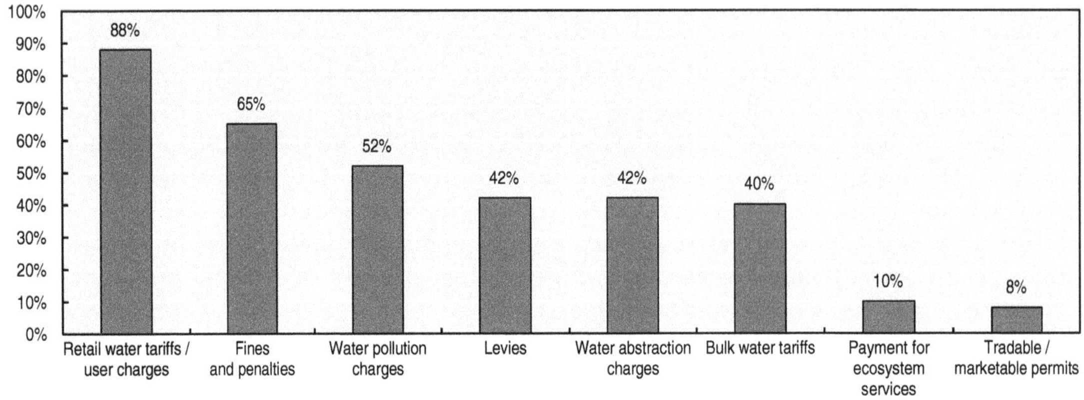

Source: OECD (2016), Water Governance in Cities, OECD Publishing, Paris, http://dx.doi.org/10.1787/9789264251090-en.

Generating higher revenues through water tariffs

Water tariffs are in use in Cebu but only limitedly and should be used more systematically. In the Philippines, many water utilities face financial difficulties because tariffs are too low to recover costs (ADB, 2013a). In terms of water sanitation, most households in Cebu particularly do not pay for septage service although MCWD plans to incorporate the cost of desludging into bills. MCWD and other LGUs of Metro Cebu, that have the authority to manage water tariffs, should enhance efforts to develop tariff for existing sanitation services and most importantly to finance and recover cost of construction of wastewater treatment plants. In terms of water supply, MCWD has adopted a block tariff structure that allows collecting revenue according to the amount of water consumed, with higher tariffs applied to larger consumers. Recently, tariff rates for the first 10 cubic meters consumed were raised by 12% to PHP 15, but residents that consume less than 30 cubic meters still benefit from subsidised rates,[1] the current cost of production from groundwater pumping being around PHP 21 per cubic meter. MCWD and other LGUs of Metro Cebu providing water supply should explore options to increase water tariffs for large consumers, especially commercial and industrial facilities. This could serve as a way to reduce excessive consumption and better manage water demands. The block tariff structure could be sharper for these large consumers, especially considering that water consumption is set to increase as economic development takes place in the Province. Such tariff increase could, in this regard, factor in the water scarcity situation in Cebu. In Manila East for instance, there is a significant leap of water tariffs for large consumers (Figure 3.6). Other LGUs in Metro Cebu should follow a similar approach. Upgrading water tariff to cost-recovery levels would encourage water utilities to borrow to finance urban infrastructure projects but also similarly encourage commercial banks and government financial institutions to lend. In contrast, the national government should adopt a common methodology for tariff review in the Philippines to facilitate such measures at the subnational level, and to further encourage investments in the water sector (ADB, 2013a).

By way of example, the Metropolitan Waterworks and Sewerage System (MWSS), in charge of water privatisation in Metro Manila, has for instance created targets and tariffs for the sanitation and sewerage programmes of the two private concessionaires of the capital city (ADB, 2013a). In Dumaguete City, the LGU enacted the required legislation to obligate households to desludge septic tanks regularly. The water district manages the facility and collects user fees from service connections that are included in monthly water bills, thus raising sufficient revenue to cover operation and maintenance expenses, and to recover capital investments over a reasonable timeframe. Fees are collected from unconnected households directly. According to both LGU and water district officials in Dumaguete, households now spend less on desludging compared to the fees charged by private operators, and have the added comfort of knowing that such waste is treated in a manner consistent with environmental regulations (ADB, 2013a). Another good case in point is Metro Vancouver, where water sales (37%) and sewer levy (27%) account for the major share of local revenues, showing the financial return that can be build out of supply and sanitation services (see Chapter 4 for more details on local revenues in Metro Vancouver). Metro Cebu should draw lessons from these examples to implement policies aiming to increase water tariffs, while working on cutting costs and optimising water treatment and supply process in order to stay competitive and so that larger customers do not turn to private suppliers, on which LGUs and the metropolitan authority should also put more pressure with stricter controls and regulations, as it is suggested further.

Figure 3.6. **Water tariff structure in selected ASEAN-5 cities**

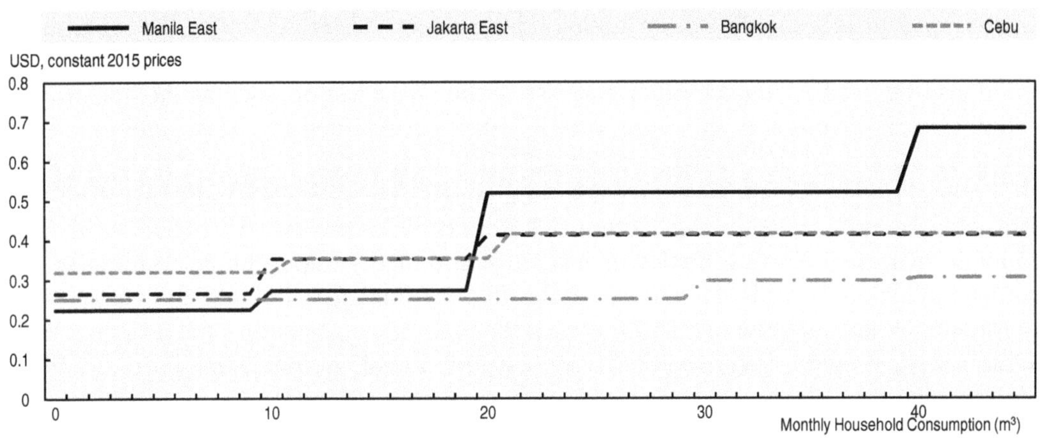

Source: Manila Water (n.d.), www.manilawater.com/downloadables/2015%20tariff%20table%20june%201.%202015.jpg (accessed 3 July 2015); PT Aetra Air Jakarta (Aetra) (2012), "Info Tariff Aetra", www.aetra.co.id/uploads/info_tarif_aetra/tarif_air_aetra_2007.pdf; Metropolitan Waterworks Authority (n.d.), www.mwa.co.th/ewtadmin/ewt/mwa_internet_eng/ewt_news.php?nid=309 (accessed 3 July 2015).

To avoid block water tariff and higher tariffs for large consumers harming poor households, MCWD and LGUs of Metro Cebu will also need to adopt flexible strategies in terms of water pricing. Also, a connected customer who sells water to an unconnected neighbour should not be penalised with a rising block tariff. As a matter of fact, 4.3% of water use for drinking and 10.5% of water used for other purposes are collected from neighbours' taps and wells in Metro Cebu[2] (JICA and MCDCB, 2015). It is therefore recommended that the number of persons served by a connection be noted on each water bill, and that the water bill for a shared connection between neighbours be adjusted to reflect it (ADB, 2014). The generation and use of water-related revenues to be invested back in water supply and sanitation systems will also require all LGUs to adopt separate budget accounts (i.e. also called ring-fencing mechanism). Ring-fencing entails separating activities, assets and revenues of a specific sector – here water – from other sectors managed by LGUs. Ring-fencing leads to more accurate information that can be used for making decisions about resources allocation, management and operational changes and improvements, and tariffs (Water and Sanitation Programme, 2009).

Making stronger use of water-related charges

Local authorities should make stronger use of water abstraction and pollution charges. In particular, there is no existing regulation from the National Water Resources Board (NWRB) to charge for private groundwater pumping in the Philippines. This encourages unsustainable consumption of water resources and opportunities to raise water revenues for MCWD and LGUs are missed, especially considering that the number of private wells is increasing at a fast rate in Cebu. This is also particularly important considering that such non-piped water collection systems (i.e. public wells, households' own wells, neighbours' wells and taps) account for 9.2% of sources of drinking water in Metro Cebu, and 33.4% of sources of water used for other purposes (JICA and MCDCB, 2015). In other words, the impact of MCWD block tariff policy only applies to a portion of the population and is not sufficient per se to raise high revenues and shape behaviour in the whole metropolitan area. Permits for water extraction should be carefully analysed by the relevant authority, taking into consideration aquifer capacities and projected water demand, and prices should be set taking into account water scarcity. The quantity of water extracted must be metered and priced accordingly. Such revenue from charges should also be used to finance other projects in the water sector, such as the construction of the Lusaran dam and the extension of pipe infrastructure. The National Water Resources Board (NWRB) has responsibilities over such matters but is currently delivering permits without such careful local analysis. The NWRB should therefore work more closely with local water authorities to regulate private water use with such economic instruments. As a matter of fact, it would also be appropriate to transfer such competency from NWRB to a local authority, for instance the newly created Cebu Provincial Water Resources Authority (PWRA) (see Section below on Water Governance). Progressively, the recourse to groundwater pumping by households and industries should be eradicated and replaced by pipe infrastructure.

Austin, Texas, also recently created through an Ordinance in the Austin City Code a "Water Well Fee" of USD 7.50 per month for all households operating and drilling a well or installing a water well pump (Austin Water, n.d.). In Southeast Asia, Bangkok stands out as a good example of use of regulations to tackle groundwater extraction. The national government and the Metropolitan Waterworks Authority for instance managed to significantly reduce groundwater extraction in the late 2000s by forbidding groundwater extraction in sensitive areas, by creating license and charging regulations, coupled with strict enforcement policies and awareness campaigns (OECD, 2015b). MCWD could adopt similar strategies for wells located within 100 metres of a pipe connection as such installation is illegal. A more moderate strategy including a fee could be set up for households and businesses using wells beyond 100 metres of a pipe connection and who are less able to access water. In addition, local authorities should explore opportunities to raise complementary charges. The City of Sacramento, California, has adopted a range of fees and charges, such as storm water drainage service fee, wastewater service fee and water development fee that can be consulted in the City Fee Database (City of Sacramento website).

Local authorities should also make stronger use of water-related taxes. Taxes can be an effective instrument to address negative externalities that affect water demand and availability, or the costs of water security (OECD, 2015a). In Cebu, there is little or no use of such economic instruments. In particular, in the case of water supply and sanitation, local authorities should develop land-development taxes (i.e. as land-value capture taxes) to cover for the cost of new needs for urban water management. The construction of new piped connections, septic tanks and wastewater treatment plants should be partly financed using such taxes to be applied to buildings benefitting from such services, in particular large industrial, commercial and residential estates, connected to municipal water distribution and treatment networks, including future sewerage infrastructure. Such taxes based on polluter-pay principles encourage water conservation and treatment at source instead of building large-scale facilities. Such taxes could be part of a carrot and stick mechanism: for instance, rebates on such taxes could be created for landowners developing individual rainwater catchment infrastructure, or septic tanks, as further incentives to develop green infrastructure. New York City has adopted interesting water re-use incentives (Box 3.1). There is high potential in Cebu for such policies as much of the land is privately owned, especially by large real estate conglomerates (e.g. SM Group) which could significantly contribute to raise water revenues. The case of Casablanca also offers a good example of such policy and has shown that it can even be tied to objectives of expanding water access to poor communities (Box 3.2). Such land-value capture tools however require a proper regime for land ownership and fiscal capacities (OECD, 2015a).

Box 3.1. **New York City's Comprehensive Water Reuse Program**

New York City's Comprehensive Water Reuse Program offers a 25% reduction on water and sewer charges for buildings that maintain a Comprehensive Water Reuse System (CWRS). A CWRS building may capture, treat and recycle blackwater (i.e. sanitary wastewater) or greywater (i.e. wastewater from lavatories, showers and clothes washers). The CWRS must achieve a 25% reduction in a building's baseline demand for potable water. Program rules establish a baseline of 60 gallons per person per day for residential buildings and 10 gallons per employee per day for indoor use in an office building.

Since its inception in 2004, this program has created an effective indirect subsidy for private water reuse systems. It has been estimated that for a large mixed residential and commercial water user, participation in the program would reduce operating costs by more than USD 1 million a year by 2012 and close to USD 3 million a year by 2015.

Source: NYC Environmental Protection (n.a.), "Comprehensive Water Reuse Program: Application and Instructions", www.nyc.gov/html/dep/pdf/waterreuse.pdf (accessed June 2017).

Box 3.2. **The financial contribution of land development taxes: Casablanca, Morocco**

Casablanca is characterised by rapid urbanisation; its population is expected to grow from 3.5 million to 5 million to 2030. Extending the water network, securing access to the resource and protecting it against frequent floods are serious concerns for the local authority, which needs to finance these projects.

The city defined a new investment programme in 2007 and contracted Lydec, a subsidiary of Suez Environnement, to provide WSS services and mitigate flood risks. Revenues from user tariffs cover operational and maintenance costs and the renewal of existing assets (accounting for 70% of total cost over the last decade).

Box 3.2. **The financial contribution of land development taxes: Casablanca, Morocco** *(continued)*

A dedicated account (*fonds de travaux*) covers the remaining costs (essentially land acquisition, network extension and social connections). Financed mainly by contributions from property developers, it has financed a growing share of total investment, from 7% in 2004 to 54% in 2014.

Property developers also cover the costs of connecting to the network and in-house equipment. Their contribution varies depending on the type of housing (social housing, villas, hotels and industrial zones), and they pay additional costs for developments that do not feature in the master plan. Contributions are waived when the developments take place in underprivileged neighbourhoods and slums. Special conditions have also been set to adjust the contribution to the pace of urban expansion, and to harness major urban developments.

The contribution is a share of the price of property when sold, ranging from 0.7% of the selling cost for social housing to 1.3% for luxury apartments and buildings.

Source: OECD (2015a), *Water and Cities, Ensuring Sustainable Futures*, OECD Publishing, Paris, http://dx.doi.org/10.1787/9789264230149-en.

The case of low-income communities and water economic instruments

Water-related tariffs (as shown in the case of shared connections), taxes and charges must be carefully used on low-income communities. A critical issue that the Province of Cebu is facing is the need to expand coverage of water distribution systems, and in particular piped infrastructure which only account for 12.5% of water used for drinking and 49.9% of water used for other purposes. MCWD plans to add 70 km of pipes by 2020 and cover 80% of the population. To date however, many low-income communities remain excluded from such service. One of the major obstacles to their expansion is the cost of connection, which is set at PHP 4 500 by MWCD. In addition, households need to pay a deposit fee of PHP 1 500. Field studies suggest that many people cannot afford to pay for this connection fee (ADB, 2014), forcing them to opt for alternative water supply systems which may be less efficient, less standardised and/or more expensive (e.g. buying water from a neighbour is usually more expensive that piped water). In addition, it prevents the water utility operators from controlling consumption accurately and raising revenues. Thus, while this type of charge, as explained previously, is overall useful to raise revenues and finance the development of water infrastructure, it can be counter-productive with regards to inclusiveness objectives. Consequently, connection fees should be eradicated for poor households only, and increased water tariffs (especially for large consumers, as discussed previously) could be used to make up for the economic losses. The case of Viet Nam, in particular the cities of Hai Phong, Binh Buong and Ho Chi Minh City, has shown that the abolishment of connection fees can bring positive benefits (ADB, 2014). An alternative could be to subsidise connection fees for low-income households, as was done in Phnom Penh, Cambodia.

Integrating progressively advanced technological solutions for water supply and sanitation in Cebu

Green infrastructure and economic instruments to improve the management of water supply and sanitation in Cebu should also be combined with technological innovation. **Smart water infrastructures (SMW)**, in particular, should be part of the roadmap for WSS in Cebu. The International Telecommunication (ITU) defines smart water management in cities as the attempt to alleviate challenges in urban water management by incorporating ICT products, solutions and systems in water management and sanitation (ITU, 2014). In particular, SMW provides benefits in terms of real-time data production, collection and analysis, and can enhance water quality and reliability, ensure proper management of green infrastructures, decrease water losses due to leakage, reduce operational costs, and improve customer control and choice (ITU, 2014). Although still fragmented, the smart water market is booming: Lloyd Owen estimates that global sales for smart water systems ranged from USD 500 000 to USD 1 billion in 2009-10; they are forecasted to rise between USD 5 billion and USD 16 billion by 2020. Smart water systems accounted for approximately 0.5%-0.9% of the global water hardware market in 2010 and look set to account for 2.9%-9.4% of the market by 2020 (OECD, 2012).

Smart water infrastructures should be included early on in the development of new infrastructures in Cebu. There will be opportunities indeed to insert monitoring devices for leakages, for instance, during the construction of new pipes and dams. Local authorities and private companies should not miss the current window of opportunity to couple "traditional" water infrastructure with SMW. The following smart water technologies could be particularly useful in the case of Cebu and should be applied to the infrastructure the JICA-MCDCB *Roadmap Study* recommended to build:

- Smart meters are the most widely adopted type of smart water infrastructure. Such metres, installed in households or in water distribution networks, can inform utility companies about leakages and help to reduce non-revenue water. They can also help customers to get information and control their individual consumption, and create a new relationship between water users and suppliers. Finally, they provide data about water consumption to the utility company and can help to refine demand forecasts and design more tailored water tariffs (OECD, 2015a).
- Pollution detectors can help local authorities monitor the quality of water in various sensitive areas, such as rivers, reservoirs, dams, and identify sources of pollution.
- Data modelling software can help to predict river and rainwater flows, and thereby improve infrastructure design. In Hamburg, the SYNOPSE projects involved developing different precipitation models and comparing the resultant digital series with real rainfall data.

Local authorities in Cebu also need to start installing advanced technological water supply and sanitation facilities. In particular, they should consider expanding desalination and used water reclamation technologies to increase water supply capacities and ease water stress in the Province. A desalination plant was built in Cebu and currently sells water at less than PHP 40 per cubic metre, which is encouraging. Solar-powered technologies have also been tested with success and show the potential of such innovation. Singapore offers an excellent example of the benefits of such technologies. The nation-state suffered from high water stress due to water scarcity until the 1990s, and decided to undertake an ambitious programme called the "Four National Taps", based on desalination, reclamation of used water, water imports and rainwater collection and storage. The support of the national government in such projects would be critical, owing to the high fixed costs of building such technologies.

Assessing and enhancing Cebu's flood resilience

Cebu's flood and typhoon risk

Floods are one of the water-related risks faced by Cebu Province. They routinely occur during the monsoon season between June and November, although average precipitation is not as high as in many other Asian cities.[3] They may also be the result of storm surges caused by typhoons, as was the case in 2013 during the super typhoon Haiyan/Yolanda, which caused many poor people to suffer from a loss of homes and livelihood opportunities (e.g. fisheries) particularly along the northern coastline. A number of other factors suggest that some areas in the Province are exposed to floods (JICA and MCDCB, 2015):

- In Metro Cebu area, it is estimated that around 42.6% of households do not have drainage systems in their neighbourhood. This figure hides significant imbalance in drainage infrastructure across LGUs: while in Cebu City, for instance, 21.1% of households do not have a drainage facility in their neighbourhood, in Lapu-Lapu City and San Fernando as much as 69.9% and 69.5% do not, respectively.
- In addition, the quality of drainage infrastructure is often suboptimal: around 21% of households with drainage facilities have reported them in bad or very bad conditions, and 62% in average condition. As reported in the drainage master plan study, drainage that was inspected revealed that more than 50% of the drainage lines are either silted or clogged by garbage. Many rivers and creeks are also filled with garbage discharged by informal settlers along riverbanks.
- Rivers in the Metro Cebu have become constricted to construction of structures on top of them.

The LGUs most affected by floods are Mandaue, Talisay, Danao and Cebu City, although only a share of households have actually experienced floods in these areas (JICA and MCDCB, 2015).[4] Another estimate made by the JICA-MCDCB study in 2015 revealed that a significant share of coastal areas, including in Metro Cebu, faces moderate flood exposure. These low lying areas extend a few kilometres inland from the coast and represent about 8% of Cebu City's total land area. Despite the small area, this land hosts approximately two-thirds of the population (JICA and MCDCB, 2015). In addition, the risk of floods is not static and the following parameters suggest that Cebu may be increasingly vulnerable to floods:

- Urbanisation and demographic growth may put a growing number of people at risk. This is even more likely if poverty in urban areas increases, which means more people with low protection and capacity to sustain a disaster are at risk;
- Economic growth, industrialisation and the increasing number of businesses and infrastructure implies that a larger number of assets can be damaged by a natural disaster, causing significant economic losses and undermining Cebu's economic growth without proper preparedness and insurance mechanisms;
- Climate change is likely to increase the Province's exposure to floods: some simulation tools already show that in 2°C and 4°C increase scenarios, the island of Mactan and the coastal areas in Metro Cebu will be flooded due to sea level rise, in a business-as-usual scenario.[5] Extreme weather events such as more severe droughts and deluges due to climate change are also more likely to occur in the

future. Although super typhoon Haiyan/Yolanda did not hit Cebu as hard as the Eastern Visayas Islands, there is no guarantee future typhoons will not primarily hit Cebu;

- Poor urban planning, lack of infrastructure and adaptive capacities are also factors of vulnerability. The increase in the share of impervious surfaces and the loss or alteration of natural hydrological systems decrease the absorption capacity of Cebu and also aquifer recharge rate, as mentioned previously. However, there is no accurate data on urban expansion and loss of natural assets in and around Metro Cebu. Settlements in flood-prone areas and coastal reclamation are also determinants of vulnerability. Obstruction of waterways owing to open dumping of solid waste and the lack of drainage and polder infrastructure in Cebu also suggest the Province's resilience is low, and is particularly vulnerable to a large-scale natural event.

If not properly tackled, such disasters can result in human losses and high economic damages. Typhoon Haiyan/Yolanda, which primarily hit the Eastern Visayas Region, near the Central Visayas Region where Cebu Province is located, is estimated to have caused economic losses at USD 13 billion. Sea level rise will also create additional costs: for instance, shoreline retreat in the United States is projected to cost between USD 270 billion and USD 475 billion for each metre of sea-level rise (OECD, 2010). Floods can also have negative consequences on the environment, if it spreads solid waste and hazardous substances which are openly dumped in a city; typhoons can also destroy mangrove forests and the whole ecosystems relying on them.

Developing robust DRRM plans at the metropolitan scale

LGUs challenges in developing DRRM plans

At the national level, the 2010 Republic Act 10121 (RA 10121) on Disaster Risk Reduction Management (DRRM) and the Disaster Risk Reduction Management Plan 2011-2028 guide resilience efforts in the country. In Cebu City, the Office for Disaster Risk Reduction and Emergency Management of Cebu was created in 2013 in order to apply national strategies. Its objectives are to i) mitigate the potential effects of the various hazards and vulnerabilities that might impact the Province; ii) implement measures aimed at preserving life and property, further minimising casualties and damages; iii) respond and manage effectively to the needs of the affected population and local jurisdictions during emergencies; and iv) provide a recovery system aimed at returning to normalcy from the consequences of natural and human-induced disasters that may impact the Province of Cebu.

In practice, however, many LGUs have not been able to craft DRRM plans (and CLUPs) or have designed weak plans which do not support a robust strategy against floods or other natural disasters. This is partly due to a lack of technical capacities and a short-sighted vision of disaster resilience. Not all LGUs possess a permanent DRRM Office, and the DRRM officers are usually not properly trained and come from the Mayor's Office, without having any specific expertise. They suffer from a lack of assistance from the national government on how to prepare the plans. Consequently many LGUs settle for a very weak DRRM plan to fulfil the conditions to receive the 5% share of the IRA, but do not build robust DRRM strategies.

Metropolitan scale DRRM planning will complement LGUs efforts

Metropolitan scale DRRM planning will greatly help LGUs in this regard. JICA and MCDCB have already developed a Roadmap for Stormwater Management in Metro Cebu, with a vision to 2050 (Table 3.2). A Stormwater Drainage Master Plan for Metro Cebu, based on the JICA-MCDCB study, is also currently in preparation with financial support of DPWH Central Office. With the Master Plan, LGUs will be able to effectively design and implement their own DRRM plans and ensure coherence with other LGUs.

Table 3.2. **JICA-MCDCB Roadmap for stormwater management in Metro Cebu**

Timeframe	Measures for stormwater management
Short-term	• Implementation of a Comprehensive Study for "A Metro Cebu Integrated Flood and Drainage System (MCIFDS) Master Plan • Cleaning rivers, creeks and drainages • Construction of small-scale rainwater storage facilities
Medium-term	• Construction of drainage facilities based on MCIFDS • River improvement projects • Embankment in inundation places in rural areas
Long-term	• River improvement projects • Construction of large-scale rainwater storage facilities

Source: JICA and MCDCB (2015), "Roadmap Study for Sustainable Urban Development in Metro Cebu", Cebu, the Philippines.

Another ongoing example is the collaboration between Cebu Province, MCDCB, the University of San Carlos and GIDRM/GIZ to facilitate the integration of scientific data in local DRRM planning through the development of a province wide multi-hazard suitability map. The suitability map supports evidence-based decision-making in local planning and budgeting (Box 3.3). There are also efforts of the Cebu Province, MCDCB and GIDRM/GIZ to jointly assist LGUs in the development and alignment of local DRRM and CCA plans. This improves their chances to access national resilience funding, such as the People Survival Fund (PSF), and implement identified DRRM priorities.

Box 3.3. **Suitability Mapping: Evidence-based and risk-informed decision making in local planning and budgeting**

In many countries specifically mandated national agencies and their national and international non-state partners make available to local governments a rich body of information on climate change and natural hazards. Mandated agencies support local governments in benefitting from this rich wealth of information by supporting in accessing, understanding, utilising and integrating this information most strategically into decision-making processes.

In support of these mandates, the GIDRM/GIZ, the Philippine National Economic Planning Agency (Neda) Region 8 and two Philippine provinces collaborated in developing a process template that helps aggregate and directly link climate and natural hazard related data from multiple sources into one aggregate surface. The suitability map approach works primarily with

Box 3.3. Suitability Mapping: Evidence-based and risk-informed decision making in local planning and budgeting *(continued)*

official local data sources and climate projections, complemented with local, national and international open data sources where available and when appropriate.

A standard suitability map covers 6 natural hazards: Rain and earthquake induced landslide, typhoon, storm surge, tsunami and fresh water flooding, weighed according to the statistical probability and the severity of their occurrence. Climate change adaptation wise it is based on a medium emission scenario using 3 global climate assumption scenarios, up to 2050. The standard resolution outlay is 1:100 000 for provinces and 1:50 000 for urban areas. The standard parameters can be adjusted based on the specific interests and contexts including the availability of data.

The special feature of the suitability map is that it translates scientific-statistical data on natural hazards and climate change into a percentage of expected damage per year. This translation in economic categories is more intuitive and facilitates the utilisation of disaster risk reduction and management (DRRM) information. It was originally developed in the aftermath of typhoon Yolanda to guide LGUs in identifying safer places for normal residential buildings. For Cebu Province, selected agricultural crops were added. Suitability mapping, above all, is not an approach to generate more data, but an approach to help consolidate and translate existing data for actual use in political decision-making.

Source: Deutsche Gesellschaft für International Zusammenarbeit (GIZ) GmbH (2015), "Residential Building Suitability Map for Leyte Island, the Philippines", www.preventionweb.net/publications/view/47118.

DRRM plans must be informed by comprehensive data on infrastructure, assets and land vulnerability

All LGUs in Metro Cebu must adopt a more comprehensive approach to flood vulnerability assessment to identify current weaknesses. The first step of any flood resilience action plan is to adopt a comprehensive approach that identifies current weaknesses. Weather and climate events, exposure (location, topography, sprawling urban development) and vulnerability (the propensity of people, infrastructure and assets to be affected) are indeed all factors of flood risk (IPCC, 2012). They are often the result of skewed development processes associated with, for example, environmental degradation, rapid and unplanned urbanisation in hazardous areas, and limited options of livelihoods for the poor (IPCC, 2012). JICA made substantial efforts to produce knowledge on Cebu's vulnerability to floods, but much remains to be done as most data produced focused on some infrastructure only and do not tackle other aspects of vulnerability. For instance, there is no estimate of the potential economic and social damages of a flood or of a typhoon. The lack of knowledge on factors of vulnerability may explain why local authorities have mostly focused on disaster response so far. To improve risk resilience in Cebu, more precise risk assessment measures also need to be in place. Currently, risks are not always measured in terms of risk probability and impact. However, including data on risk probability and impact would provide for a more comprehensive approach in tackling vulnerability. This can help LGUs implement more targeted policy measures.

LGUs in Cebu should assess and map the vulnerability of residents, businesses and infrastructure based on the recent and potential impacts of a flood or a typhoon on infrastructure and the local economy. Assessment of potential future damages is critical to factor in climate change impacts on the resilience of Cebu. The Paris region

(Ile-de-France) offers a good practice of flood vulnerability assessment, in this regard. The national government has successfully involved governmental and relevant non-governmental stakeholders to assess the potential impacts of a 100-year flood6 on infrastructure (power distribution, local transport systems, water supply and heat distribution), hospital and school capacities and operations, government buildings and operations, and business and economic performance. For each of the critical urban utility systems, a map of vulnerability has been created and helps to visualise more clearly the different types and different urban areas at risk (Box 3.4). The same OECD study (OECD, 2014b) that reports on these initiatives in the Paris region also details methodologies to calculate the macroeconomic and microeconomic impacts of a flood event. LGUs in Cebu could use them as guides to strengthen their flood and typhoon risk assessment mechanisms. The national government and an organisation such as Earthquake Megacities Initiative (EMI), based in Quezon City, could provide assistance through frequent capacity-building training on vulnerability assessment.

LGUs in Cebu could also take example from Bogor, Indonesia: local authorities have collected data on families to assess their vulnerability to floods (i.e. if they have been affected and how much assets lost in the past) and have built GIS maps of vulnerability. A comprehensive plan has been designed based on such data and also tackles preparedness aspects on the ground, in schools in particular. Such data will provide useful information for the Metro Cebu Integrated Flood and Drainage System Master Plan and each LGU's DRRM plan. It is also critical to collect data and design a plan at the watershed level and integrate it with strategies in Metro Cebu, since floods have a strong urban-rural linkage (many low-lying areas of Metro Cebu are affected by flash floods originating in mountainous areas such as Lusaran, for instance). The newly created Provincial Water Resources Authority (PWRA) could play a critical role in this regard, but this will require an acknowledgement of its role in the legislation (see Section 4).

Box 3.4. **Flood vulnerability assessment in the Seine Basin region (Paris Ile-de-France)**

By dint of its location at the confluence of the various Seine tributaries, Île-de-France and its heartlands are particularly vulnerable to a major Seine flood. Extensive flooding of underground spaces and cellars in the urban area and its impact on critical networks, including electricity, water, communications and transport, means that major flooding would have effects beyond the flood-prone area. The various works carried out since the beginning of the 2000s by the General Secretariat of the Paris Defence and Security Zone (*Secrétariat Général de la Zone de Défense et de Sécurité de Paris*, SGZDSP) have made it possible to actively involve network operators and other stakeholders in the flooding issue and to evaluate a number of impacts as follows, under a 100-year flood scenario:

- Power distribution would be substantially affected with almost one-quarter of power sub-stations either flooded or cut off as a precaution (DRIEE, 2012). ERDF, the French electricity distribution network operator, estimates that, in an extreme case, more than 1.5 million domestic and business customers, including 377 000 in Paris, would experience power cuts as a result. The area that would potentially be affected by the power cut is around 50% greater than the flooded area.

Box 3.4. **Flood vulnerability assessment in the Seine Basin region (Paris Ile-de-France)** *(continued)*

- A significant proportion of public transport could be affected with almost 140 of the 250 kilometres of the underground network closed as a precaution. The rail termini of Lyon, Austerlitz and Saint-Lazare are also in the flood-prone area and would experience service disruption.
- The road network could be closed at many points: the bridges across the Seine would be closed to traffic, due to their weakened structure, making it impossible to travel from the right to the left bank. Five motorways and several major highways, especially along the Seine, would also be inaccessible.
- The drinking water supply could be disrupted in the outskirts of Paris where more than 5 million customers could suffer extended water cuts and 1.3 million a deterioration in quality in the worst case scenario. It is estimated in total that the power outages, water cuts and the disruption to transport networks would have significant impacts on the daily lives of over 5 million people. For each of the critical urban utility systems, a map of vulnerability has been created and helps to visualise more clearly the different types and different urban areas at risk.
- Flooding is a direct concern for 55 700 businesses and 622 000 jobs in the floodplain (IAU, 2011). The businesses' premises and means of production may be damaged and some or all of their stock destroyed. Consequential operating losses may also be exacerbated by disruption to the electricity, communications and water services; outages will also affect a more extensive area and, therefore, many more businesses. Heavy disruption to the metropolitan public transport network will also prevent many workers from getting to work. Small and medium-sized enterprises (SMEs) account for 85% of businesses in the flood-prone area, and a persistent flood and its consequences could severely affect them. Moreover, the activities in these business quarters focus on computerised services, finance and business services, all areas for which functional telecommunications systems are essential. The impact of major flooding on tourism could also be serious, as this sector is the source of many jobs in the region. 13% of hotel rooms in the region are in the flood-prone area, of which 30% are in an area of electrical vulnerability.
- All of the water treatment plants in the Paris urban area are alongside the river, and the protection measures in place could be overtopped, not only causing them to stop working and therefore discharge effluent directly into the river, but also flooding effluent storage areas. More than 40 million m^3 of untreated water was discharged directly into the natural environment due to Hurricane Sandy (Kenward et al., 2012).

Source: OECD (2014b), "Assessment and recommendations" in *Seine Basin, Île-de-France, 2014: Resilience to Major Floods*, OECD Publishing, Paris, http://dx.doi.org/10.1787/9789264208728-4-en; DRIEE (2012), "Approvisionnement électrique du Grand Paris", Seminar, 6 March 2012, www.driee.ile-de-france.developpementdurable.gouv.fr/IMG/pdf/Seminaire_du_6_mars_2012_-_Presentations_Approvisionnement_electrique_du_Grand_Paris__cle2dcb2f-1.pdf; IAU (2011), "Économie francilienne: Quelle robustesse face à une inondation majeure?", *Note rapide Économie*, No. 534, Institut d'Aménagement et d'Urbanisme, Paris, https://www.iau-idf.fr/savoir-faire/nos-travaux/edition/economie-francilienne-quelle-robustesse-face-a-une-inondation-majeure.html; Kenward et al. (2012), "Sewage Overflows from Hurricane Sandy, Climate Central, Princeton", New Jersey, www.climatecentral.org/pdfs/Sewage.pdf.

Green infrastructure: the connections between WSS and stormwater management

In the past decades, the development of hydraulic infrastructures, improved flood risk management plans and better risk preparedness (among other efforts) have allowed many OECD countries to reduce their flood risk vulnerability, despite increased exposure from economic growth and urbanisation. However, recognition of the limitations of such traditional, engineer-based approaches to flood control has led to the gradual emergence of a new paradigm over the last 10-15 years, based on a more integrated and landscape-based approach to flood risk management and a stronger emphasis on ecosystem-friendly strategies (OECD, 2015a). "Green infrastructures" in this regard contribute both to water supply and sanitation, as elaborated previously, and also flood resilience.

Despite traditional facilities being necessary for Cebu, it is also worthwhile to look for complementary and more flexible infrastructure options, taking into account climate change. Green infrastructures in particular are more adaptive solutions that allow "making space for water", a concept increasingly popular and widely adopted in flood-prone countries such as the Netherlands. Such an example can be found in the city of Portland, Oregon (United States). One of its key policies, in the city's 2005 Watershed Management Plan (PWMP), is the use of plants and soil to slow, filter and infiltrate runoff close to its source, in a way that strengthens and mimics natural functions/processes (OECD, 2012). In Malmö (Sweden), a system has been put in place to drain rainwater from rooftops and other impervious surfaces and channel it through canals, ditches, ponds and wetlands before it arrives in a sub-surface conventional sewer system. The objective was to avoid further overflow in the traditional drainage network (Naumann et al., 2011). Therefore, while the potential of green infrastructures is recognised, it is also important to note that traditional approaches, combined with adaptive green infrastructures, provide complementarities that could tackle the issue of flood management more effectively.

In Cebu, local authorities have already started to recognise the importance of green infrastructures. Many existing drainage pipes are located underground and therefore not easy to maintain, and for this reason tree planting activities have been organised, as some trees flourish on wet terrain, having draining properties and thus helping absorbing groundwater seepage. However, they only take place at a small scale and do not have much impact yet. Local authorities should explore the relevance and feasibility to build the following green infrastructure in combination with the traditional "grey" infrastructure prescribed in the JICA-MCDCB Roadmap Study:

- **Large-scale rainwater retention facilities:** water retention ponds, wetlands, and river and creek catchment areas should be created in both urban and rural areas: depending on the origins of water run-off, this could be an efficient and cheap policy option for Cebu. The use of agriculture soil for water retention should also be promoted. This will require a strategic management that includes both rural and urban areas of Cebu Province. In Metro Cebu, the JICA-MCDCB *Roadmap Study* recommends the creation of large-scale rainwater storage facilities, in particular river and creek catchment areas, although it is difficult to find proper space due to urbanisation (JICA and MCDCB, 2015). There may however be opportunities on vacant land in urban areas, especially those identified as unfit for urbanisation (see Section 2). Wetlands and reservoirs are currently protected through Environmental Impact Assessment (EIA) methods, and some of them benefit from the status of "protected areas" and registered under the National Integrated Protected Area System (NIPAS) Act. Zoning regulations issued by LGUs are also means utilised to safeguard such areas from development;
- **Household rainwater storage facilities:** Republic Act 6716 "Water Wells, Rainwater Collectors, and Spring Development" (1989) requires the Department of Public Works and Highways to construct rainwater collectors and develop springs in every barangay (similar to a subdivision of a city). Republic Act 7160 providing the Local Government Code (1991) extended the requirement to local governments. Such measure is therefore already encouraged at the household level in Cebu, but the implementation is plagued with difficulties, despite petition from the civil society.

MCDCB and the future MCDA, if created, should create ordinances making it mandatory for each household. Economic instruments could support such objectives (see Section 2); and

- **Permeable pavements.** Installing semi-permeable surfaces on secondary roads and pavements and newly developed ones can also yield high retention rates.

Economic instruments could be used to facilitate the implementation of such infrastructures, as already explained in the previous section. Land-value capture tools could be used in development that occurs in flood-prone areas. Strict land-use regulations should however be applied in catchment areas, wetlands and retention ponds if such infrastructures are to be created. Likewise, a tax could be created on impervious surfaces, such as large commercial and industrial spaces and parking lots. Such mechanisms are already in place in France, for instance (Box 3.5). Installing green infrastructure will also require local authorities to make a significant effort in producing data on local water resources and dynamics. Indeed, in order to create the right infrastructure in the right locations, capacities to measure, compute and model river flows will be necessary (see OECD, 2015a).

Box 3.5. **Financing urban rainwater management in France**

The failure to manage rainwater properly affects the capacity of French local authorities to achieve the "good ecological status" mandated by the European Water Framework Directive. Thanks to a dedicated fiscal instrument introduced in 2011, French local authorities have the capacity to set up a new public service dedicated to urban rainwater management. This new service can be financed in full or in part by earmarked revenues from a dedicated tax.

The tax is based on impervious surfaces, in urban areas or future development areas, whether or not the surfaces are connected to a drainage system. It is paid by the owner of the land or property, when the property is larger than a minimal area set by the local authority. The tax rate is set by the local government and cannot exceed EUR 1 square metre per year (EUR/m2/year). It can be reduced, in full or in part, where facilities are in place to reduce run-off; the reduction is meant to reflect the decreased run-off. Several adjacent property owners can join the mechanism, if they build and operate a common facility.

This new tax principally aims to create incentives for managing rainwater close to the source and limiting run-off by implementing measures that mitigate the consequences of impervious surfaces. It also aims to raise revenues, earmarked for long-term urban rainwater management. In the long term, the revenues generated by the tax are bound to decrease as the objectives are met – a trend that local authorities need to anticipate and factor in.

Local authorities have the opportunity when engaging in feasibility studies to reflect on the level of ambition of their urban rainwater management policy and the policy packages (zoning, standards, information, tax, etc.) they wish to implement. Stakeholder consultation should feature prominently in the process.

Source: OECD (2015a), *Water and Cities, Ensuring Sustainable Futures*, OECD Publishing, Paris, http://dx.doi.org/10.1787/9789264230149-en; CERTU (2012), "Taxe pour la gestion des eaux pluviales urbaines", Ministère de l'Écologie, du Développement durable, des Transports et du Logement, Paris.

Flood-resilient land-use and building codes for Cebu

Land-use should be recognised as an anchor of diverse strategies to enhance Cebu's resilience to floods. Land-use policies can first of all avoid settlements in flood-prone areas. The Civil Code of the Philippines (Republic Act 386) provides that "the banks of rivers and streams, even in case they are of private ownership, are subject throughout their entire length and within a zone of three meters along their margins, to the easement of public use in the general interest of navigation, floatage, fishing and salvage." The

Water Code and the National Building Code of the Philippines provide similar regulations. The Forestry Reform Code also protects mangrove forests and swamplands from development by 20 metres. In practice however this is not implemented and it is very unclear how LGUs identify flood-prone areas beyond these broad national regulations, and therefore the land-use decisions may be inappropriate in this regard. There is no specific office to deal with this particular issue. From this perspective, risk screening should be applied to areas where new development is likely to occur, and land-use regulations (e.g. zoning, building permits) could be used to create disincentives to develop such lands to avoid creating new zones at risk. In France, local prevention plans delineate areas at various levels of risk based on previous floods, but also according to predictions for the future. These measures should reinforce or complement economic interests (e.g. tourism) by taking flood risks into account.

Building codes and local development plans should also contain regulations to encourage flood-resilient design and the use of green infrastructure. In Bangkok for instance, a Floor-Area-Ration (FAR) Bonus System was set up for developers who build rainwater storage facilities and green spaces juxtaposing the new building. If the capacity of the rainwater storage is not less than 1 m^3 per 50 m^2 of the project area, the extra FAR will be 5%. The extra FAR can be increased proportionally up to 20% of the restricted FAR, if the capacity is more than 1 m^3 per 50 m^2 (OECD, 2015b). LGUs and the national government, if its involvement is necessary, could consider amending current regulations to integrate such carrot and stick mechanisms.

The benefits of insurance mechanisms and business resilience strategies

Insuring disaster-related losses must be a critical instrument of flood resilience, complementing infrastructure protection and flood-resilient urban planning. Compensating farmers when their land is flooded can for instance be more cost-effective than building dykes, which are less flexible and may become ill-adapted to future risks (OECD, 2015a). The mega disaster Haiyan/Yolanda typhoon, which caused economic damage estimated at USD 13 billion in 2013, revealed weaknesses in the insurance schemes for disasters, which were insufficient to recover from the damage. The scarcity of disaster funds that could be paid immediately to damaged parties, the insufficiency of finance schemes that could cope with large-scale restoration and the lack of funds for the most vulnerable communities and parties were particularly pointed out. As a result, many companies went bankrupt and the rural poor were hit hardly by the typhoon (Government of Japan, 2015). These weaknesses are observed at the national level and could also affect Cebu Province in case of major flood or typhoon.

In the recent years, a number of proposals to enhance the resilience of the Philippines' economy to natural disasters were formulated under the leadership of a few international organisations (Government of Japan, 2015):

- A **Catastrophe Bond** ("CAT-BOND") and a **Catastrophe Deferred Drawdown Option** (CDDO), proposed by the World Bank, aims to provide immediate assistance at the early recovery stage directly after a disaster. Similarly, a stand-by-loan mechanism called **SECURE** (Stand-by Emergency Credit for Urgent Recovery) was proposed by JICA to fund needs immediately after a disaster.
- To protect the private sector, a compulsory catastrophe insurance pool for small and medium-sized enterprises and medium-sized residential units has been proposed by the Philippine Insurers and Reinsurers Association (PIRA).

A **business continuity management (BCM) credit rating system** was set up to provide a signal to the insurance and the credit market on the resilience of private companies, thereby creating an incentives for them to enhance the resilience of their own facilities through business continuity plans;

- Finally, complementary insurance scheme for Local Government Units (LGUs) are being explored and developed, and could directly benefit LGUs in Cebu Province. LGUs can receive cash payments from the Government Service Insurance System (GSIS) two to three weeks after a disaster. Recently, the United Nations Office for Disaster Risk Reduction (UNISDR) has partnered with global insurance companies Willis Re and Munich Re to propose the **Philippines Risk and Insurance Scheme for Municipalities (PRISM)** to the Philippines government. The objective of PRISM is to provide a fast track way of budgetary support to LGUs through payments made not based on actual losses – which can take days or weeks to calculate – but rather when specific triggers are met, such as a certain level of rainfall. This should help to unlock and channel funds to LGUs much more quickly and increase the response capacity at the local level. However, the adoption of such a scheme by the government has not yet been confirmed.

Such measures would be critical to recover and unlock resources after a disaster but government authorities must also make sure that reconstruction efforts do not perpetuate past mistakes that make infrastructure vulnerable. In this regard, risk-financing mechanisms could be combined with risk reduction mechanisms: more incentives could be given to developers and builders to "build back better" (e.g. by increasing access to public transport, nearby shopping centres, restaurants and recreational opportunities, and providing green public spaces) after a disaster, to avoid simply rebuilding and exposing housing to the same risks. The national government could subsidise insurance compensations or provide matching funds based on such efforts (OECD, 2014a).

In addition, there is a need to reform the insurance market to integrate disaster risk insurance mechanisms directly in the development process. Currently, insurance premiums are not based on actual risks but based on a flat rate which is not affordable to many developers. Developing insurance premiums against natural disasters, based on actual risks, would be a win-win situation, as it would help to protect both the economy and private assets. This would also help to generalise the purchase of such insurance premiums, as currently insurance scheme are only delivered to a few developers on a case-by-case basis. This will require efforts to develop data on vulnerability, as mentioned previously. Also, such premiums could be provided in CLUPs and would give incentives to private developers to recognise the importance of such plans.

Business continuity planning and awareness efforts should also be scaled up. In particular, all LGUs and MCDCB could raise awareness on the above insurance schemes and help companies develop their own business continuity plans. The Greater London Authority has developed a Business Preparedness Checklist available online, and a five-step strategy to assist the private sector in business continuity planning. This includes: i) analyse the business; ii) assess the risks; iii) plan and prepare; iv) communicate the plan; and v) test the plan. Each of the five strategies is adapted according to the size of the business at risk (small, medium or large). The Greater London Authority also features key actions to be taken in case of a shock, and pools knowledge on best practices for urban resilience worldwide (Greater London Authority, n.d.). In Florida, the Business Continuity Information Network helps to connect businesses and their employees with local governments before and during a disaster. It allows the company to stay connected after a disaster, to share critical reports about facilities and monitor the condition of the community where the business operates (Business Continuity Information Network, n.d.). Local authorities in Cebu can learn from such examples and replicate similar mechanisms to enhance the resilience of its economy.

Developing innovative financing options for enhancing Cebu's flood resilience

Strategies to unlock finance for UR-DRM are critical. The budget of the 13 LGUs in Metro Cebu is PHP 3.4 billion in total in 2014, which is low compared to the registered population. There are opportunities first to raise own revenue, which only account for 31% of total local revenue on average, in particular tariffs and user charges that can simultaneously promote green growth objectives. In addition, the national government's transfers should be better aligned with green growth objectives. Attracting private investment should also be emphasised: FDI inflows have been lower in the Philippines than in all other countries of the Southeast Asian region, in particular because of the strong restrictiveness imposed by the government. Restrictions could be loosened in opportunity areas for green growth and Public-Private Partnerships should be encouraged at the subnational level.

An option for Cebu is to explore local private finance. It is not known precisely what percentage of Cebu's climate-resilient infrastructure investments are being made with local sources of private finance or through domestic capital markets. However, it is clear that Cebu's political and community leadership understands the importance of forming public-private partnerships, and is actively embracing collaborative actions and building coalitions between the private and public sectors with full civil society engagement for that purpose, as evidenced by the continuous dialogue taking place among local stakeholders in the government, private sector and civil society represented on the MCDCB. A possible further role of the MCDCB is to increase the banking and investment communities' awareness of the role they can play in supporting climate-resilient investments and initiatives. Businesses and the investors who finance them realise that they can't operate profitably in isolation from their surrounding environments and labour forces, and know they depend on public services like roads and the electric power grid to function normally. They increasingly realise that they have as much as, if not more, to lose in disasters than Cebu's citizens. The MCDCB can function as a catalyst in this regard to increase the awareness of local business leaders and investors and connect the public and private sectors.

Another innovative way to attract UR-DRM funding is a new form of financing called social impact investment. Through an environmental branding of its projects aiming to improve resilience, Cebu could attract 'impact investors' who may be willing to invest in UR-DRM in Cebu. It appears that Cebu's current political leadership has already begun to pursue this type of innovative financing approach. It would be useful for the governments in Cebu to increase transparency by disclosing fiscal situations in an internationally comparative way.

Enhance disaster response through local community engagement

In developing countries, floods tend to disproportionately affect the urban poor and deepen poverty and inequalities. The urban poor tend to settle in vulnerable areas such as canals and riverbanks. In Metro Cebu, poor communities can be found near the shoreline and at the estuary of rivers, which are also exposed to floods. At the same time, the important role that is played by communities and individuals acting as "first responders" of natural disasters should be emphasised. During the Great Hanshin Earthquake of 1991 in Kobe, Japan, more than 27 100 people were rescued by their neighbours, as compared with only 7 900 by the Kobe Fire Department (IFRC). The 2011 mega flood in Bangkok also showed the critical importance of community engagement to limit the damage of such a disaster and to compensate for the lack of capacity of local and national governments to respond to such large-scale emergency situation. Local community engagement should therefore be an important element of Cebu's resilience strategies, in order to avoid disproportionate impact on the poor and to mobilise a broader spectrum of the civil society in disaster preparedness and response.

Mechanisms to allow civil society organisations (CSOs) to participate in the design of disaster action plans should be reinforced, so that they can make contributions based on their knowledge and experience of practical and viable community-based responses to disasters. Local authorities could encourage the establishment of community-based resilience committees at the district level and provide them with capacity-building training. With other technical and logistical support, they could carry out simple vulnerability assessments and develop threat or risk maps, and establish some priorities among actions to enhance their resilience. These could then be proposed to MCDCB (or the future MCDA) and the provincial government for approval and funding. An example of community-based input system is offered by the city of Kitakyushu (Japan), which had also experienced periodic flood disasters. The city developed co-ordinated response mechanisms between civil society and local government. The local government set up frequent meetings with citizens living in vulnerable urban areas to exchange information and experience on both sides ("shared learning dialogues"). It allowed the city to come up with improved safety measures for residents, and raise awareness about the need to settle in safer areas of the city.

Schools and churches that offer large open spaces that can act as emergency shelters are natural centres for community action and organisation, especially in Cebu and the Philippines, When it comes to building greater resilience and adaptive capacity to prepare for, respond to and recover from shocks and crisis, physical and social assets and attributes go hand in hand. A major threat to flood resilience is a lack of social capital on the ground, which can lead to inaction when a disaster occurs. School programmes and religious centres can raise awareness of flood risks, and include practical workshops to build knowledge on how to manage floods at the household and community levels. They can also serve as efficient communication channels assisting district administrations, and provincial and national governments. If they deploy early warning systems in the neighbourhoods where they are located, they can inform the population about the imminence of a flood. Likewise, they can be critical "first responders" and "safe havens" to complement local authorities' action to protect local communities and assets in case of disaster.

Enhancing governance in the water sector

The quality of the water governance system in place in the Province of Cebu is a critical implementation parameter for existing strategies and the recommendations contained in this chapter. The scope and responsibilities of municipal, metropolitan and provincial water government bodies, their capacity to monitor, manage and reform water supply, sanitation and resilience systems, and co-ordination with the national government agencies and departments are critical governance aspects to be addressed.

Creating and empowering metropolitan and provincial water government bodies

Typical water governance problems of cities between 1.5 and 5 million inhabitants in the OECD area are municipal fragmentation, lack of relevant scale for investment, lack of incentives for co-operation, lack of staff, difficulties in raising tariffs, and limited information sharing (OECD, 2016). Very similar issues are found in Metro Cebu and beyond at the scale of the Province and constrain the ability of LGUs to effectively manage water resources and risks.

Territorial fragmentation is the first type of governance challenge observed in Cebu. Metro Cebu Water District (MCWD) covers eight LGUs of the Metro Cebu. The five other LGUs constituting Metro Cebu are therefore managed by a different authority operating completely separately, either the LGU alone, the LGU in co-operation with water associations, private service providers, or by a private service provider alone. Even in the MCWD service area, MCWD is supported by complementary water associations or private vendors, and only supplies 56% of the population (JICA and MCDCB, 2015). The impact of such fragmentation should be carefully analysed, in particular on economies of scale. Overall, the cost of production tends to be lower for non-integrated districts, due to lower need for costly hard infrastructure (e.g. water pipelines), but potential gains from increased production are larger for integrated districts. In addition, increased scale of operations for a single water operator is likely to improve access to financing (ADB, 2013a).

Apart from these economic considerations, the fragmentation of water utilities in Cebu creates management failures and incapacities. The population of Metro Cebu benefits from the same hydrological resources but their use is uncoordinated: there is no metropolitan authority supervising the management of water systems at the scale of the entire urban area. This mismatch has consequences on the effectiveness of service delivery and investment, and contributes to the unsustainable increase in water consumption. Such disorganisation indeed implies fragmentation of financial and technical capacities, a lack of data and vision at the metropolitan scale, and also regulatory obstacles for metropolitan investment. Moreover, systematising water pricing mechanisms between the different suppliers can be employed as a way to encourage water conservation by consumers.

Territorial fragmentation may also be an obstacle when considering water management in co-operation with rural areas, which is necessary in many cases. A survey of OECD cities showed that flood control mitigation and water quality often generate interdependencies between rural and urban areas, along other parameters (Figure 3.7). LGUs in the Province of Cebu should recognise the potential need to expand the metropolitan governance of water into adjacent rural areas. This is already the case regarding current plans to build dams and reservoirs, but other challenges should be considered. Flood control mechanisms and the preservation of watersheds, in particular, have strong urban-rural linkages in Cebu. Currently, there is no government body to address DRRM at the watershed level and there is no watershed management plan (for water supply and sanitation) that integrates the whole ecosystem boundaries "from ridge to reef". MCWD for instance only covers part of Metro Cebu and the corresponding watershed. The Department of Natural Resources and Environment (DENR) is also supposed to be involved in the management of watersheds, considering its oversight responsibilities, but it lacks capacities to do so. The issue also lies in the absence of a legal framework to address water challenges at such a scale specifically.

Figure 3.7. **Issues generating interdependencies between cities and surrounding areas in OECD cities**

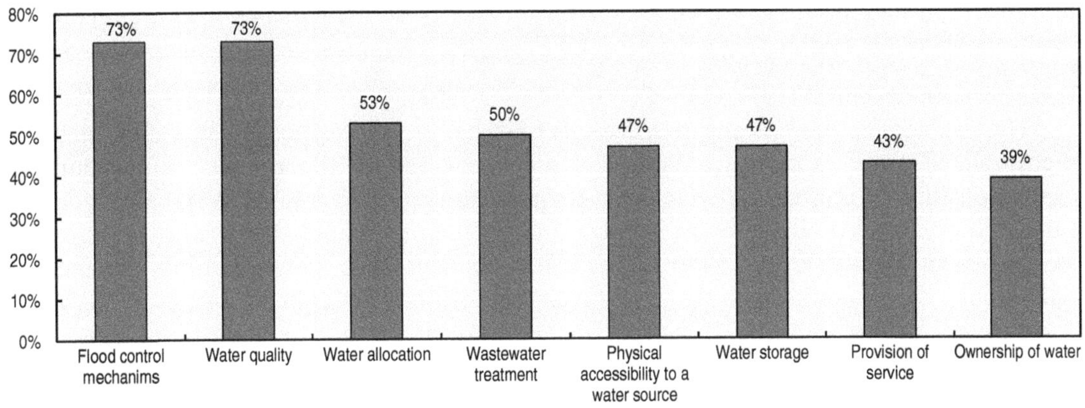

Note: Results based on a sample of 30 respondents who indicated the issues as being "very important" and "important"

Source: OECD (2016), *Water Governance in Cities*, OECD Publishing, Paris, http://dx.doi.org/10.1787/9789264251090-en.

Water governance in Cebu is also affected by high **sectoral fragmentation of water-related tasks** and raises obstacles for the adoption of holistic approaches for water management. A survey of OECD cities revealed that 50% of those examined reported this aspect as a prominent obstacle to policy coherence (OECD, 2016). In fact, in the case of Cebu, all water authorities mentioned above mainly manage water supply. For example, MCWD has not been actively engaged in septage and sewage until recently. There is almost no centralised water sanitation system, since septic tanks are the primary means of wastewater sanitation. However, in 2016, MCWD has launched a Septage Management Program in the city of Lapu-Lapu, after the city approved its septage and sewerage management ordinance in 2015. MCWD also established a septage treatment plant in Cordova town with a capacity of 150 cubic meters of sludge per day.[7] A more comprehensive approach at the metropolitan level is needed for all the water providers including MCWD, where services such as access to potable water (in light of the increasing demand), septage and sewerage management as well as reduction of loss of non-revenue water are considered altogether.

Flood management also requires concerted and coherent efforts across government agencies at each level of government. Some LGUs have recently created DRRM offices, but others have not and several departments may share the main responsibilities in this field (e.g. Planning and Development Office, Engineering Office, Building Office, Economic Affairs), due in particular to loose national policy framework on this matter. This means that there is no co-ordinated legislation and infrastructure to optimise together water supply, sanitation and flood resilience systems. Such sectoral fragmentations at national and subnational levels limit incentives for the diffusion of comprehensive water management solutions. More generally, the lack of co-operation between water bodies and other departments can be problematic: who is in charge of – or accountable for – a particular issue is not always clear, especially when the issue cuts across such domains as urban planning, the environment and economic development. For instance, it is difficult to know how permeable surfaces used for parking slots or streets should be defined in the context of urban drainage – as water related equipment or as transport infrastructures?

Who is in charge of managing them? Who is responsible for failures (OECD, 2015a)? An example of overlapping responsibilities and its negative consequences is the management of the river system in Metro Cebu, which has no clearly defined agency in charge for both the overall river system (e.g. LGUs, DPWH, DENR) and even within each LGU (e.g. Municipal Engineering Office, Environment Office) (JICA an MCDCB, 2015).

The lack of policy framework for WSS and flood resilience, and the lack of metropolitan water governance body are also reflected in the **unclear allocation of responsibilities between government corporations (LWUA, MCWD) and LGUs.** Local experts in Cebu have reported several times the uncertainty about who is supposed to undertake the different aspects of water management, i.e. planning, financing, operations, data monitoring etc. For instance, efforts have been made to regulate wastewater pricing in Cebu but problems of co-ordination and unclear allocation of responsibilities between different stakeholders have created difficulties. Generally speaking, this hinders policy preparation and implementation for WSS and flood resilience.

The territorial and sectoral fragmentation at the metropolitan and watershed levels can be tackled by the creation and empowerment of governance bodies that encompass wider territories than existing institutions (i.e. MCWD, LGUs). Recent developments in the institutional landscape of Cebu precisely go into this direction and offer opportunities to reform in depth the inefficient water governance system currently in place. Indeed, the creation of the **Provincial Water Resources Authority (PWRA)** in 2016, on the one hand, and the submission of the **Mega Cebu Development Authority (MCDA)** Act to the Congress (in 2016 as well), on the other hand, are timely decisions. One of the objectives of the PWRA in particular is to create a Cebu Water Code, inspired by the Water Codes of California and of Singapore. It could be an opportunity to recognise the need to address water management at the watershed level, to encourage water governance across jurisdictions when necessary and to develop a vision for the whole Province with concrete objectives of improvement of water supply and sanitation systems, and of enhancement of flood resilience, all supported by investment plans in the short, medium and long terms.

The MCDA, if created, will be supported by several corporations, including a Water District for the 13 LGUs of Metro Cebu (JICA and MCDCB, 2015). The Water District will have responsibilities in water supply and sanitation, and drainage, in particular "Water, septage and sewerage, and storm water management, which includes the formulation and implementation of policies, standards, plans, programmes and projects for water supply and water resources management; integrated storm water management, drainage and flood control; and septage and sewerage management system". The creation and empowerment of MCDA would fall in line with the national government's previous attempts to reform water governance in the Philippines, through the Angara Bill or Water Sector Reform Act 2011.

In the current context, there is however no certainty that these institutions will sufficiently help to tackle the water governance issues in Cebu. The creation of the MCDA is suspended to the decision of the Congress and the responsibilities and resources of the PWRA remain unclear. Government authorities should make sure that both entities have sufficient capacities to manage water resources and risks in Cebu, in particular:

- The ability to issue metro-wide or provincial ordinances and regulations on most matters that affect water supply, sanitation and DRRM in Cebu. For instance, permits for groundwater extractions could be managed by the PWRA that has an oversight responsibility on the entire watershed, or if deemed appropriate, such responsibility could be incumbent to MCDA. A smart allocation of responsibilities between PWRA and MCDA is necessary so that there is no governance failure. PWRA should only have authority on matters in MCDA's jurisdictions when the issue may affect the whole watershed. MCDA's Water district and PWRA should also closely collaborate to ensure smooth co-ordination with other provincial departments. MCWD for instance regularly faces difficulties in obtaining excavation permits from DPWH to expand the water pipe infrastructure, and PWRA could help to raise awareness to other provincial departments on the need to increase Level III connections in the Province and deliver such permits quickly;

- The necessary funds to enforce regulations and to implement projects. This can be achieved through increased water revenues (see discussion in Section 1), further transfers or direct support from the national government (see discussion below), and in the case of Metro Cebu a significant share of budget allocation from MCDA. Currently, LGUs in Metro Cebu tend to not pay enough attention to water issues and do not have a holistic approach of water management. The creation of a metro-wide corporation supported by a supra-municipal authority should help to bring the water agenda upfront; and
- Technical capacities to formulate comprehensive water management strategies and projects. This includes dispositions to monitor and analyse data at the scale of the provincial and metropolitan areas. Such technical capacities can be increased through larger funds, but also technical assistance from higher levels of government (see discussion below). For instance, the national sewerage and septage management programme of the national government includes a mechanism for local projects to be supported at 30% by the central government, but LGUs in Cebu lack capacities to propose sound and credible projects for application. In terms of urban resilience, the PWRA and MCDA should also integrate and make greater use of the League of DRRM Officers existing in Cebu, and which is constituted of representatives from each LGU. The League is a form of knowledge-sharing and collaboration platform: for instance, a mechanism for sharing assets in case of disaster (e.g. human resources, technical knowledge) was created within its framework. As each member has a position in Cebu's LGUs, PWRA and MCDA should rely on these officers to increase capacity with the objective of ensuring that each LGU designs robust DRRM plans, and to integrate them coherently in metropolitan, watershed and provincial DRRM plans.

Metropolitan areas in other parts of the world can be a good inspiration for MCDCB and LGUs in building a metro-wide water authority and in understanding its potential benefits. The cases of Barcelona, Nantes and Vancouver are particularly inspiring, as well as Singapore which showed that institutional reforms are often necessary to design and implement comprehensive water management policies (Box 3.6). The case of Singapore also showed that metropolitan arrangements for water management also encourage innovation. The Public Utilities Board (PUB) which manages the different aspects of water management also leads the Environment and Water Programme Office (EWI), an inter-agency created in 2006 that promotes research and development in the water sector, and which notably aims to reinforce the water cycle system put in place in Singapore and combines water supply, sanitation and stormwater facilities together. These examples are also relevant for the PWRA, as they show the benefits of integrated governance and management of water systems across multiple jurisdictions or at the watershed level.

Box 3.6. **Examples of metropolitan water governance**

Area Metropolitana Barcelona, Spain

The metropolitan area of Barcelona is formed by 36 municipalities of which Barcelona is the largest. From a hydrological point of view, the 36 municipalities are managed as a unique territory by the Metropolitan Authority (AMB). The AMB has regulatory and statutory authority. In the water sector the AMB approves regulations governing the integrated water cycle (supply, purification, distribution and sanitation) and the discharge of wastewater to the metropolitan sewage. It also approves tax ordinance to regulate the fees connected with the services and carries out administrative activities. The AMB has jurisdiction over most of these activities, which promotes integrated management of water supply and sanitation in the metropolitan area.

In the metropolitan area, there are seven wastewater treatment plants and three reclaimed water plants. Managing urban waters at the metropolitan level has fostered an integrated perspective of the water cycle level, as well as shared infrastructure and expenses. The AMB encourages customers' involvement to learn about different territorial needs and expectations. Next steps for AMB include looking at alternative sources for water and strengthening the water cycle management. Aguas de Barcelona was created in 2013, jointly with a large metropolitan utility, to manage drinking, reclaimed and wastewater for all the metropolitan territory.

Nantes Métropole, France

Nantes Métropole has prerogatives over the water policy in the 24 municipalities of its territory. This policy covers the entire water cycle: drinking water and collective sewage and wastewater, but also restoration of aquatic environments and storm water management. Since 2001, Nantes Métropole has been managing infrastructure that supplies drinking water and sanitation for nearly 600 000 inhabitants and chose the mix of management models in its territory. Nantes Métropole is in charge of the organisation of general public water services (collective and non-collective), and has the title of Organising Authority that sets the level of tariffs, defines the pricing policy for water and sanitation, and evaluates operators' performance.

Metro Vancouver, Canada

Metro Vancouver: the regional government, operating under the name "Metro Vancouver", provides services through four corporate entities, one of which is the Greater Vancouver Water District. It has a role in watershed management, water treatment, water transmission, wholesale distribution to municipalities, monitoring and reporting on Metro Vancouver water quality, and planning for Metro Vancouver water system's sustainability.

Singapore

Institutionally, the Public Utilities Board (PUB) currently manages the entire water cycle of Singapore. Earlier, PUB was responsible for managing potable water, electricity and gas. On 1 April 2001, the responsibilities for sewerage and drainage were transferred to PUB from the Ministry of Environment. This transfer allowed PUB to develop and implement a holistic policy, which included protection and expansion of water sources, stormwater management, desalination, demand management, community-driven programmes, catchment management, outsourcing to private sector specific activities which are not core to its mission, and public education and awareness programmes.

Source: OECD (2016), *Water Governance in Cities*, OECD Publishing, Paris, http://dx.doi.org/10.1787/9789264251090-en; OECD (2015a), *Water and Cities, Ensuring Sustainable Futures*, OECD Publishing, Paris, http://dx.doi.org/10.1787/9789264230149-en; Marest, P., Blanche, M., Guillard, M., Gouriten, Y., L'Honoré, O. and Perrouin, J-L. (2012) "Sustainable water management, the choices of Nantes Métropole" (article provided by the respondent of the Survey); Tortajada, C. (2006), "Water management in Singapore", *International Journal of Water Resources Development*, Routledge, Vol. 22, pp. 227-240.

The problem of sectoral fragmentation is also a consequence of institutional fragmentation at the national level: indeed, the National Water Resources Board (NWRD), the Department of Environment and Natural Resources (DENR), the Department of Public Works and Housing (DPWH) (which controls the Local Water Utilities Association, LWUA), the Department of Health (DOH) and the National Housing Authority (NHA) are all major stakeholders involved in water governance in the Philippines and affecting water management in Cebu. The co-ordination between these governmental bodies is weak, although the problem is well-recognised (ADB, 2013a). In addition, some issues do not benefit from sufficient attention: the only unit at the DOH addressing sanitation issues is the Environmental and Occupational Health Office of the National Disease Control and Prevention Centre, the mandate of which in sanitation is limited to policy formulation and monitoring of laws and policies (ADB, 2013a). This lack of institutional clarity and leadership is an obstacle to the creation of clear water policy frameworks (for supply, sanitation and flood resilience) for the entire country including clear allocation of responsibilities at the local level. The creation of a National Water Resources Management Office to manage water more comprehensively and effectively was in discussion recently, but no concrete action has been taken by the national government hitherto.

Devolving the proper responsibilities at the local level and enhancing vertical co-ordination

Water management in Cebu is also characterised by a vertical fragmentation of responsibilities and a lack of co-operation across levels of governments, which is a major obstacle to sound management of water resources and risks. Similarly to OECD cities, national legislations typically define cities' responsibilities, powers and, crucially, revenue sources, but attention to the basic legislative framework for cities is overlooked. In the Philippines, the Clean Water Act was adopted in 2006 and the National Sewerage and Septage Programme is in development, but there is no specific legislative framework for water supply, sanitation and flood resilience in cities (ADB, 2014), despite the existence of the Local Water Utilities Administration (LWUA) that supervises the various local water utilities of the country, and is attached to the Office of the President. In addition, there is a lack of water policy at the national law that comprehensively addresses supply, sanitation and flood issues. LGUs therefore do not have sound legislative framework and necessary financial support to ensure water security.

While the national government should improve its strategy for water security and clarify the role to be played by LGUs, a critical issue lies in the financial resources to support the necessary infrastructure projects. As mentioned previously, LGUs must raise revenues from water services, but this will not be sufficient especially to finance large projects such as the Lusaran dam, and the numerous responsibilities that they take on currently. MCWD in particular had been given more responsibilities than previous waterworks utilities but without proper investment capacities to achieve its objectives. Proper allocation of resources should be devolved at the same time as a policy framework for urban water supply, sanitation and flood resilience is made available nationally. In addition, the national government should also support LGUs' efforts more directly. Currently, there is no subsidy from the central government to LGUs in Metro Cebu for water projects. Such financial support would be particularly helpful to support some large infrastructure projects with high fixed costs such as dams, desalination and wastewater treatment plans, and solar-powered water systems. The expansion of pipe infrastructure or reduction of non-revenue water could also be the object of specific development programmes financed by the national government, since these are also costly undertakings. The PWRA and MCDA could be privileged recipient as they can encourage holistic and cross-jurisdictional projects and therefore deliver higher impacts. In addition, it can be a solution to circumvent the fact that the national government cannot legally invest directly in territories administered by independent cities (i.e. Cebu City, Lapu-Lapu and Mandaue). The central government should also help subnational governments increase their capacity to attract external sources of finance. Neither the Province nor cities and municipalities have the power to issue green bonds, for instance, while a study has recently shown that stormwater and water supply are the two most attractive sectors and are increasingly growing in the fixed income market (DuPont et al, 2015).

In parallel, the national government can develop programmes to empower LGUs if competences are new and their capacity is limited. When dealing with new competences in water, as a result of early stages of decentralisation, subnational governments may indeed lack expertise. Central governments may "empower" subnational ones through capacity building tools that favour learning and dialogue (e.g. contracts across levels of governments) (OECD, 2016). This is particularly critical for flood risk assessment. While there are national laws for DRRM and climate change adaptation to be mainstreamed in CLUPs, in practice this is not achieved because of a lack of technical capacities at the municipal level and lack of awareness about national plans. As mentioned previously, many LGUs do not develop robust DRRM plans but instead just settle with weak plans to fulfil the conditions to receive the 5% share of the IRA. The national government should create mechanisms for technical assistance not only targeted at municipalities individually but also encouraging metropolitan and provincial wide action. It could also directly finance such capacity-building activities.

Finally, in some cases the sheer allocation of responsibilities should be carefully assessed, and PWRA and MCDA should be considered as good candidates to undertake some responsibilities that so far lie in the hands of the national government. Indeed, because of the complex situation on the ground, the national government lacks the specific knowledge about Cebu that would help to make proper decisions. National agencies also have inadequate financial and technical capacity for their oversight roles: LWUA monitors more than 500 water districts, at least half of which have less than 3 000 service connections. The NWRB has to oversee several thousand domestic water service providers such as the private developers, homeowners' association, water co-operatives, and other small water utilities, and the Department of Interior and Local Government (DLIG) oversees about 1 000 LGU-run water utilities (ADB, 2013a). A good example is the uncontrolled extraction of groundwater from private tiers that leads to a dangerous depletion of water resources in Cebu. The National Water Resources Board is the agency responsible for delivering such permits but in practice is loosely regulating the process, without assessing the capacity of local aquifers. Many persons and businesses easily get an extraction permit from NWRB, even though they dig within 100 metres of a pipe connection, which is illegal. This is one of the responsibilities that should be devolved to the PWRA or to the future Water District of MCDA. Other competencies, if they do not affect water management beyond the provincial level, could be delegated to LGUs in Cebu. It would fit well in the portfolio of the PWRA or 'MCDA's Water District, and would allow for a holistic management of water by such authorities.

The data challenge: monitoring and evaluation for a better management of water resources and risks

Managing water requires a good monitoring system. Currently, local authorities in Cebu possess too little data to understand the policy and investment needs, which results in a lack of incentives to act and potentially wasteful investment. Lack of up-to-date, integrated, harmonised, and comprehensive data on the sector continues to handicap both planning of developed water and sanitation infrastructure, and assessment of development gaps, in Cebu and in the Philippines (ADB, 2013a). Most existing data in Cebu have been produced through the JICA-MCDCB Roadmap study and focus on the Metro Cebu area. The following data issues, for instance, are critical:

- Lack of accurate water consumption data in all areas of Metro Cebu;
- Lack of data on unaccounted-for-water or non-revenue water outside MCWD service area;
- Lack of accurate data on the quality and continuity of water supply;
- Lack of data on the number of wells and abstraction of ground water;
- Lack of accurate data on the number of households possessing septic tanks; and
- Lack of data on past and potential economic damage of floods.

One reason for the lack of accurate data, not only in Cebu Province but also generally speaking in the Philippines, is the presence of many different water service providers (WSPs), including water districts, community-based small-scale WSPs such as co-operatives, rural waterworks and sanitation associations (RWSAs), barangay water and sanitation associations (BWSAs), homeowners associations, and property developers that supply water. A majority of them are not registered with the NWRB, nor are they attached to a national agency (ADB, 2013a). The lack of technical capacities and the fragmentation of responsibilities in WSS and disaster risk management (horizontally and vertically) are also responsible for these issues. The future MCDA and its Water District, in this perspective, will be instrumental in regulating and raising capacities to produce and monitor comprehensive data on WSS and flood vulnerability at the scale of Metro Cebu. It should ensure that the above challenges are tackled and that performance standards or monitoring and benchmarking performance be set up for water utilities. Such standards should also be established by the national government for the whole country (ADB, 2013a), and reiterated in the Cebu Water Code in preparation by the PWRA. Requiring WSPs to collect accurate and comprehensive data on water will be an option to raise awareness on the real cost and benefits of WSS policies and investment for better decision making.

Stakeholder engagement

Many of the WSS and flood / typhoon problems discussed previously are already well known of LGUs in Cebu Province. In fact, one of the most important governance elements to address is the lack of awareness among the population about the solutions to poor water management and the lack of popularity of some reforms among policymakers. Many laws and regulations also go in the right directions but are not well implemented. Increases in water tariffs, for instance, are often unpopular among citizens and therefore elected officials are unwilling to touch upon this aspect. However, sustainable consumption, and financially sound water utilities will have positive green growth benefits by increasing the capacity of service providers, in the long term, to improve coverage and quality of centralised water systems. Also, raising awareness is critical to implement such measures as decentralised rainwater collection systems and generally speaking reduce unnecessary water consumption in households.

In this regard, it is extremely important that LGU officials including MCDCB / MCDA, and PWRA take a leadership role in raising general public awareness about water supply, sanitation and resilience issues. A civil society more aware of the threats of water scarcity, water pollution and climate change impacts will be a powerful incentive for political leaders to encourage and implement ambitious water development programmes.

Conclusion: Strengthening the water governance system and support a more comprehensive approach to water management

The Province of Cebu is facing great challenges in the water sector, in particular water scarcity in a context of increasing consumption due to population and economic growth, low coverage and efficiency of water distribution systems, sanitation issues affecting surface and ground water resources, and periodic floods. This chapter has demonstrated that the three aspects of supply, sanitation and resilience to floods are closely interrelated, and that policy synergies can be found to address water management in a comprehensive manner. Green infrastructures, for instance, provide ecosystem services which can help to refill groundwater, which ensure quality of water and increase the absorption capacity of urban areas in case of floods (Table 3.3). LGUs in Cebu should consider these options alongside or as alternative of harder and more costly infrastructure projects prescribed in the JICA-MCDCB Roadmap Study (e.g. dams). While dams, reservoirs, wastewater treatment plants are necessary given the high infrastructure gap in the Province, local authorities should be careful not to overinvest in such solutions, given their high cost and low flexibility. Green infrastructure, and also economic instruments and Information and Communication Technologies (ICT) (i.e. smart city tools) are more flexible, often cheaper and quicker solutions for water management. The case of Singapore also shows how green infrastructures can complement advanced technologies in creating a "water loop" that encourage water conservation and protection of ecosystems.

Table 3.3. **Green infrastructure solutions for water resource management**

Green infrastructure solution	Urban water management issue							
	WSS (including drought)	Water quality regulation			Moderation of extreme events (floods)			Protection of ecosystems
		water purification	biological control	water temperature	reverine flood control	urban stormwater	coastal flood (storm)	
demand management	x							x
local processing of black or grey water	x	x	x					
wetlands restoration/conservation	x	x	x	x	x			x
constructing wetlands	x	x	x	x	x			x
water harvesting	x					x		
green spaces	x	x		x		x		x
permeable pavements	x	x				x		x
green roofs						x		x
protecting/restoring mangroves, coastal							x	x
Corresponding grey infrastructure (primary								
dams, groundwater pumping	x			x				
dams, levees				x	x			
water distribution systems	x							
water treatment plant		x	x					
urban stormwater infrastructure						x		
sea walls							x	

Source: OECD (2015a), *Water and Cities: Ensuring Sustainable Futures*, OECD Publishing, Paris, http://dx.doi.org/10.1787/9789264230149-en.

The links uniting the different aspects of water management call for a better integration of water authorities and responsibilities in Cebu but more generally speaking in the Philippines. The high sectoral fragmentation of water-related task and the fragmentation of water "jurisdictions" between water districts, LGUs, private providers, local associations etc. prevent quick and efficient reforms in water tariffs and charges, investment in large-scale supply and sanitation infrastructure, solid data collection mechanism at the provincial and metropolitan levels, and a holistic approach to flood resilience. For these reasons, all levels of government must be involved in reforming the water sector. In Cebu, PWRA and MCDA appear to be good candidates to promote such approach to water security at the watershed and metropolitan scales, and tackle the great challenges coming ahead for Cebu.

Main policy recommendations

- Develop and encourage **green infrastructures** more aggressively, such as rainwater collectors on buildings and retention ponds, green spaces in vacant land deemed unsuitable for development.
- Make greater use of **economic instruments to manage water demand**, such as increased block water tariffs, charges for water abstraction, and carrot and stick mechanisms to encourage developers and households to build or use green infrastructures.
- In parallel, adopt a specific economic instrument strategy for low-income households, in particular **abolish connection fees**, to expand standardised pipe infrastructure.
- Progressively install **smart water technologies**, in particular smart water metres, pollution sensors in water streams and runoff simulation tools to assess flood risk.
- **Scale up efforts to build robust DRRM plans in Cebu's LGUs, supported by a thorough assessment of the vulnerability** of businesses, industries, critical infrastructure and low-income households to floods. Develop corresponding flood risk maps and under different flood scenarios.
- **Establish a protection and rehabilitation plan for Cebu's watersheds**, which are vital in providing a sustainable water supply to the urban area, **by increasing the** human, material and financial **means of the Central Cebu Protected Landscape** and **through co-operation with local communities.**
- Take a stronger leadership in **promoting strategies for the resilience of businesses and industries**, such as continuity plans, regular communication channels on assets and employers at risk, and local insurance mechanisms, with the support of the national government and international organisation.
- Ensure, through PWRA and MCDA, means to **regulate and harmonise water governance in Cebu**, in particular flood control mechanisms, tariffs and charges (e.g. water abstraction), water production and supply, and water sanitation, and supported by **investment plans**.
- Clarify and build more coherence and synergies between water supply, sanitation, and resilience **policy frameworks** at the national level. Set up **national mechanisms for financial subsidies** to large infrastructure projects in Cebu such as dams, wastewater and desalination plants, solar-powered water systems, and expansion of pipe connections.
- Develop **metropolitan and provincial capacities to produce, collect and harmonise data on water supply, sanitation and flood risk.**

Notes

1. www.philstar.com/cebu-news/2014/12/02/1398190/mcwds-new-water-rates-take-effect-january-1.

2. The JICA-MDCDCB Roadmap study provides the figures for neighbours' wells and taps together, so the specific figure for neighbours' taps is unknown.

3. The average precipitation during this period is around 148 mm per month, against a mean of 105 mm per month year-round. In comparison, the average precipitation in London is around 50 mm per month. This is however lower than other Asian cities such as Tokyo (127 mm per month), Singapore (195 mm per month), and Bangkok (137 mm per month).

4. This information is based on a sample survey undertaken by JICA for the JICA-MCDCB Roadmap Study (2015). It is based on data referring to how many households (in percentage) experience flooding every year in each LGU of Metro Cebu.

5. http://choices.climatecentral.org/#12/10.3070/123.9222?compare=temperatures&carbon-end-yr=2100&scenario-a=warming-4&scenario-b=warming-2

6. A 100-year flood refers to a flood that statistically has 1% chance of occurring in any given year.

7. A JICA grant package is making it possible for MCWD to replicate the project through the rest of its service area. The grant will provide three septage treatment facilities that will serve the remaining 6 LGU's under MCWD service areas namely Cebu City, Talisay City, Mandaue City, Consolacion, Liloan and Compostela. The programme is still under the feasibility stages with completion set for 2019.

References

ADB (Asian Development Bank) (2014), *Urban Water Supply and Sanitation in Southeast Asia: A Guide to Good Practice*, Arthur C. McIntosh, Mandaluyong City, the Philippines.

ADB (2013a), *Philippines: Water Supply and Sanitation Sector Assessment, Strategy, and Road Map*, Mandaluyong City, the Philippines.

ADB (2013b), *Asia Water Development Outlook 2013, Measuring Water Security in Asia and the Pacific, Asia-Pacific Water Forum,* Mandaluyong City, the Philippines.

Austin Water (n.d.), Water Wells Program, www.austintexas.gov/department/water-wells-program (accessed 15 March 2017).

Business Continuity Information Network (n.d.), "How it works", www.bizrecovery.org/How-It-Works (accessed 15 January 2015).

City of Sacramento website (2016), www.cityofsacramento.org/Utilities/Services/Water-Service (accessed 6 September 2016).

CERTU (Centre d'études sur les réseaux, les transports, l'urbanisme et les constructions publiques) (2012), "Taxe pour la gestion des eaux pluviales urbaines", Ministère de l'Écologie, du Développement durable, des Transports et du Logement, Paris.

DRIEE (2012), "Approvisionnement électrique du Grand Paris", séminaire du 6 mars 2012, www.driee.ile-de-france.developpementdurable.gouv.fr/img/pdf/seminaire_du_6_mars_2012_-_presentations_approvisionnement_electrique_du_grand_paris__cle2dcb2f-1.pdf.

DuPont, C.M., J. Levitt and L. Bilmes (2015), "Green Bonds and Land Conservation: The Evolution of a New Financing Tool", *Faculty Research Working Paper Series*, Harvard Kennedy School of Government.

European Commission (2013), "Green Infrastructure (GI) – Enhancing Europe's Natural Capital", COM/2013/0249 final, European Commission.

GIZ (Deutsche Gesellschaft für International Zusammenarbeit) GmbH (2015), "Residential Building Suitability Map for Leyte Island", the Philippines, www.preventionweb.net/publications/view/47118.

Government of Japan (2015), "Sustainable Disaster Risk Finance in the Philippines: Restoration Activities after Typhoon Haiyan", Ministry of the Environment, Tokyo, Japan.

Granert, W. (2017), "Protecting Central Cebu Watershed", www.sunstar.com.ph/cebu/opinion/2017/03/20/tell-it-sunstar-protecting-central-cebu-watersheds-532153.

Greater London Authority (n.d.), “Preparing your business”, www.london.gov.uk/mayor-assembly/mayor/london-resilience/preparing-your-business (accessed 17 January 2015).

Grey, D. and C.W. Sadoff (2007), “Sink or Swim? Water security for growth and development”, *Water Policy*, Vol. 9, pp. 545-571.

IAU (Institut d’Aménagement et d’Urbanisme) (2011), “Économie francilienne: Quelle robustesse face à une inondation majeure ?”, *Note rapide Économie*, No. 534, Institut d’Aménagement et d’Urbanisme, Paris, www.iau-idf.fr/fileadmin/newetudes/etude_791/nr_534_web_01.pdf.

Intergovernmental Panel on Climate Change (IPCC) (2012), “Summary for policymakers” in: *Managing the Risks of Extreme Events and Disasters to Advance Climate Change Adaptation*, A Special Report of Working Groups I and II of the Intergovernmental Panel on Climate Change, Cambridge University Press, Cambridge, United Kingdom, and New York, pp. 1-19.

IPCC (2007), “Climate Change 2007: Synthesis Report, An Assessment of the Intergovernmental Panel on Climate Change”, www.ipcc.ch/pdf/assessment-report/ar4/syr/ar4_syr.pdf.

ITU (International Telecommunication Union) (2014), “Technical Report on Smart Water Management in Cities, International Telecommunication Union”, Geneva.

JICA (Japan International Cooperation Agency) and MCDCB (Metro Cebu Development and Coordination Board) (2015), “The Roadmap for Sustainable Urban Development in Metro Cebu”, http://open_jicareport.jica.go.jp/pdf/12235529.pdf.

JMP (2012), “Progress on Drinking Water and Sanitation”, The WHO/UNICEF Joint Monitoring Programme for Water Supply and Sanitation, www.unicef.org/media/files/JMPreport2012.pdf.

Kenward, A., D. Yawitz and U. Raja (2012), “Sewage Overflows: From Hurricane Sandy”, Princeton, New Jersey, www.climatecentral.org/pdfs/Sewage.pdf.

Manila Water Company Inc. (n.d.), www.manilawater.com/downloadables/2015%20tariff%20table%20june%201,%202015.jpg (accessed 3 July 2015).

Marest, P., Blanche, M., Guillard, M., Gouriten, Y., L’Honoré, O. and Perrouin, J-L. (2012), “Sustainable water management, the choices of Nantes Métropole” (article provided by the respondent of the Survey).

Marsden Jacob Associates (2006), “Securing Australia’s Urban Water Supplies: Opportunities and Impediments. A discussion paper prepared for the Department of the Prime Minister and Cabinet”, Australian Government, Department of the Environment and Energy, www.environment.gov.au/system/files/resources/a4c27c83-6edd-4fc5-84a2-70e38b183fc4/files/urban-water-report.pdf.

Metropolitan Waterworks Authority (n.d.), www.mwa.co.th/ewtadmin/ewt/mwa_internet_eng/ewt_news.php?nid=309 (accessed 3 July 2015).

Naumann, S. et al. (2011), “Assessment of the potential of ecosystem-based approaches to climate change adaptation and mitigation in Europe”, Final report to the European Commission, DG Environment, Contract No. 070307/2010/580412/SER/B2, Ecologic Institute and Environmental Change Institute, Oxford University Centre for the

Environment, http://ec.europa.eu/environment/nature/climatechange/pdf/EbA_EBM_CC_FinalReport.pdf.

NYC Environmental Protection (n.a.), *Comprehensive Water Reuse Program: Application and Instructions*, www.nyc.gov/html/dep/pdf/waterreuse.pdf (accessed June 2017).

OECD (2016), *Water Governance in Cities*, OECD Publishing, Paris, http://dx.doi.org/10.1787/9789264251090-en.

OECD (2015a), *Water and Cities, Ensuring Sustainable Futures*, OECD Publishing, Paris, http://dx.doi.org/10.1787/9789264230149-en.

OECD (2015b), *Green Growth in Bangkok, Thailand*, OECD Publishing, Paris, http://dx.doi.org/10.1787/9789264237087-en.

OECD (2015a), "Policies to Support Smart Water Systems, Lessons from Countries Experience", OECD Publishing, Paris.

OECD (2014a), *Boosting Risk Assessment through Innovative Governance*, OECD Publishing, Paris, http://dx.doi.org/10.1787/19934106

OECD (2014b), "Assessment and recommendations", in *Seine Basin, Île-de-France, 2014: Resilience to Major Floods*, OECD Publishing, Paris, http://dx.doi.org/10.1787/9789264208728-4-en.

OECD (2013), *Water Security for Better Lives*, OECD Publishing, Paris, http://dx.doi.org/10.1787/9789264202405-en.

OECD (2010), *Cities and Climate Change*, OECD Publishing, Paris, http://dx.doi.org/10.1787/9789264091375-en.

PT Aetra Air Jakarta (Aetra) (2012), "Info Tariff Aetra", www.aetra.co.id/uploads/info_tarif_aetra/tarif_air_aetra_2007.pdf.

The City Government of Baguio (2016), Republic of the Philippines, "MOA to protect Buyog watershed forged", http://baguio.gov.ph/content/moa-protect-buyog-watershed-forged.

Tortajada, C. (2006), "Water management in Singapore", *International Journal of Water Resources Development*, Routledge, Vol. 22, pp. 227-240.

UN ESCAP and UN HABITAT (2015), "The State of Asia-Pacific Cities 2015: Urban transformations Shifting from quantity to quality", Bangkok, Thailand, www.unescap.org/sites/default/files/the%20state%20of%20asian%20and%20pacific%20cities%202015.pdf.

Walton B. (2012), "America's water infrastructure shows its age – the national debate about how to pay for repairs", *Circle of Blue*, 5 March.

Water and Sanitation Programme (WSP) (2009), "Guide to Ring-Fencing of Local Government-Run Water Utilities", Manila, the Philippines, www.wsp.org/sites/wsp.org/files/publications/Ring_Fencing.pdf.

WEF (World Economic Forum) (2014), "Strategic Infrastructure: Steps to Operate and Maintain Infrastructure Efficiently and Effectively", World Economic Forum, Geneva.

Chapter 4

Governance for green growth in Cebu, Philippines

Chapter 4 examines governance strategies to tackle green growth implementation in the Province of Cebu. This chapter is structured into the following four sections: 1) Enhancing vertical and horizontal policy co-ordination between government bodies; 2) Financing urban green growth; 3) Optimising the impacts of international co-operation for urban green growth; and 4) Enhancing local governments' capacities to undertake urban green growth.

Key findings

- Local Government Units (LGUs) in Cebu have faced great difficulties in undertaking sustainable growth and infrastructure development that could foster urban green growth. There is **a significant gap, in particular, between national policy objectives and concrete action taken by LGUs on the ground.** A lack of national policy frameworks in some key sectors, particularly water management, results in an absence of explanation of the role of LGUs. In parallel, the translation of existing national legislation and policy frameworks at the local level is relatively inefficient. There seems to be an over-reliance on regulatory approaches rather than outreach, collaboration, and capacity building.

- **The lack of horizontal policy co-operation and co-ordination between the 13 LGUs composing Metro Cebu** hampers the development of green growth in Cebu. Initiatives and policies need to take into account the urbanisation rates and growth of Metro Cebu. These challenges have been a major driver in the formation of **Metro Cebu Development and Coordinating Board (MCDCB),** a consortium all LGUs of Metro Cebu, regional line agencies of the national government, private sector representatives and civil society organisations. MCDCB however remains limited in terms of financial and legal power, and government authorities should make sure the creation of the **Mega Cebu Development Authority (MCDA)** is designed to efficiently tackle both horizontal and vertical governance issues.

- **Strategies to unlock finance for urban green growth will be critical.** The total revenues of the 13 LGUs in Metro Cebu has significantly increased from PHP 8.3 billion in 2012 to PHP 10.4 billion in 2014, but participation of LGUs in public expenditures and investment remains low compared to OECD countries. There are opportunities to further **raise own revenue**, in particular tariffs and user charges. Attracting private investment should also be emphasised: **FDI** inflows have been lower in the Philippines than in other countries of the Southeast Asian region, in particular because of the strong restrictiveness imposed by the central government. Opportunities also lie in **Public-Private Partnerships (PPP)** which are currently encouraged at the subnational level through the PPP Centre of NEDA; however, the impact of such initiative is not yet visible in Cebu.

- International co-operation can further bridge the finance gap for urban green growth. Between 2002 and 2014, **the Philippines has been the third largest recipient of official development finance in Southeast Asia**, with around USD 30 billion, including USD 1.8 billion of environment-related commitments to cities. The benefits for Cebu, however, have been small and targeted at water supply and a Bus Rapid Transit System. LGUs in Cebu and the national government should collaborate more systematically to channel down such sources of finance to the local level. In addition, there is a need to address the lack of capacity at both the national and local levels to apply for the range of development funds available.

- Finally, there is a critical need to build local capacities to undertake green growth. In particular, **the lack of skills and strategies to collect, produce and analyse** is a serious obstacle. There is no data, for instance, on air quality, GHG emissions, and natural assets in Cebu, or about commuting, making it impossible to apply the OECD methodology on Functional Urban Areas (FUAs). In some cases, the data is only available in some sectors, and not in others (e.g. non-revenue water). In other cases, the type of data is not consistent across jurisdictions, or owned by private companies but not communicated to LGUs. Local universities and research institutes in particular, as well as local communities should be more actively engaged in the data production process.

Enhancing the quality of co-operation between government bodies in Cebu

Creating more efficient governance linkages between LGUs and the national government

The Local Government Code 1991 has empowered Local Government Units

There is a complex government structure in place in the Philippines. Below the national government, the country is divided into **Local Government Units (LGUs)** of four categories, as prescribed by the Local Government Code of 1991: i) provinces, ii) cities, iii) municipalities, and iv) barangays. There are 81 provinces in the Philippines regrouped into 17 administrative regions, and one autonomous region (the Autonomous Region of Muslim Mindanao). The island of Cebu is one of the three provinces of Region VII (Central Visayas), along with Bohol and Siquijor. Each province is governed by an elected legislature called the Sangguniang Panlalawigan and by an elected governor. Cities are governed by the own specific charters in addition to the *Local Government Code*, and categorised as follows:

- *Cities independent from the provinces in which they are located*; they are not under the jurisdiction of the province and can be considered 'at the same level' in the governance hierarchy. There are two types of independent cities: i) highly urbanised cities, defined as a population of at least 200 000, and ii) independent component cities, which have not attained the "highly urbanised" status yet. In Cebu Province, there are three highly urbanised cities (Cebu City, Mandaue City and Lapu-Lapu City) and no independent component city; and
- *Component cities*; like municipalities, they fall under the jurisdiction of the Province in which they are located. There are six component cities in the Province of Cebu, namely: Bogo City, Carcar City, Danao City, Naga City, Talisay City and Toledo City.

Municipalities are also under a Province's jurisdiction. They can, upon attaining certain requirements, including a minimum population size and annual revenue, opt to become a city. Cebu Province comprises 44 municipalities. Finally, municipalities and cities are composed of barangays, the smallest independently elected LGUs; there are over 42 000 throughout the Philippines and 1 096 in the Province of Cebu alone. Metro Cebu, specifically, is composed of 13 LGUs in total, including three independent cities, four component cities and six municipalities.

Cities and municipalities serve as the primary planning and implementing unit of government policies, plans, programmes, and activities. The 1991 Local Government Code devolved to LGUs the responsibility for delivery of basic services that previously had been the responsibility of the national government, and also considerable discretion over local taxes. It granted LGUs regulatory powers and increased available financial resources. Efforts to enhance governance and LGUs capacities are continuing: the National Economic Development Agency's (NEDA) Philippine Development Plan 2011-16 has an entire chapter dedicated to good governance and the rule of law. It prioritises empowering LGUs via capacity building to improve their ability to deliver public services and promoting public accountability. It also elaborates on the desire and intent to connect government, reduce corruption, enhance transparency, reduce redundancies, standardise quality of service, and enhance partnership structures and international linkages.

But LGUs lack capacities and need stronger collaboration with the national government

In practice however, the governance system is plagued with problems and LGUs in Cebu have faced great difficulties in undertaking sustainable growth and infrastructure development that could foster urban green growth. There is a significant gap, in particular, between LGUs' responsibilities, their budget and capacity, and legal authority is still largely held by the national government in the opportunity areas for green growth developed in Chapter 2. While some factors may lie in the character of decentralisation, which has been mostly political (LGUs have elected representatives) but not advanced with regard to local financial and legal power, other factors lie in the poor vertical co-operation and co-ordination between all levels of government.

First of all, there is a lack of national policy frameworks in some key sectors for urban green growth, which creates policy gaps including an absence of explanation of the role to be played by LGUs, and prescribing their resources to do so. This is particularly an issue for water management. There is no policy framework guiding water supply and sanitation, nor flood management, at the local level and even at the national level. At the national level, responsibilities are shared between the National Economic and Development Authority (NEDA), Local Water Utilities Association (LWUA), the National Water Resources Board (NWRB), the Department of Environment and Natural Resources (DENR), the Department of Health (DOH), the Department of Public Works and Highways (DPWH), without any official co-ordinating body. In the case of flood management, the absence of NEDA in committee meetings of the Environment Management Bureau, despite the obvious role this Authority could play, reveals the gaps existing in national policy frameworks. At the local level, the allocation of responsibilities between water districts and LGUs is sometimes unclear and not efficient, and there is no appointed body for disaster risk reduction in LGUs, creating a lot of inconsistencies across jurisdictions about the management of this issue. In addition, even in existing national legislation, the role dedicated to LGUs is often unclear and not well supported: despite the existence of the Clean Water Act (2004) and a national law for Risk Management and Climate Change Adaptation, which are supposed to be mainstreamed into local plans, there is no effective implementation of the prescribed policies on the ground in Cebu, due to the lack of details on subnational responsibilities and resources. The creation of national policy frameworks would help to clarify responsibilities, especially for LGUs, while giving them appropriate resources.

Such national policy frameworks should allow LGUs to play a greater role in the opportunity areas for green growth. The Local Government Code of 1991 put LGUs in charge of the provision of basic services, including agriculture (power to reclassify agricultural land), health, social services, public works (enforcement of the National Building Code, power to close and open roads), and environment and natural resources. However, responsibilities are often not well defined and incomplete, therefore limiting local actions. Taking down a tree requires the approval of the national government, for instance. As a result of the lack of a clear national policy framework and well-defined responsibilities, LGUs have taken some critical responsibilities in the management of urban utilities, such as water supply, without efficient legislative framework. For instance, the NWRB is the agency responsible for delivering water extraction permits in the whole country, but does not have the capacity to monitor the sustainability of its own decisions. As a consequence, many permits have been delivered without proper analysis of the local aquifer capacities in Cebu. Therefore, in order to ease the burden on NWRB, such roles could be given to local water utilities or LGUs. Ideally, this responsibility should be given to an authority whose jurisdiction corresponds to the surface of the aquifer in use. In the future, it could be Mega Cebu Development Authority (MCDA, see below) in Metro Cebu; another alternative is to create a provincial office of the NWRB in Cebu, so that it can have a view on the use of water resources in the whole province. The same recommendation also applies to the transport sector: the Department of Transport has no provincial office and co-ordination with LGUs of Metro Cebu to develop sustainable transport systems is very weak (see below discussion on BRT).

In parallel, national legislation and policy frameworks should be supported by **efficient technical assistance mechanisms** between the national government and LGUs including provinces and MCDCB/MCDA. The Central Visayas Region's (Region VII) Policy Formulation and Planning Division is responsible for co-ordinating the development and implementation of the Regional Development Plan (2014-2016) and Regional Physical Framework Plan (2003-2030), and for providing technical assistance to LGUs on plan and policy formulation. Region VII recently completed a set of guidelines intended to assist LGUs in completing their Comprehensive Land Use Plans (CLUPs). The mandate of cities and municipalities to prepare, implement and enforce land use plans resides in the Philippine constitution and provisions of the 1991 *Local Government Code*. The CLUP and its implementation instrument, the zoning ordinance, are intended to regulate land use as part of a set of plans that span all levels of government. LGUs are required to complete CLUPs and update them every six years. Yet despite the legislative requirement and the guidelines created by Region VII to assist LGUs in developing CLUPs, there is not one completed, updated CLUP.

Regional office staffs have an outreach mandate and regularly conduct workshops with LGUs, industry and others to communicate their guidelines and work. Some LGUs have however stated that the guidelines are overly technical for local government application. In addition, there is no binding mechanism to force LGUs to implement the CLUP guidelines. There seems to be an over-reliance on regulatory approaches rather than outreach, collaboration, and capacity building. As such, more efforts on the outreach aspect should be made. Strong linkages among completed CLUPs, the Mega Cebu vision, and the nationally prepared Regional Physical Framework Plan should be ensured. The Department of Interior and Local Government must first recognise and ensure that authorities involved in city planning and engineering are up-to-date on existing CLUPs. Relevant authorities, for instance, the Department of Public Services (DPS) and the Housing and Land Use Regulatory Board (HLURB), should then consult LGUs on their specific local contexts, and then work together to ensure effective implementation of the CLUP. This could either be done through outright requirement for alignment in legislation, coupled with an outreach and capacity-building programme to make it happen, or through an instrument such as the "regional context statement" as in British Columbia, Canada (Box 4.1). All 13 LGUs have adopted the JICA Mega Cebu Roadmap study as the regional vision, which is a strong statement of support. It will be important to embed that support in the local CLUPs and upward into the Regional Physical Framework Plan, and to ensure that the alignment is kept up to date and renewed.

Box 4.1. **Canada's British Columbia's regional context statement**

In British Columbia, prior to 1983, all local plans had to be consistent and aligned with regional plans. In 1996, new legislation softened the regional role and strengthened that of municipal government in relation to the regional growth management plan. The legislation instituted what is called a 'regional context statement', which essentially is a linking document housed in the municipal Official Community Plan (OCP), that demonstrates how the OCP is aligned with, and supports, the regional growth strategy, or how it will be made more consistent over time. The regional context statement is adopted as part of the OCP by the municipality and must be submitted to the regional district Board of Directors for acceptance. It is an agreement. There is a dispute resolution process prescribed if the two parties are unable to agree. The regional context statement must be submitted to the regional district within two years of a new regional growth strategy being adopted, and must be renewed every five years.

However, there is no recourse described in the legislation if the regional context statement is not submitted. Metro Vancouver, as the largest regional district in the province of British Columbia, focuses on collaboration, early and frequent communication, moral suasion, and ensuring a good value proposition in its regional planning function and relationship with member municipalities. To date, four and half years after the adoption of the most recent regional growth strategy, 18 out of 20 regional context statements have been successfully completed and accepted.

Metro Vancouver's Board of Directors is made up of elected officials from all member municipalities – it is a federation, and as such, Metro Vancouver staff are the stewards of the regional vision created by that federation.

Source: Peer reviewer report submitted to the OECD (2016).

Further enhancing horizontal co-operation among LGUs in Metro Cebu

Metro Cebu Development Co-ordinating Board: a promising platform but with limited means and power

In addition to vertical policy alignment and co-ordination, another critical aspect of governance that should be addressed to foster green growth in Cebu is **the lack of horizontal policy co-operation and co-ordination between the 13 LGUs composing Metro Cebu**. Rapid growth in Metro Cebu has shed light on the fact that escalating development problems associated with the provision of clean water, septage, solid waste, transportation, environmental management and disaster risk reduction, and public and project financing cannot be addressed effectively by one LGU alone. In addition, there seems to be no easy means for horizontal integration and information sharing among existing LGU planners and no means to co-ordinate CLUPs and local planning across borders. This has resulted in many isolated initiatives and policies in critical sectors for green growth that have not addressed the metropolitan size of urbanisation and growth in Metro Cebu, and also in incoherence and management failures due to inconsistent policies across jurisdictions.

An example of this problem is the current development of the Bus Rapid Transit (BRT) system supported by the French Development Agency (AFD). The BRT is only being designed and implemented in Cebu City. Even though Cebu City is the largest LGU of the metropolitan area, Metro Cebu would benefit much more from a bus network that reaches out to adjacent LGUs, as many residents commute from these areas to Cebu City, or vice-versa. In addition, the current expansion of the metropolitan area towards its outskirts (the fastest growing LGUs are Carcar and Danao City) create increasing demand for public transport system in these areas. The BRT system is relatively flexible compared to a metro system but not building it right from the start and letting adjacent LGUs expand their built-up areas without including BRT will nonetheless create an infrastructure lock-in that will be difficult to circumvent in the future. Similarly, road widths are not being maintained across LGU boundaries, which precludes good, co-ordinated transportation (and land use) planning. The same types of problems can be observed in other sectors, such as water supply and sanitation (see Chapter 3).

The challenges associated with horizontal co-operation among LGUs seem to have been a major driver for forming **Metro Cebu Development and Coordinating Board (MCDCB),** a consortium of the 13 LGUs of Metro Cebu, regional line agencies of the national government, private sector representatives and civil society organisations (Box 4.2). The MCDCB has been successful in developing and expressing a strong and coherent regional vision, synthesised in the JICA Mega Cebu Roadmap study, and as such has set the stage as a strong advocate to the national government in terms of capital funding, policy implementation, and LGU capacity building. MCDCB has also sown the seeds of success in terms of collaborative planning and trust amongst LGUs. While it is still 'early days' in terms of buy-in and trust, the MCDCB continues to actively demonstrate success in collaborative dialogue and advancing plans and projects in a way that co-ordinates, but does not prejudice the autonomy of affected LGUs. The MCDCB model is also unique in its explicit engagement with, and leadership from, the private sector and civil society. This model of having both the private sector and civil society at the Board level of a regional organisation can be seen as a means to institutionalise innovation, accountability and transparency.

MCDCB is also supported by other initiatives of the Ramon Aboitiz Foundation Inc. (RAFI) – one of the founders of MCDCB – which is developing PACT programme to encourage LGUs to develop projects – even small ones – in line with Metro Cebu, by providing some funding and technical expertise. This is also a strategy to build a constituency on the ground and give more visibility to such metropolitan forms of action.

Box 4.2. **Metro Cebu Development Co-ordinating Board (MCDCB)**

The **Metro Cebu Development Co-ordinating Board (MCDCB)** is a co-ordinating body for metro-wide planning and development that was created on April 1, 2011 through a Memorandum of Agreement (MOA). It is a consortium of the 13 LGUs composing Metro Cebu (7 cities -Cebu, Danao, Mandaue, Lapu-Lapu, Naga, and Carcar and 6 municipalities – Compostella, Liloan, Consolacion, Cordova, Minglanilla, and San Fernando), regional line agencies of the national government, private sector representatives and civil society organisations. The key objectives of the MCDCB are to:

- Act as a co-ordinating body and platform for inter-jurisdictional challenges and responsibilities;
- Be a platform for inter-jurisdictional co-ordination between the public and private sectors and local and national governments;

Box 4.2. **Metro Cebu Development Co-ordinating Board (MCDCB)** (*continued*)

- Be a launch pad for collective action and impact (recognising the importance of collaboration in developing policy and priority coherence, improving capacity etc.); and
- Be a vehicle for regional, national and international co-operation.

The MCDCB model is unique in its explicit engagement with, and leadership from, the private sector and civil society. This model of having both the private sector and civil society at the Board level of a regional organisation can be seen as a means to institutionalise innovation, accountability and transparency. The private sector offers resources and is a main driver of economic growth and in bringing in technology and innovation. Having the private sector at the table as a co-chair sends a clear message in terms of integration and in providing an environment conducive to business and investment. Having the idea for co-ordination stem from the private sector also facilitates broad local government engagement in that it project ownership is seeded more broadly, rather than with one or two local governments or officials. However, there is some question as to the role of the private sector in establishing public policy where elected officials must be responsible for implementation (e.g. zoning, parking restrictions etc.).

Source: Authors.

Independent financial resources and power of MCDCB are however limited, which impedes a strong impact of the promising dialogue and outreach initiative it represents. Currently, operations of the MCDCB are supported through non-specific financial contributions from the member LGUs as well as through grants, donations, national government appropriation, and other sources. In addition, LGUs are still the units in charge of adopting the CLUP, and MCDCB only pushes them to follow through. There is only a Memorandum of Understanding (MoU) between MCDCB and LGUs, but not regulatory relationship. Because LGUs cannot afford a planning department staffed by professional planners, and therefore cannot fulfil the obligations to complete a CLUP, the impact of the support of MCDCB to prepare CLUPs has been limited so far. Also, the MCDCB has undertaken a strong branding and outreach programme, with brochures, videos and other tools. However, anecdotal evidence, after speaking with a number of residents in Cebu, is that there is still relatively little broad based awareness or understanding of the Mega Cebu initiative or efforts for co-ordination among LGUs.

Continuing to develop an understanding of, and broad support for, the initiative may help increase political traction at all levels. Metro Vancouver's 'regional federation' derives its authority from a legislated basis coupled with a commitment to collaborative governance. Strong communication among members and Metro Vancouver as well as between the federation and other stakeholders is essential. Metro Vancouver's collaborative governance model precedes the creation of regional districts by the Province of British Columbia in 1965. Since 1886, the communities of Metro Vancouver have co-operated in the development and delivery of services essential to the growing region. Members continue to deliver the services best provided at the local level, while Metro Vancouver as a collaborative governance platform, allows members to work together in areas where there are economies of scale or value in speaking with a collective voice.

Mega Cebu Development Authority: using the window of opportunity to create the most efficient metropolitan governance system in Metro Cebu

The current attempts to create the Mega Cebu Development Authority (MCDA) should be an opportunity to strengthen metropolitan governance mechanisms initiated by MCDCB and should take into account the current limitations of the Board.

MCDCB prepared and submitted to the provincial Congress in 2015 a bill to create the **Mega Cebu Development Authority (MCDA)**. The MCDA bill is based on the Metropolitan Manila Development Authority created in 1975 and influenced by the regional district model created through British Columbia's Local Government Act (Parts 6, 8 and 13). The main purposes of the creation of MCDA are: i) to recognise a more institutional approach to metropolitan and integrated development planning; ii) to foster co-operative relations between and among metropolitan and surrounding cities and towns; iii) to ensure active participation by the private, business, and civil society sector; and iv) to implement a national government-approved Metropolitan Cebu Roadmap and other subsequent and related metro-wide roadmaps and plans. If the bill is enacted, MCDA would administer the affairs of MCDCB. Its responsibilities, as stated in the bill, would be as follows (Republic of the Philippines, 2015):

- Formulate, co-ordinate, regulate and monitor the short, medium, and long-term plans, policies and programmes for the sustainable development and integration of Metropolitan Cebu Area;
- Render services that have multi-LGU or metropolitan wide coverage and impact, transcending local geopolitical boundaries or entailing substantial expenditures including, but not limited to: integrated and infrastructure development planning; transport and traffic management; solid waste disposal and management; water, septage, sewerage and storm water management; and disaster risk reduction. Public Service Commission (PCs) would be created in each of these five initial sectors;
- Ensure that plans, policies, programmes and services are pursued for the purpose of realising the Mega Cebu 2050 Vision of a Wholesome, Advanced, Vibrant, Equitable, and Sustainable Cebu;
- Ensure continuing research, evaluation, and monitoring to enhance plans, policies, programmes, services and efforts to anticipate or respond to the dynamic and changing realities and needs of metropolitan development; and
- Perform other related functions required to achieve the Mega Cebu 2050 Vision and objectives of the MCDA, including delivery to services to the LGUs.

The draft Mega Cebu Development Act will enable the MCDA to assume the planning function for the whole Province through the development of a 'technical research and planning unit'. This co-ordinated planning function will enhance planning capacity and allow the Mega Cebu 2050 Vision priorities to be identified and advanced. The MCDA would be headed by the Governor while the two co-chairpersons will be from the public and private sector (modelled strongly on the existing MCDCB). The governing board (Mega Cebu Development Board, not to be confounded with MCDCB) will also be composed, among others, of the Mayors of the 13 LGUs of Metro Cebu and Directors of Region VII National Government Agencies in relevant sectors mentioned above (Republic of the Philippines, 2015).

The bill is structured to ensure there is no loss of autonomy for LGUs. A similar approach was undertaken in British Columbia, where the legislation guiding the role and authority of regional districts around regional planning clearly speaks to a collaborative relationship, but authority over land use planning at the local level. The 'soft' relationship is both successful in terms of partnership and collaboration and shared vision, but challenged by an inability to require the vision to be implemented. If the MCDA approach is not efficient, alternative options could be explored to improve implementation of metropolitan policies. In Iskandar Malaysia, service level agreements have been set up by the Iskandar Regional Development Authority (IRDA) to encourage collective action into concrete projects on the ground.

While MCDA will surely be a powerful institution to enhance horizontal governance in Metro Cebu, the drafting and development process of MCDA should also be an opportunity to tackle the vertical and finance governance issues mentioned previously. The draft legislation still reflects a disconnect between a required relationship with the national government in terms of the dependencies on that level of government to implement LGU priorities (e.g. approvals, inclusion of Mega Cebu development plans and investment programmes in the Philippines Development Plan and Public Investment Programme) and the level of authority granted to national level officials in the proposed MCDA administrative structure (i.e. a Director of the Regional Office sits on the Board "as may be necessary to pursue the mandate and scope of services of MCDA" with one vote). It is not clear where the value proposition is for national government buy-in to the MCDA as proposed in the bill. The bill is also focused on the relationship between LGUs, and does not really address the challenges of implementing national level regulations or policies. A stronger focus on vertical integration and co-ordination is needed. This challenge manifests in the clauses that speak to:

- The importance of the Metropolitan Cebu Roadmap without acknowledging its fit with national policies, nor approval from the national government; and
- The intent to submit "to the NEDA Board MCDA plans, programmes, projects and activities to enable adoption, endorsement, approval, integration and or progressive roll out of integrated and system-wide plans". It is not clear from the bill by what process the translation from MCDA to national government plan and implementation will occur.

Government bodies and stakeholders involved in the MCDA creation process should explore a stronger national level government role in the MCDA to ensure good integration with national regulations, policies and funding. A co-chair role or final level of approval at the national level may be appropriate as well as a higher level national government representative (not a representative of the regional office) on the Board, for example the Director General of NEDA. The bill would also benefit from greater clarity on the relationship between MCDA and the national government more generally in terms of alignment with the national regulatory and policy frameworks as well as with the Philippines Development Plan and Public Investment Programme. In addition, MCDA should explore a stronger relationship with the Regional Development Council (RDC) of the Central Visayas to ensure proper co-ordination, policy complementarity and coherence across all sectors. For instance, regular consultations between MCDA and the RDC will help to ensure that short, medium and long term plans formulated by the MCDA are in line with regional economic and social development efforts, and this will help to ensure that uneven development in the region is avoided.

Finally, there is little substantiation offered in the draft legislation in terms of the requested start up budget (1 PHP billion) for the MCDA, nor for ongoing funding, which is noted simply as "thereafter, the National Government shall appropriate annually and include in the General Appropriations Act the funds as may be necessary for MCDA personnel, capital expenditures, maintenance and other operating expenses". It is also not clear how the funding for the MCDA interacts with other funding for LGUs, for example the Internal Revenue Allotment (IRA) (see Section on Financing). A more realistic costing of needs should therefore be carried out to make the business case for MCDA.

Financing urban green growth in Cebu

Enhancing opportunities and capacities for public investment in urban green growth

Public investment is one of the two critical financing sources that can be mobilised to meet green growth objectives in Cebu. Sustainable infrastructure, in particular, faces great financing gaps that should be addressed urgently. Two main channels of finance should be enhanced to boost the quantity and quality of public investment: local financial sources and national investment in Cebu.

Revenue gap and disparities amongst Metro Cebu's LGUs

The combined revenues of the 13 LGUs in Metro Cebu was PHP 10.4 billion in total in 2014, including PHP 4.7 billion for the City of Cebu alone. The revenues of the provincial government were PHP 2.5 billion in 2014. The total revenues are still low compared to the registered population: on average, LGUs in Metro Cebu raised annual revenues to around USD 227 per inhabitant in 2014. Wide disparities are observable in the metropolitan area: the municipality of Liloan has the highest revenues per inhabitant, at USD 474, followed by the largest LGU, Cebu City, with revenues of USD 291 per inhabitant. At the other end of the spectrum, the municipality of Cordova only raised revenues at around USD 88 (Figure 4.1). In comparison, revenues per inhabitant in Davao City, Quezon City and Makati City were of USD 210, USD 318 and USD 1 229, respectively (Department of Finance website). Revenues in Metro Cebu are also low relatively to standards of other major Southeast Asian cities: in terms of purchasing-power-parities, the City of Bangkok for instance benefitted in 2012 from revenues estimated at around USD 1 075 per inhabitant; the City of Bandung from revenues at around USD 653 in 2016 and the City of Hai Phong from revenues at around USD 3 340 in 2014 (OECD, 2015, 2016a, 2016b).

Nonetheless, the total revenues of cities and municipalities in Cebu have significantly increased over the past few years. From 2009 to 2014, in Region VII, provinces' revenues have increased from PHP 4.4 billion to PHP 6 billion, cities' revenues have increased from PHP 9.1 billion to PHP 14 billion, and municipalities' revenues have increased from PHP 7.3 billion to PHP 9.7 billion. In Metro Cebu, total revenues have increased from PHP 8.3 billion in 2012 to PHP 10.4 billion in 2014. This reflects national trends: at the country level, from 2001 to 2013, provinces' revenues have increased from PHP 33.7 billion to PHP 90.2 billion, cities' revenues have increased from PHP 57.1 billion to PHP 168.3 billion, and municipalities' revenues have increased from PHP 47.3 billion to PHP 141 billion (Department of Finance website).

Figure 4.1. **Revenue per inhabitant in LGUs of Metro Cebu**

USD, PPP

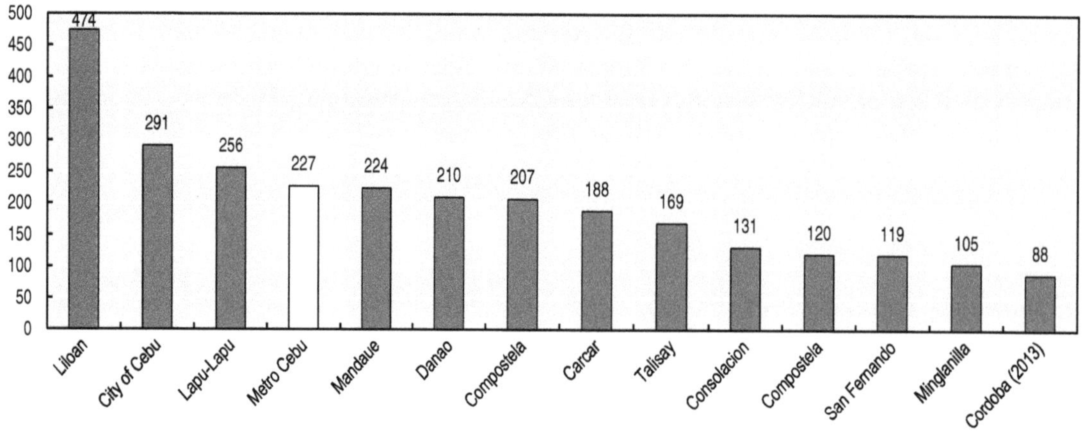

Source: Department of Finance website.

LGUs' revenues are constituted of a certain number of items which can be classified into three main categories: i) locally-raised revenues, ii) transfers from the national government (Internal Revenue Allotment, IRA), and iii) other revenues (tax sharing from the national government, inter-local transfers, grants and donations). In Metro Cebu, locally-raised revenues account for around **51% of total revenues on average, and the IRA around 40% of total revenues**. These figure however hide wide disparities, again, from one LGU to another, and in particular from the three independent cities (Cebu City, Lapu-Lapu and Mandaue), where locally-raised revenues account for around 59% of total revenues on average, and other LGUs (component cities and municipalities), where locally-raised revenues only account for around 31% of total revenues on average (Figure 4.2). This is mainly due to the different status and tax authority of LGUs in the Philippines. Independent cities have much wider tax collection authority than component cities and municipalities, which are much more dependent on transfers from the national and provincial governments. For instance, independent cities collect and retain their own property tax, while municipalities only get a share of the property tax which is collected by the provincial government. Revenues of the provincial government of Cebu are also strongly constituted by the IRA, at around 80%, while locally-raised revenues account for 18% of its total revenues (Department of Finance website).

Figure 4.2. **Revenue profile of LGUs in Metro Cebu**

Fiscal Year 2014

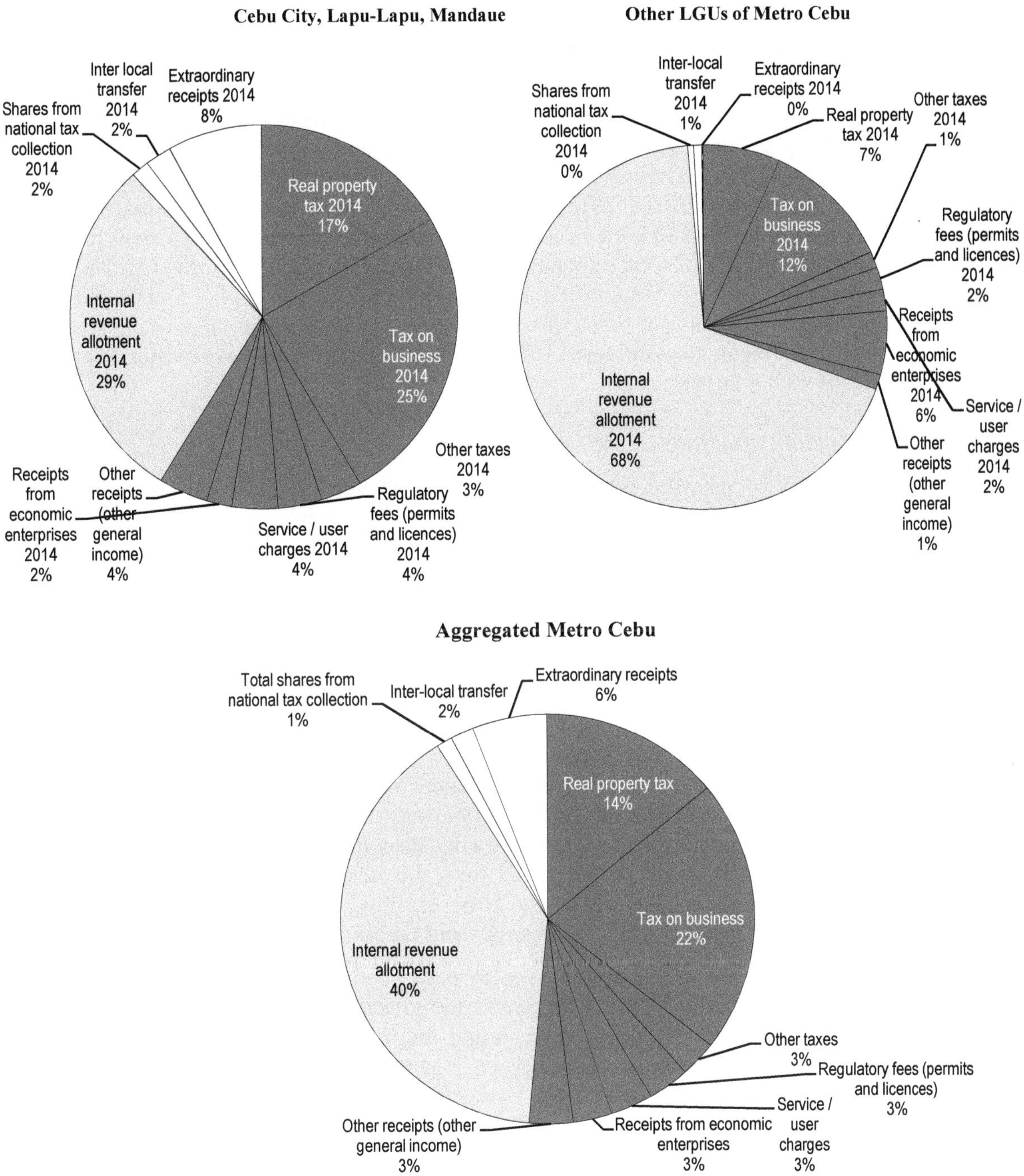

Note: Locally sourced revenues are marked in blue; national transfers are marked in light grey; other revenues are marked in white. Figures "Other LGUs of Metro Cebu" and "Total Metro Cebu" do not comprise data for the municipality of Cordoba.

Source: Department of Finance website.

In terms of expenditure, the 1991 *Local Government Code* has not resulted in expected benefits either. LGU expenditure remains very low by international standards.

LGUs represent nearly 17% of total government expenditures and around 14% of public investment, compared to 40.2% and 58.8% in OECD countries, respectively (OECD, 2015b). Total LGU spending increased from an average of 1.6% of GDP during 1985-91 to about 3% in the late 2000s, against 16.6% of GDP in the OECD area in 2015 (OECD, 2015b). While the central governments still undertake major "hard" public infrastructure investment (e.g. major roads, ports, airports), LGUs nonetheless have substantial expenditure responsibilities, for instance in the environment sector (e.g. solid waste disposal, water supply systems, seawalls and dikes, drainage and sewerage, flood control) (Department of Finance, 2015). However, LGUs have very limited ambitions for funding infrastructure development (OECD, 2015). In Metro Cebu, total expenditures reached around PHP 8.7 billion in 2014 (83.7% of total revenues); most of expenditures went for general public services (54% of total expenditures), followed by social services (22.7%) and economic services (16.7%). Around PHP 0.9 billion were spent in capital investment in Metro Cebu, which accounts for 9.8% of total revenues in the metropolitan area.[1] On average, capital investment account for 13.2% of local governments' expenditures in OECD countries (OECD, 2016b).

Enhancing financial capacities at the local level

One of the causes of insufficient revenues is the inefficiency of the tax collection system and outdated tax rates. In 2013, total tax revenues only represented 16.2% of the Philippines's GDP, while this share is around 34% on average in OECD countries (OECD, 2015c). The inability of LGUs to collect taxes efficiently, in particular, has been pointed out by the LGU Tax Watch, an initiative of the Department of Finance and the Bureau of Internal Revenue. This particularly affects the Real Property Tax. Between 2010 and 2012, it is estimated that provinces and cities in the Philippines forewent up around PHP 9.4 billion and PHP 20.3 billion, respectively, in real property taxes (Philippines Department of Finance, 2015). In Region VII, only 86% of the targeted revenues from the Real Property Tax were collected. In addition, four in every five cities use outdated tax bases which are not properly indexed on market values. The City of Mandaue, for instance, still used the tax bases of 1991 until it recently received support from The World Bank to update them, and Cebu City uses the tax base of 2002.[2] As a consequence, more revenues could be perceived from the Real Property Tax. In Metro Cebu, the first source of local revenues is the Business Tax. LGUs however lack the capacities to calculate the market value of properties and the issues is politically sensitive.

The national government has a pivotal role to play in expanding and diversifying local own sources of revenue and raising capacities to undertake programmes which can foster urban green growth. In particular, they should facilitate cost sharing at the local level through levies or utility fees in critical green growth sectors. In Metro Cebu, fees and charges accounted for only 6% of all LGUs' revenues combined in 2014 (Figure 4.2), against 14.9% for subnational governments in the OECD area (OECD, 2016b). In Liloan municipality, the solid waste management fee was only recently applied to households. In addition, they do not target green growth services sufficiently. Such tools can indeed directly promote urban green growth: water extraction charges, taxes on impervious surfaces, development charges in middle to high income areas and land value capture tools along public transport networks are all instruments that could help to raise local finance and guide the development of Cebu towards green growth. A charge for ecological services for watersheds could also be considered, as watersheds provide a range of environmental benefits such as purification of water and biodiversity conservation but. Once in place, the local capacity will help LGUs gain a sense of ownership over planning and implementation of infrastructure projects. In many cases, this will require the involvement of the national government, to give more autonomy to LGUs in managing such financial instruments. The *Local Government Code* may need to be reviewed, because it specifies the conditions in which such fees and charges can be perceived and such conditions may be too restrictive. For instance, the amount of the environmental fee is fixed and does not accurately take into account the size of industries of the type of activities. A solution could be to base the environmental fee on floor area or to transform the environmental fee into an environmental tax.

Careful consideration also needs to be given to land use changes. In most cities where BRT has been implemented, land values of properties around the corridor increased as demand for properties rose given the improved accessibility (Salon and Shewmake, 2011). Two major benefits can be reaped from this. Firstly, LGU's in Metro Cebu could use land value capture tools to raise revenue from the direct and indirect benefits generated by the BRT to finance urban transport expansion. Land value capture enables the mobilisation for the benefit of the community the land value increments generated by the actions of others besides the landowner (Smolka, 2016). Cities such as Tokyo, Seoul and Hong Kong have used different mechanisms of land value capture to finance their sustainable urban development (Suzuki et al., 2015). In Seoul, prices of land within 300m of BRT stops went up by a premium of up to 10% for residences while properties within 150m shot up by more than 25% (Cervero and Kang, 2011). Secondly, Metro Cebu could capitalise on encouraging higher density developments around the corridor. Intensive land uses such as the conversion of single family to multifamily residential uses have taken place in a number of cities along BRT routes (EMBARQ, 2013). Cebu learning from this practice could develop in a compact way to accommodate its increasing population, while simultaneously increasing its own source of revenue.

This expanded revenue generation capacity will also facilitate LGU ability to actively support realising the Mega Cebu vision they have signed on to. MCDA, in this perspective, can play a key role by channelling up LGUs' financing obstacles to the national government. In addition, one of the powers of the MCDA is the imposition and collection of fine and penalties. Progressively, MCDA should be granted increasing fiscal authority on numerous matters that require metropolitan management, in particular mobility, solid waste and water management. Giving more weight to MCDA in managing finance in Metro Cebu could also help to ease the negative effects of revenue inequalities as shown in Figure 4.2. As an example, Metro Vancouver's revenues are mostly built through water sales (37%), sewer levy (29%) and solid waste tipping fee (12%) (Box 4.3). Similarly, 43% of Barcelona Metropolitan Authority's (AMA) budget – at around EUROS 280 million – are built through the waste management tax and the mobility tax, and 13% from PPPs for water supply and night bus service. *The Local Government Units Public Financial Management (LGU PFM) Reform Roadmap and Implementation Strategy*, an initiative launched by the national government in 2015, could consider this particular topic.

In terms of investment, LGUs should also obtain more flexibility in borrowing to finance green or sustainable infrastructure. LGUs are authorised to go into loans but only individually: two LGUs cannot make a loan together, a process that could also encourage inter-governmental co-operation between them. Given the horizontal fragmentation of LGUs in Metro Cebu and the need to develop infrastructure across the whole metropolitan area (e.g. water, transport), this is a critical obstacle to finance urban green growth. The creation of the Mega Cebu Development Authority (MCDA) should therefore go hand-in-hand with the establishment of a Mega Cebu Investment Board, as recommended by the MCDCB-JICA roadmap study. The Board should be entitled to borrow from banks and on markets to make the necessary investment to carry out the functions devolved by the *Local Government Code*.

Box 4.3. **Metro Vancouver revenue system**

Metro Vancouver's core utility functions (water, sewerage and solid waste) date back to the early 1900's when municipalities saw the benefits of working together and pooling resources for utilities infrastructure. By legislation, Metro Vancouver districts are required to operate balanced budgets and any deficit must be repaid immediately the following year. Each utility generates revenues via user pay that reflect the costs of managing the infrastructure in the region. Vancouver's revenue sources in 2015 are indicated in the figure below:

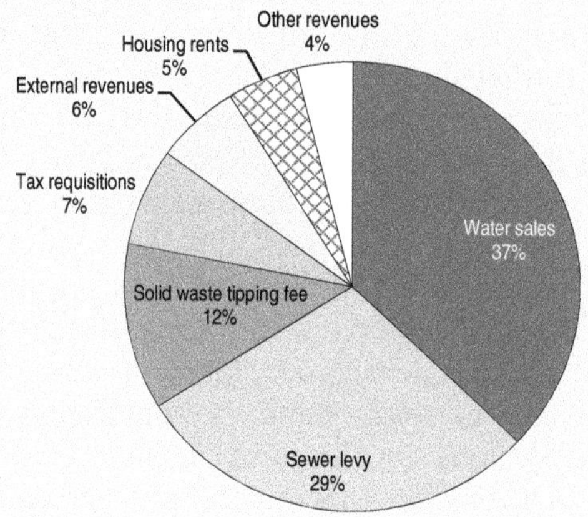

Metro Vancouver's annual budgets are driven primarily by the costs of delivering fundamentally important utility services, in partnership with member municipalities, to the region's citizens and businesses. Drinking water supply, sewerage and management of solid waste represent the majority of both operating and capital budgets, and are financed through utility fees. Property taxes account for a small portion of the regional budget, and support the Regional Parks system, as well as other services including Air Quality Management and Regional Planning activities. The Metro Vancouver Housing Corporation is financed almost entirely through rents paid by tenants. The budget represents a CAD 427 annual cost to the average regional household.

Source: Peer reviewer report.

Reducing dependency on national transfers

The national government has a critical role to play in enhancing local finance in metro Cebu. While the fiscal mandate of LGUs was broadened by the *Local Government Code 1991* to include revenue assignments, devolvement of expenditure responsibilities, intergovernmental transfers, and subnational debt/credit financing (Department of Finance, 2015), fiscal decentralisation has been limited in practice and authority and resources remain highly centralised: the proportion of total tax revenue collected by LGUs in the Philippines remains low at around 5.2% in 2013, and has not evolved since 2000. In Indonesia, the proportion of total tax revenue collected by local governments was only 3.2% in 2000 but increased to 9.6% in 2013 due to decentralisation reforms. On average, the proportion is around 12% in OECD unitary countries, and is as high as 25% in Japan (Table 4.1).

Table 4.1. **Attribution of tax revenues to sub-sectors of general government as percentage of total tax revenue in selected countries and regions of the world**

	Central government			State or regional government			Local government			Social security funds		
	2000	2010	2013	2000	2010	2013	2000	2010	2013	2000	2010	2013
Federal countries												
Malaysia	94.7	94.3	95.2	..	..	..	3.4	4.0	3.3	1.9	1.7	1.5
OECD	56.5	53.8	54.5	15.3	16.3	16.5	6.9	7.9	7.6	21.1	21.8	21.3
Unitary countries												
Indonesia	96.8	92.8	90.4	..	..	..	3.2	7.2	9.6	..	..	..
Philippines	81.5	82.2	82.2	..	..	..	5.3	5.2	5.2	13.2	12.7	12.7
Japan	38.7	33.0	33.7	..	..	..	26.1	25.9	24.7	35.2	41.1	41.6
Korea	68.2	60.4	58.2	..	..	..	15.1	16.7	15.5	16.7	22.8	26.3
OECD	66.5	63.4	62.9	..	..	..	11.0	11.9	12.0	22.3	24.4	24.8

Source: OECD (2015c), *Revenue Statistics in Asian Countries 2015: Trends in Indonesia, Malaysia and the Philippines*, OECD Publishing, Paris, http://dx.doi.org/10.1787/9789264234277-en.

Currently, the national government is the largest public investor in the country and such investment is often made directly by the lead national agency. The national government of the Philippines' investment in infrastructure is guided by the Public Investment Program (PIP) 2011-2016. Infrastructure development has the largest share among eight key areas of investment, with planned infrastructure investments of about USD 13 billion from 2013 to 2016. The national government shoulders about two thirds of the investment program including official development assistance grants, followed by private sector investment at an 18.5% share of the cost. LGUs will supply about 1.1% of the investments. Recent studies show that the outlay for infrastructure are increasingly sourced from local funds rather than foreign assistance at a ratio of 84-87% to 13-17% since 2008, but foreign investment remains a critical factor (Navarro and Llanto, 2014). The largest portfolio of infrastructure investment is transport.

As mentioned previously, the national government contributes indirectly to local finance through transfers to LGUs, in particular the Internal Revenue Allotment (IRA). All levels of LGUs in the Philippines get a separate allotment based the class of the city/municipality, population and land area. The IRA is intended to fund basic services and facilities, particularly those that have been devolved by the national government. The aggregate IRA of LGUs is set at 40% of the actual internal revenue tax collections of the central government three years prior to the current year. In effect, it comprises about 15-20% of the national expenditures. In 2014, the IRA and other national transfers accounted on average for about 80% of provinces and municipalities' revenues, against 43.5% for cities. In Metro Cebu, the IRA accounts for 40% of LGUs' revenues on average, and accounts for a particularly large share of component cities and municipalities' revenues (around 68%), against only 19% of the three independent cities' revenues (Figure 4.3). Interestingly, the dependency of LGUs to the IRA has decreased overall since 2009, except for component cities. LGUs must set aside no less than 20% of their IRA for development projects as directed by the Local Government Code, including 5% for disaster mitigation and further 3% on other areas deemed as national priorities (OECD, 2015). The Region VII office of NEDA recently published a guidebook compiling funding institutions that may be accessed for funding projects (NEDA, 2013).

The national government should aim to increase LGUs' capacities to raise local revenues, with the objective to make them less dependent on the IRA in the future, reflecting upon the three independent cities. A heavy reliance on the IRA may make LGUs too dependent on this transfer and discourage them from making efforts to develop their own financial sources. In parallel, the national government could set up earmarked transfers in green growth opportunity areas, backed up by concrete development plans (public transport development, wastewater treatment facilities etc.). This would create coherent public investment frameworks where all levels of government are involved in achieving common green growth goals (see below).

Figure 4.3. **IRA (Internal Revenue Allotment) Dependency of LGUs in Metro Cebu**

Fiscal year 2014

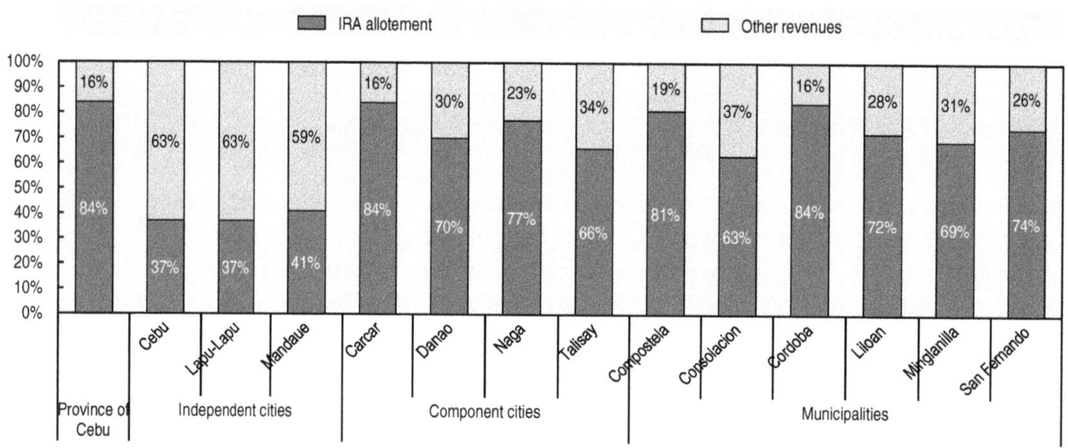

Note: Inter-local transfers and grants / aids were excluded from the graph, due to their very minor share of revenues in each LGU category

Source: Philippines Department of Finance website.

The national government should also create local priority funds to finance specific local initiatives in green growth related sectors. In Sweden, a national programme (KLIMP) provides local governments of all sizes financial support to manage greenhouse gas (GHG) emissions and adapt to climate change. Local governments can apply for national subsidies that can be used to promote local investment to reduce emissions and improve energy efficiency and independence. Examples of funded municipal activities include removing disincentives for individuals to reduce emissions, such as eliminating free parking, and subsidising the cost of retrofitting filling stations to add a pump to supply renewable biofuels (Corfee-Morlot et al., 2009). Such system should be developed and tailored to green growth/sustainable development/climate change objectives in the Philippines. There are some similar mechanisms already in place, but they are not very effective owing to lack of local capacities to propose well-crafted projects for funding. In addition, there is a problem of co-ordination between national line agencies: LGUs are required to go through two different processes to validate a project: one for the contents themselves, and one to get the funding. This is a big discouragement for LGUs which already suffer from under capacity issues. Vertical co-operation and co-ordination is all the more important in this perspective. The national government should take an active role in the creation and management of the MCDA and work with all relevant LGUs even before the application process to ensure full success of the application. Collective efforts should be particularly concentrated on the priority projects identified in the present report and also the MCDCB-JICA roadmap study.

Creating a public investment framework for urban green growth

Urban green growth in Cebu requires a significant amount of public investment across levels of government. Local governments need funding tools, capacity building in terms of effective public investment, and planning professionals need a working knowledge of how to prioritise and implement the plans they develop. In addition, the reliance of LGUs on national grants through the IRA, as well as the weakness of the proposed MCDA legislation regarding financing, indicates a real need for a more robust funding strategy and understanding of how to successfully achieve integrated public investment across levels of government. In this context, creating a more effective public investment framework is crucial (Box 4.4). For example, central government's earmarked transfers could be better aligned with CLUPS for the entire Metro Cebu, so that national funds contribute coherently to local strategies.

Box 4.4. **OECD Recommendation on Effective Public Investment Across Levels of Government**

In 2014, the OECD adopted a *Recommendation of the Council on Effective Public Investment Across Levels of Government*. This is an OECD instrument adopted by the Council. Recommendations are not legally binding, but practice accords them great moral force as representing the political will of member countries.

Subnational governments, defined as federated states, regions and other municipalities, undertook 72% of total public investment in 2012 throughout the OECD area in terms of volume. Variations across countries are important, as subnational public investment ranges from 31% in Greece to 91% in Canada. More effective public investment has a critical role to play to address inequalities, rebuild trust, restore growth and enhance well-being. The impact of public investment depends to a significant extent on how governments manage this shared competence across levels of government. Effective public investment requires substantial co-ordination across levels of government to bridge information, policy or fiscal gaps that may occur, as well as critical governance capacities at different levels to design and implement public investment projects.

The purpose of these principles is to help governments assess the strengths and weaknesses of their public investment capacity in a multi-level governance perspective and set priorities for improvement. An Implementation Toolkit provides guidance with details for all countries (www.oecd.org/effective-public-investment-toolkit).

Source: OECD (2014b), *Recommendation of the Council on Effective Public Investment Across Levels of Government*, OECD, Paris, www.oecd.org/gov/regional-policy/Principles-Public-Investment.pdf.

Efforts to facilitate private investment should be strengthened

Need to improve FDI attractiveness in the ASEAN region

Foreign Direct Investment (FDI) is potentially an important source of private external finance that can help to reduce the green infrastructure gap in the critical urban utility systems. However, FDI inflows have been lower in the Philippines than in all other countries of the Southeast Asian region. They accounted for only 1.4% of GDP between 2005 and 2014, against 2.1% in Indonesia, 3% in Thailand, 3.4% in Malaysia and 6% in

Viet Nam. Since 2010 however, there has been a steady increase in the FDI's share of GDP in the Philippines, while the evolution has been negative or unstable in Malaysia, Viet Nam and Thailand (Figure 4.4).

Figure 4.4. **Foreign direct investments in ASEAN countries, net inflows (% of GDP)**

2005-2014

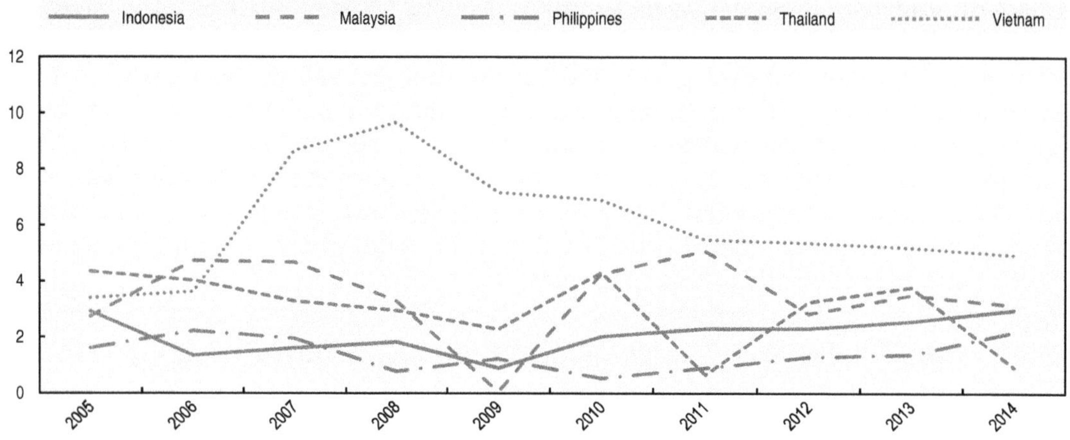

Source: Word Development Indicators.

The low amounts of FDI in the Philippines are strongly correlated with the high restrictiveness imposed on FDI in the country (Figure 4.5). Indeed, the OECD FDI Regulatory Restrictiveness Index ranks the Philippines as the worst performer among the countries in its database, at around 0.4. The ASEAN-9 average Index is around 0.22 and the OECD average Index around 0.07, in comparison (Figure 4.6). In the land and transport sectors, in particular, the Constitution of the Philippines restricts ownership to Filipinos and Filipino companies: foreign investors can only own up to 40% of land or transport companies, and only where leases are permitted (OECD, 2014a). While this could be seen as a means to avoid speculation on land from foreign companies, as it has happened in Iskandar Malaysia, this does not prevent domestic speculation or poor urban planning and management. In the transport sector, such restrictions are problematic to develop public transport networks; currently, the domestic market for public transport, in particular mass transit, is weak and inefficient, and the restrictions prevent the necessary investment that such infrastructure requires. The national government should therefore consider loosening such restrictions in critical sectors that can foster green growth. In order to make sure that FDI well-contribute to green growth, sustainability standards or conditions should be created in these sectors.

Figure 4.5. **FDI Index scores vs. FDI stocks as a share of GDP in ASEAN-9 members**

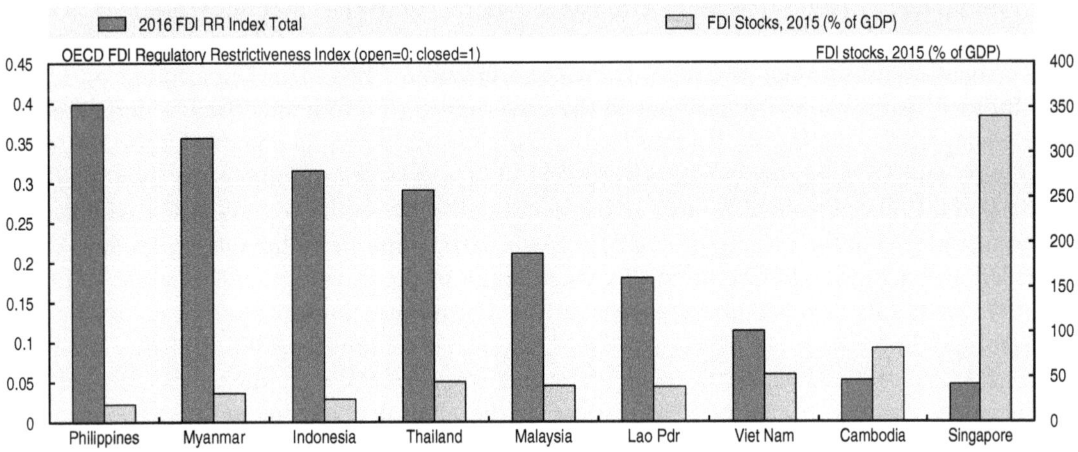

Source: OECD (2014a), Southeast Asia Policy Investment Perspectives.

Figure 4.6. **OECD FDI Regulatory Restrictiveness Index**

2016 FDI RR Index

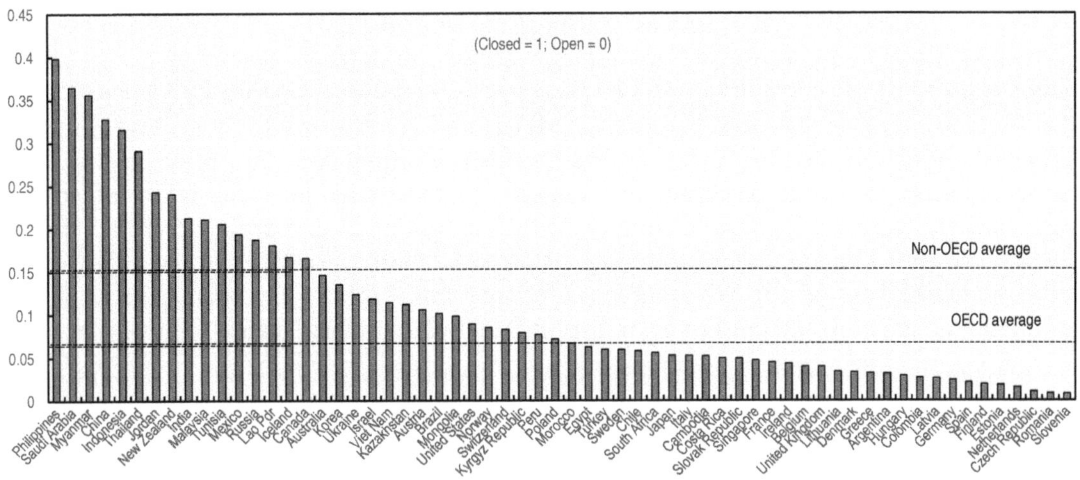

Source: OECD (2014a), Southeast Asia Policy Investment Perspectives.

Encouraging Public-Private-Partnerships for green growth at the metropolitan level

In parallel, public authorities should encourage private investment through Public-Private-Partnerships (PPP). PPPs provide a tremendous opportunity to leverage private sector innovation and capability towards meeting the public interest. As demonstrated in Cebu by FDR Integrated Resource Recovery Management Inc., which was originally a construction company, now diversified and providing waste management services for local governments, PPPs are effective not only for infrastructure (design / build / operate), but also for service agreements. This company enters into 20-25 year agreements with LGUs in order to collect, process and treat non-hazardous solid waste from households, commercial and industrial sectors.

The policy context is increasingly favourable to such forms of public procurement in the Philippines. In 2010, a new emphasis placed on PPPs was identified as a key component of an overall growth strategy by the national government and was translated into critical organisational and legal reforms to promote PPPs. The Department of Trade and Industry is now a board member in the governance of a unit specifically dedicated to PPP management, the Public-Private-Partnership Centre, which is chaired by the National Economic and Development Authority (NEDA). These changes have been fruitful: prior to 2010, the Philippines had limited experience with PPPs with only six solicited projects being completed in the period 1992-2010. Since 2010, nine PPPs have been tendered and awarded and a further 14 are at an advanced stage in the development pipeline (OECD, 2015b). Most PPP project interventions in the Philippines have so far been led by the national government. For instance, in Cebu, the extension and upgrading of the Mactan-Cebu International Airport (the second largest airport in the country and hub of the southern regions) is a priority PPP project of the central government; undertaken with GMR Megawide Cebu Airport Corporation (SPV), with financial support of the Asian Development Bank.[3]

The central government is now advocating the mainstreaming of PPPs at the local level through the PPP Centre's Capacity Building Programme for Local Government Units (LGUs), created in 2013. The Internship Programme and Partnerships with selected Local Capacity Building Institutions has also been created with the aim to provide assistance to LGU-PPP programmes and projects (KPMG, 2015). The PPP Centre has promoted the PPP initiative and invited expressions of interest from LGUs, provided training for LGU officials, has produced a comprehensive three volume PPP Manual[4] and has engaged with a few LGUs seeking advice and internships to help develop PPP proposals (OECD, 2015b). The Centre is also working on the creation of PPP Subcommittees in Local Government Councils, to "assist in the formulation of action plans and strategies to the implementation of PPP programmes and projects" (PPP Centre, 2012). The PPP Manual defines the types of projects eligible for PPPs at the LGU level. Sectors related to green growth include environment and solid waste management, land-use (land reclamation and dredging), transport, and water and sanitation.

Nonetheless, the PPP Centre's initiatives at the LGU level are very recent and have not resulted in tangible achievements yet, except in Tanauan City (OECD, 2015b). Still, very few LGUs show interest in PPPs. In addition, a number of obstacles to the implementation of PPPs persist at the LGU level, in particular (OECD, 2015b):

- **The preference for projects with high potential for cost recovery**, such as commercial and industrial development. Indeed, wastewater, solid waste tipping and transport fees and charges tend to be under-used in cities, in particular due to the reluctance of local governments to touch upon such sensitive issues. This is also the case in Cebu, and this undermines the attractiveness of such sectors for private investors;
- **The technical challenge of PPPs and the limited timeframe** of the local chief executives to complete their projects. While some capacity-building initiatives have been undertaken by the PPP Centre, many LGUs still struggle to cope with some technical challenges such as calculating the equity participation of LGUs in a project. The fragmented size of LGUs and the presence of many small municipalities, including in Cebu Province, is also a challenge to develop skills and resources to undertake PPPs;

- **The inability of many LGUs, especially municipalities, to borrow** has particularly hindered public investment at the local level and prevented them from spending and borrowing for PPPs. The high reliance on the IRA, also, has had perverse incentives; in particular the reluctance of LGUs to invest in public infrastructure and an over-reliance on special pleading to the national government; and
- **The difficulty to undertake PPPs across jurisdictions at the metropolitan level** in order to match investment with the right geographical scale. There is a lack of incentives and regulations to tackle the inability of two or more LGUs to enter into a binding contract with private sector actors. This is particularly relevant in the case of Metro Cebu.

The MCDA, in this perspective, can be instrumental in facilitating PPPs. It will be an opportune level of governance to explore PPPs because of the dispersal of risk and ability to pool resources among 13 LGUs in partnership with the national government. OECD (2015b) indeed recommends that alliances of LGUs be given a legal status to do joint PPP projects. In this regard, the MCDA should be able to sign PPP contract, involving several LGUs of Metro Cebu. In the future, it will be critical to develop PPP projects in green growth opportunity areas that will spread over or involve multiple jurisdictions (BRT, metro system, drainage and recycling facilities etc.). Likewise, by comprising big cities such Cebu City and smaller municipalities, the establishment of MCDA should help to integrate municipalities with lower tax authority and borrowing capacities into metropolitan projects with the private sector. In parallel, MCDA should also work with each LGU to explore options to raise cost recovery capacities in critical green growth opportunity areas mentioned above, by raising charges and fees for environmental services. Finally, OECD (2015b) recommends narrowing down the number of sectors in which PPPs should be carried out at the LGU level. The national government should try to align and integrate better the list of sectors with environmental / green growth / climate change national objectives to establish a clearer framework for public investment in infrastructure. Water, for instance, is an urgent issue in the whole country, including in Cebu Province.

Undertaking PPP at the local level is not only a challenge in the Philippines. In Canada, there is a growing but cautious municipal enthusiasm for PPPs. There are a number of obstacles for local governments that have led to a lower number of PPP projects than for provinces, including lack of financial resources, greater political risk, lack of familiarity with PPP delivery and smaller project sizes. To improve uptake of PPPs, a change of the national P3 Canada Fund funding formula to provide funding as a share of total project costs rather than as a share of capital costs is under consideration. This would provide an additional incentive to package the operations and maintenance phase with the design build phase, which is of interest for many municipalities. The Philippines PPP Centre could replicate such Fund and mechanisms. Also, some Canadian municipalities are banding together to create economies of scale in operations (e.g. sharing staff among several wastewater facilities). However, this is often difficult without a co-ordinating body, another benefit that the MCDA would provide. Canadian companies have developed their own PPP expertise that has allowed them to increasingly participate and even lead PPP projects.

Creating incentives for green finance at the national and local levels

Attracting green investment is a complementary instrument that LGUs in Cebu should use to finance the cost of green infrastructure and realise green growth objectives. The example of Solid Waste Corporation Inc., a private company working in Naga, Minglanilla and Carcar, shows that the private sector can bring a decisive contribution to the management of critical urban services. SWC assists LGUs in providing advice on ordinance, structuring garbage fees and generally speaking in building capacities of LGUs for solid waste management. However, such initiatives remain too timid in Cebu and infrastructure and services needs are still largely unmet. Incentives should be created both at the national and local levels to encourage green investment in Cebu.

Green lending and investment should be first and foremost encouraged at the national level. The only noticeable effort was the adoption of a national renewable energy programme in some RE sectors. Policies to attract green finance should be more aggressive and comprehensive. The Philippines could take some inspiration from the case of Indonesia, a pioneer in the region on this matter. One of the flagship policies of the Government of Indonesia and which is very innovative for a developing country was the creation of the SRI-KEHATI Index and the SRI-KEHATI-ETF, which are sustainability ratings for the stock markets. The Ministry of Finance is also considering green weighting for capital requirements, which could significantly encourage green finance (UNEP, 2015). Another policy with potentially high impact is the development of the Roadmap for Sustainable Finance in Indonesia by the Ministry of Finance, which may include a binding regulatory framework for green finance which could include the establishment of compulsory environmental and social management systems and reporting in both capital and stock markets (UNEP, 2015). Similar mechanisms could be designed in the Philippines, as many banks still do not consider developing green lending capacities as a priority. It is especially important that the Ministry of Finance takes such initiative so that all financing institutions are on an equal footing, and not to leave individual initiatives suffer from competition with other institutions. Similar for green investment incentives that could be developed include differentiated reserve requirements with lower required reserve rates for green assets and differentiated capital requirements for green lending. Such measures should be applied in all areas of opportunities for green growth, in particular transport, water supply and sanitation, disaster risk reduction, and solid waste management.

Finally, at the municipal level, LGUs and MCDA can create simple incentives such as tax breaks targeted at companies willing to invest in opportunity areas for green growth. However, to date there is still low awareness and interest in such mechanisms which have not been set up. In the future, they should also start to make use of green bonds to attract institutional investors. LGUs in Cebu do not at present issue municipal bonds, but could develop capacities to do so with the support of the national government and/or international financial institutions, such as the World Bank Group, which has now issued close to USD 12 billion since its inception in 2008 and whose growth is accelerating rapidly. This type of financing mechanism presents another opportunity for Cebu to raise additional finance for green growth projects. Such an instrument could help attract private investors and alleviate the (actual or perceived) financial risks associated with investments in some key green growth projects. The city of Gothenburg (Sweden), with the support of the World Bank, has issued green bonds since 2013 to leverage finance for climate change mitigation and adaptation projects and other environment-related activities (Climate Bonds Initiative, n.d.). In Bandung, this strategy could be further explored in the area of energy use and transport, for instance, where private investors are not yet effectively involved. Co-operation and co-ordinated action with the national government would be highly advantageous. The Roadmap for Sustainable Finance in Indonesia should include regulations allowing local governments to issue green bonds, in particular, so that local governments do not face legal obstacles to do so.

Potential benefits of international co-operation for green growth in Cebu

Green growth targeted official development finance needs to be scaled up

The Philippines is the third highest recipient of official development assistance in Southeast Asia...

International co-operation plays a non-negligible role in the development of the Philippines. One of the forms it takes is official development finance, in particular Official Development Assistance (ODA) and non-concessional other official flows (OOF), such as the Clean Technology Fund (CTF) and the Climate Investment Fund (CIF). Between 2002 and 2015, the Philippines have received around USD 32 billion in the forms of official development finance,[5] which makes it the third highest recipient in the whole Southeast Asian region. Indonesia and Viet Nam, however, have received much larger amounts of official development finance during this period. Among all funds committed to the Philippines, USD 4.8 billion (i.e. 15% of total official development finance) – committed through a total of 2 474 projects – targeted either or simultaneously the environment, climate change mitigation, climate change adaption, biodiversity and desertification (i.e. the objectives set by the Rio Conventions)[6] (Figure 4.7). Amounts of environment-related ODF have also significantly increased from USD 0.2 billion in 2002 to USD 1.5 billion in 2014. The increase is particularly sharp since 2012.

Figure 4.7. **Total and environment-related official development finance committed to ASEAN-5 countries**

2002-2015, USD billion, constant 2015 prices

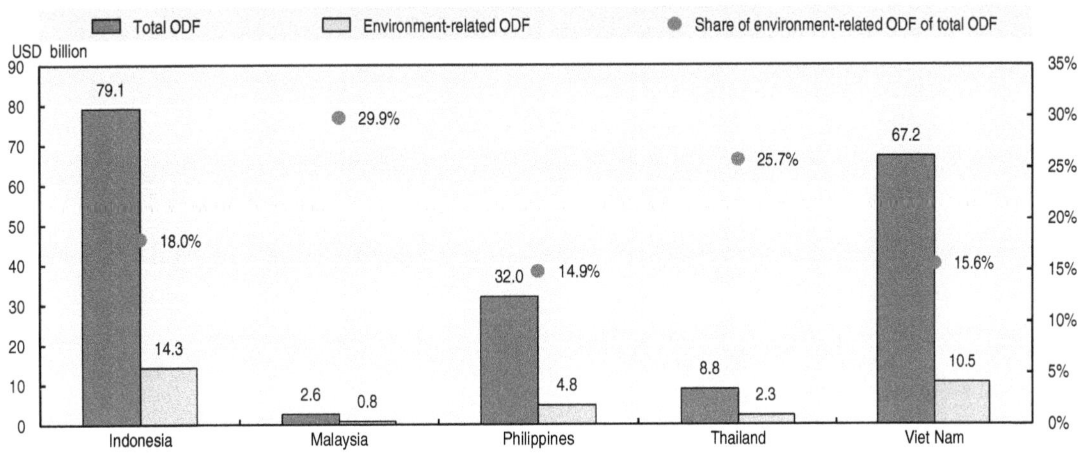

Note: ODA includes both bilateral and multilateral commitments.

Source: OECD (2016), "Aid activities targeting Global Environmental Objectives", DAC Creditor Reporting System (database), https://stats.oecd.org/index.aspx?datasetcode=riomarkers (accessed 23 November 2015).

...But Cebu has not significantly benefitted from such funds

Among those, 212 projects totalling USD 1.8 billion (i.e. 30% of total environment-related official development finance) were specifically and clearly committed to cities, including only USD 11.9 million for Cebu (i.e. only 0.2% of all environment-related funds committed to the Philippines) (Figure 4.8). Therefore, so far, the contribution of international public finance to Cebu's green growth has been rather low, especially with respect to its significant economic growth importance it is to take in the Visayas' regional development. This contrasts with a city such as Bangkok which received during the same period around USD 2.3 billion for environment-related projects (OECD, 2015), and the city of Hai Phong, which received around USD 500 million (OECD, 2016), while the latter has a comparable population size. Until 2014, most of the official development finance (USD 9.4 million) committed to Cebu targeted the water supply and sanitation sector. More recently, a Bus Rapid Transit (BRT) system project[7] has been supported through a loan by the French Development Agency (AFD) and the Clean Technology Fund (CTF), with a total commitment of USD 118 million[8] (Figure 4.9). Some nationwide ODA may also target to environmental objectives in Cebu, but the extent of the contribution is difficult to know as such projects are not specific to Cebu.[9]

Figure 4.8. **Number of official development activities and funding for urban and rural areas in the Philippines for environmental purposes (including Rio Conventions)**

2002-2014, USD billion, constant 2013 prices

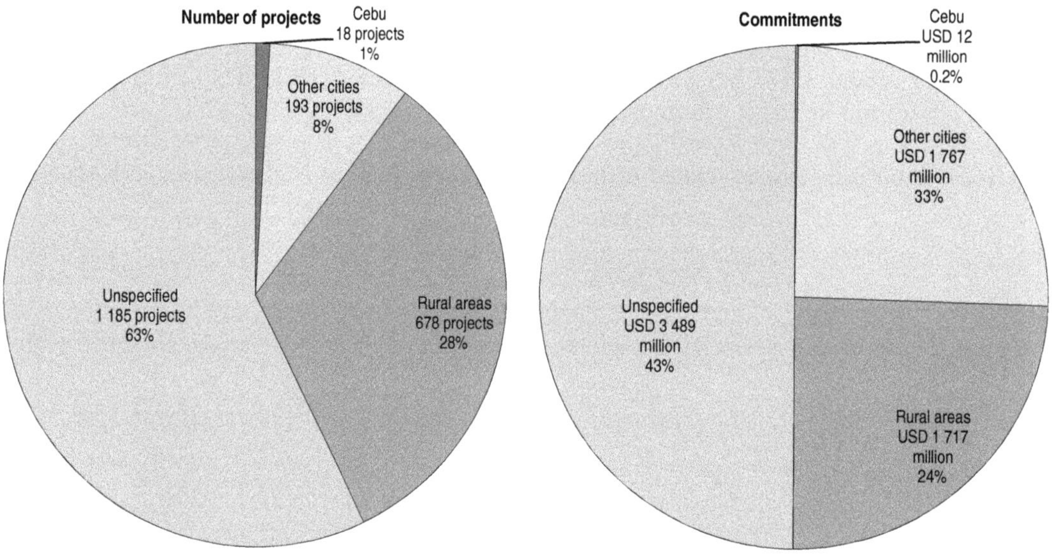

Source: OECD (2016), "Aid activities targeting Global Environmental Objectives", *DAC Creditor Reporting System* (database), https://stats.oecd.org/index.aspx?datasetcode=riomarkers (accessed 4 February 2016).

Figure 4.9. **Number of official development activities and funding for Cebu for environmental purposes (including Rio Conventions), by sector**

2002-2014, Constant 2013 prices

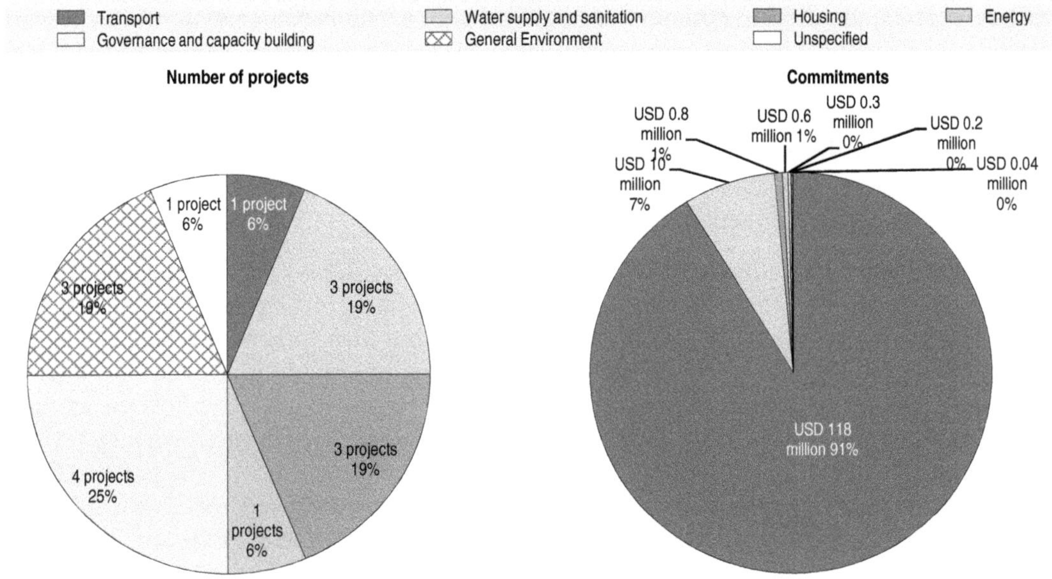

Source: OECD (2016), "Aid activities targeting Global Environmental Objectives", DAC Creditor Reporting System (database), https://stats.oecd.org/index.aspx?datasetcode=riomarkers (accessed 4 February 2016).

Among environment-related official development finance that was committed to Filipino cities, 58% (in terms of funds) supported Metro Manila's development alone, in particular disaster risk resilience objectives. Generally speaking, many projects and a significant share of environment-related official development finance were committed to the Government of the Philippines to support disaster prevention, preparedness and recovery. Such funds were almost always allocated to the national government with no indication on the specific beneficiaries at the local level, which partly explains why a large share of finance is classified as "unspecified". Likewise, a certain number of projects supporting renewable energy development are difficult to tag as "rural" or "urban". While the concrete infrastructure may be built in rural areas, the benefits may nonetheless largely go to cities.

Building capacities to access and apply for official development finance and ensuring aid effectiveness

The above analysis reveals that not only the amounts of official development finance committed to the Philippines should be enlarged, but also that secondary cities such as Cebu are "left behind" or are not the object of major targeted projects supported by international aid. While the national government should seek more aggressively to get official development finance – especially because they are called to increase substantially in the post-COP21 agenda – it should also play a critical role in ensuring that local governments outside of Metro Manila, including Cebu, benefit more concretely from these sources of finance. This is all the more important that national governments are almost always the contact points of international financial schemes application. In Viet Nam, the large amounts of international finance received in Hai Phong for port development, although the city is only medium-sized, are an obvious consequence of the strong involvement of the national government in the local port modernisation projects. In this regard, the national government should co-operate more efficiently with provincial and local authorities in Cebu, but also international funders, to design and propose well-crafted projects, identifying concrete needs to achieve urban green growth. In the past for instance, local authorities in Cebu were unable to benefit from a loan within the Clean Development Mechanism (CDM) scheme from a German Bank because of the lack of capacity of local authorities in Cebu to propose a good project and a lack of capacity of the Land Bank of the Philippines to review the submitted proposals from the LGUs. All levels of government could use the JICA-MCDCB roadmap and the present study as a basis to design projects collectively.

A potentially interesting option is to set up a local investment fund for urban development in Cebu (and other Provinces). It could be an opportunity to attract more easily official development finance at the local level but also to give the LGUs – and in particular the MCDA if created – a more important role in attracting international finance to realise urban green growth objectives. Such local mechanism has already been set up in several main cities in Viet Nam, with support of the French Development Agency (AFD). Such initiative could be supported by the national government, and in particular the Philippines Development Bank and the Land Bank of the Philippines. MCDA could play a critical role, also, in facilitating land acquisition and LGU-related issues, which are common official development projects implementation obstacles in the Philippines (NEDA, 2015).

In parallel, enhancing the effectiveness and quality of aid that reaches Cebu will be critical otherwise the potential benefits of international support will be nullified. One of the aspects to be improved is the appropriate targeted area of support. The current fragmentation of LGUs within the same metropolitan area of Metro Cebu indeed makes metropolitan wide projects hard to design, agree on and implement. As a consequence, projects tend to be limited to a single LGU's jurisdiction. The current Bus Rapid Transit (BRT) project in discussion with the AFD for instance is only designed for implementation in the City of Cebu, excluding all other 12 LGUs of Metro Cebu, even though commuters frequently cross local jurisdictions. While the BRT system can in theory be expanded to adjacent LGUs in the future, land availability restrictions and infrastructure lock-in make it even more difficult than in the current context. The creation of the MCDA, in this perspective, would be a great opportunity to co-ordinate implementation of official development assistance in the whole metropolitan area from the start. In the future for instance, an organisation like AFD should privilege the MCDA as its first interlocutor for development projects. The MCDA bill states that "MCDA shall also co-ordinate and interface with foreign assistance and other agencies for the purpose of obtaining financing and technical assistance" (Republic of the Philippines, 2015). The Province of Cebu should also be involved, especially if such projects involve or affect surrounding rural areas.

Continuing Cebu's efforts to mobilise international partners

In addition to official development finance, Cebu should also develop partnerships with international organisations to achieve urban green growth. The importance of such partnerships is already well-recognised by the local government. The main projects involving international partners are listed in Table 4.3. MCDCB in particular has been particularly active in reaching out international partners. JICA, as mentioned already in this report, has been a critical to develop the extensive Roadmap for Sustainable Urban

Development in Metro Cebu, which contains extensive analysis of the development context and strategic recommendations for the next 25 years.

Table 4.2. **List of major projects undertaken with international and foreign partners in Cebu**

Name of partner	Description of the project
JICA	Roadmap Study for Sustainable Urban Development in Metro Cebu (2015) Construction of Mandaue-Mactan Bridge (1972)
AFD and CTF	Construction of a BRT system in Cebu City
City of Yokohama	Construction of a wastewater treatment plant
The World Bank	Update of Mandaue's property tax base
APEC	Low-carbon model town in Mandaue
GIZ	Promotion of Green Economic Development (ProGED)
GIDRM/GIZ	Alignment and strengthening of Cebu DRRM-CCA planning & budgeting processes Inter-LGU co-operation on public safety in Metro Cebu

Source: Authors.

Numerous potentially useful initiatives could benefit Cebu, and the local governments and MCDCB should pursue their efforts to reach out to the international community. International partners could play a more active role in supporting local and national applications for international climate funds, for instance.

Capacity-building for green growth in Cebu

Enabling green growth in Cebu will require boosting the capacity of LGUs and MCDCB/MCDA. In many cases, implementation obstacles do not lie in the willingness of government authorities to design policies that can contribute to green growth, but rather their capacity to collect data, design policies correctly and mobilise all relevant stakeholders for implementation. Capacity should be raised within LGUs, but also through the involvement of local communities and universities and research institutes.

Increasing capacities of the local administration

First, as mentioned in the first section of this Chapter, capacity for planning has to be improved at the local level to enable better harmonisation among LGUs and with provincial and national plans and objectives. The medium term Philippine Development Plan alignment, in which there are strong policy statements about PPPs and links to climate change, is critical, in particular. This will require efficient vertical co-operation between LGUs, MCDCB/MCDA, and the national government (see Section 1). Capacity building is also needed in linking planning with investment and implementation. Ideally, the programmes, projects and activities proposed in the CLUP should be prioritised as part of an investment programme and incorporated into the budgets for implementation. However, few of the priorities identified are actually implemented and project implementation tends to be influenced by political considerations rather than evidence-based planning. Spot zoning is for instance rampant in the absence of completed CLUPs to guide land-use. Likewise, while 5% of the IRA must be dedicated to disaster risk reduction planning by LGUs, in practice local authorities lack technical capacities and the long-term vision to do so. Many plans are short-sighted and only developed to receive the 5% share of the IRA. In Cebu Province, a League of Disaster Risk Reduction Officers is supposed to assist LGUs in doing so, but many of them are not sufficiently trained (see

Chapter 3). DRR officers in each LGU also tend to be close to the Mayor with no specific training. Consequently, many LGUs in Metro Cebu have not completed their DRR plan and risk map, and have not integrated them in their CLUP.

The lack of completed of local plans, and subsequent lack of alignment between local planning and regional and national planning, is partly due to a lack of qualified personnel, especially professional planners in LGUs, as well a lack of understanding of green growth (or sustainable development) principles and practices in existing planning. CLUPs are often done by consultants due to the lack of qualified in-house personnel. There is a lack of understanding and buy-in to important sustainability concepts such as the benefits of densification, mixed use development, and redevelopment of existing sites rather than simply striving for greenfield development, in achieving complete, walkable communities with a good range of amenities that are more efficient and cheaper to serve in terms of the provision of urban infrastructure (e.g. utilities and transit).

LGUs should in this regard make the completion of all CLUPs a priority, and ensure that building capacity within the LGUs is a key part of that process. The draft Mega Cebu Development Act calls for the institution of a regionally based Technical, Operations and Planning Office intended to assume the planning function for the Metro Cebu area and to facilitate capacity building and integration of LGU CLUPs. Both of these initiatives are strong endeavours to rectify the lack of qualified personnel and professional planners required to support the Mega Cebu vision and strive toward alignment among local, regional and national land use plans. The Mega Cebu Development Act provisions should be used to develop such Office to guide this work. Also, Region VII office needs to refocus efforts to not just communicate completed guidelines aimed at getting LGUs to complete CLUPs, but also engage with local planners and officials to build capacity and understanding of key planning principles and practices. They would benefit from a formal outreach and engagement strategy that is focused on collaborative implementation rather than top-down requirements being communicated to LGUs (see also Section 1). Current collaboration with the University of San Carlos to build LGU's capacities through Mega Cebu's Government-Academe-Private Sector (GAP) partnership programme should also continue under the programme of the Technical, Operations and Planning Office of the future MCDA.

Mobilising local communities to undertake urban green growth

Considering the burden placed on LGUs, and the amount of efforts needed to foster green growth in Cebu, LGUs and MCDCB/MCDA should involve local communities more systematically in the design and implementation of policies in opportunity areas for green growth. It can be a pragmatic solution especially to tackle issues affecting the urban poor. It is estimated that 30% of families in Central Visayas were affected by poverty (OECD, 2014a). In particular, LGUs should make greater use of the *purok* system. The *purok* system is a micro-structure of a barangay that promotes empowerment of communities and effective governance at the sub-village level (urban or rural). This system has been first set up in the Camotes Islands and later used in Liloan and Carcar municipalities in Metro Cebu to manage solid waste and clean rivers, in particular. The "Our Cebu Scorecard" developed by the Ramon Aboitiz Foundation, Inc. and the Province of Cebu to assess LGUs' governance performance tends to indicate that LGUs using this system perform better than those without it. LGUs and MCDCB/MCDA should make use of the *purok* system more systematically, by integrating them in the solid waste management strategy, for instance. Such vertical governance strategy would echo Surabaya's successful solid waste management programme which mobilised local communities to tackle rampant solid waste pollution (Box 4.5). Also, LGUs and MCDCB/MCDA should make efforts to formalise the *purok* system: currently, the system is not accountable because the mandate and salary of its members are not defined by the law. Local authorities could develop some legal framework to support the *purok* system and unlock some resources for its functioning.

Box 4.5. **Surabaya's community involvement for solid waste management**

Surabaya is the capital of the East Java Province and the second largest city in Indonesia. Rapid and uncontrolled urbanisation resulted in a range of environmental issues in the city by the mid-2000s, including solid waste pollution due to unsorted garbage and open waste disposal. The city also suffered from lack of clean water supply and wastewater treatment system, and periodic floods, creating critical health hazards such as dengue fever and diarrhoea.

To address these problems, the City of Surabaya engaged into an ambitious solid waste management programme based on community involvement. The creation of a waste bank and 24 composting houses in the city were two important measures taken by the municipality, but raising public awareness was the keystone of the programme. It was carried out community education programmes on waste management. These programmes promoted the use of simple and appropriate technologies at the household level, such as the Takakura Box. The programme insisted on how to sort out organic waste and other procedures of waste management.

In order to facilitate implementation, 420 Environmental Facilitators were appointed and trained by the local government. They were recruited from community leaders, young generation and cadres of the Family Welfare Programme (PKK). They role is to further raise awareness of the population about the need to preserve the environment and drop habits that result in local pollution, such as open waste dumping. The Environmental Facilitators also trained environmental cadres at a lower level in the whole city. The City of Surabaya has gradually expanded training of Facilitators and provided aid supplies and finance to support their community activities. Environmental cadres operate at a lower level than the Facilitators, but carry the same functions of raising awareness among urban residents. They come from diverse background (e.g. students, office workers) and each accompanies a group of ten houses. Around 28 000 cadres were recorded in 2012, which represents a significant manpower for the local government to implement on the ground its solid waste management principles.

In addition, the City of Surabaya was assisted by a network of NGOs to disseminate the new solid waste management techniques, which were then integrated into the city administration (Office of Cleanliness and Gardens of Surabaya).

Source: APEKSI (2012), *Best Practices of Indonesian Cities*, 8th Edition, Jakarta, Indonesia.

Community engagement can also bring benefits in other opportunity areas for urban green growth. Managing floods, for instance, can be enhanced by involving local communities in implementing diverse measures. It will be necessary, for instance, to develop rainwater storage devices at the household level to ease the pressure on aquifers and void runoff during the storm, and to react efficiently during a major typhoon and avoid panic from lack of preparedness. The major floods that hit Bangkok in 2011 showed that the help of volunteers can be a decisive element to ensure the resilience of a city to such a climatic event (OECD, 2015a). Another opportunity area where community and stakeholder engagement can bring high benefits is the transport sector, especially in view of the creation of a BRT and hypothetically a rail system in the future. Planning the BRT system was challenging because of the opposition of some jeepney operators, and the fragmentation of the jeepney industry. More efforts could be spent to integrate the jeepney routes with the BRT system, and to convince jeepney drivers to accept the new bus lanes (see Chapter 2). MCDCB/MCDA should encourage community involvement and not leave the initiatives to LGUs and Barangays only, so that community initiatives are given a clear framework at the metropolitan and are coherent with regional strategies for flood management.

Another means of involving communities is the dense network of churches that characterises the Philippines. Indeed, 86% of the country's population is Roman Catholic and churches play a very important social role in the everyday life of most citizens. In this regard, churches could be privileged interfaces between the population and the government. Currently however, some parishes undertake some projects but these are timid and not aligned with government initiatives to promote policies that can encourage green growth. The Basic Ecclesiastical Community (BEC) for instance helps people affected by disasters. LGUs and MCDCB/MCDA should be more aggressive in reaching out to these networks, directly or through barangays (which has stronger ties with parishes), to raise public awareness about resilience and even green growth principles. This would help to shift behaviour and provide LGUs support from citizens in the medium to long terms.

Building capacity through sound data collection and monitoring mechanism

One of the recurrent problems faced by LGUs in Cebu is the lack of data and the lack of capacity to collect, analyse and monitor them in order to assess performance and progress towards green growth. There is no data, for instance, on GHG emissions, and natural assets in Cebu. In some cases, the data is only available in some areas of the metropolitan area, and not in others (e.g. non-revenue water or air quality). In other cases, the type of data is not consistent across jurisdictions, or owned by private companies but not communicated to LGUs (e.g. the transportation data which is collected by the Department of Transportation on a "per request" basis). The main indicators related to green growth performance which are currently missing are listed in Table 4.3.

Table 4.3. **Main green growth data missing in Metro Cebu**

Sector	Data
Social	• Slum population • Gini coefficient
Economic	• Employment and GDP output in the Environmental Goods and Services (EGS) sector • Size of the informal economy
Land-use	• Recent land-use map • Location of slums
Transport	• Commuting by trips and distance • Modal split (including walking and cycling)
Solid Waste	• Coverage of the solid waste collection system • Solid waste recycled by industries and informal "scavengers"
Water	• Quality of rivers and other water bodies
Energy	• Final energy consumption in households, industries and businesses and by type of energy (here mainly electricity, and heating if appropriate) • CO_2 emissions • Renewable energy production potential
Other	• PM2.5 concentrations in the ambient air • Health impact of air pollution • natural disasters Vulnerability to by urban area • Status of major fauna and flora species (including coastal mangrove)

Source: Authors.

Some initiatives have been taken at the metropolitan level, such as the development of the Metro Cebu Development Index by RAFI and the Province of Cebu, an attempt to integrate several criteria to evaluate the social, economic and environmental needs of Metro Cebu. However, some initiatives are too isolated and generally speaking efforts still need to be scaled up and integrated with the Metro Cebu roadmap. The Metro Cebu Development Index, for instance, does not include indicators on disaster risk resilience. There is a need to develop a metropolitan observatory to collect and monitor data on green growth more systematically and for the whole metropolitan region, and ensure that such observatory is well connected to policymakers from LGUs and the future MCDA. A recent example of such observatory is the Iskandar Malaysia Urban Observatory (IMUO), whose objective is to raise capacity building at the metropolitan level for data collection for implementation of the regional comprehensive plan (Box 4.6). Such an observatory could be placed under the direction of the MCDA, as one of the functions of MCDA would be to ensure continuous research, evaluation and monitoring to enhance policies. It would ensure that the observatory is well connected to policymakers in all LGUs constituting the metropolitan area, and that critical departments and agencies, and private companies, which possess data on Cebu's development, also participate. An important task of such an observatory is to define Functional Urban Areas (FUAs) in Metro Cebu. A harmonised definition of urban areas as "functional economic units" would be useful in designing and implementing green growth strategies according to functionally integrated areas, rather than administrative entities. It would also increase comparability of metropolitan areas, and therefore Metro Cebu can learn draw positive lessons from best practices in other FUAs, thereby encouraging more effective co-ordination. Smart city solutions may also help to create more channels for governance linkages between LGUs. The observatory, by collecting and sharing data with all the LGUs in one location, will function as a platform which eliminates silos in urban and metropolitan management and makes it easier to address common issues such as transport, flood risks, air and pollution and waste management. The Bandung Command Centre in Bandung, Indonesia, can be a good model (Box 4.7).

Box 4.6. **Iskandar Malaysia Urban Observatory**

Iskandar Malaysia Regional Authority (IRDA) has ambitious development plans that can foster green growth but also face significant implementation obstacles. Currently, a lot of data is missing that is needed to assess the environmental status and performance of the region (e.g., there is no recent air quality data available, while increasing commuting trips and motorisation suggests air pollution may become more severe in the near future). In addition, where data is available, it is often only at the scale of local authorities, or at the broader scale of the Johor State, which is insufficient for any accurate analysis of the policy needs.

To respond to these problems, the Iskandar Malaysia Urban Observatory (IMUO) was created in 2015 to tackle these problems. The IMUO is one of the catalytic projects of the Comprehensive Development Plan ii, completed in 2015, and consists of:

- A Central Data Centre as the focal point to collate, update, analyse, manage and disseminate data and information about IM;
- A Knowledge Hub that will improve the region-wide evidentiary base of urban knowledge about IMER. It will also be the physical repository of all documents related to urban planning such as Local Plans, State Structure Plans, and other studies;
- A Monitoring and Assessment Centre that will monitor the progress of IMER in

Box 4.6. **Iskandar Malaysia Urban Observatory** *(continued)*

implementing the CDPii as well as its urban status and trends. It will undertake "Development Impact Assessments" periodically to ensure sustainability;

- A Technical Services Division to develop tools and methods to monitor programmes and provide capacity-building efforts to implement policies at the local level.

Source: OECD (forthcoming), *Green Growth in Iskandar Malaysia*, OECD Publishing, Paris.

Box 4.7. **Bandung Command Centre**

The Bandung Command Centre is Bandung City's flagship project for its vision to become a smart city. It was initiated in early 2015, in partnership with IBM and Institut Teknologi Bandung (ITB), one of the top universities in Indonesia, and is similar to other existing command centres in Japan and Korea, aiming to improve public services. The centre consists of a digital control board that allows city staff to remotely monitor traffic and manage crisis situations in the city (in case of accidents, crime, etc.). Fifteen operators from the Bandung Telecommunication and Information Agency work permanently in the Command Centre, but it is also accessible to other city departments, such as fire brigades, police officers and transport agencies. It collects information from the street level to make informed decisions to improve such public services as ambulances, fire fighters and police intervention. The information is shown on a digital screen in the Command Centre.

Some of the information gathered by the Command Centre is also accessible to the public. The data collected through GPS devices in school buses can be viewed by the local population, so they can make an informed decision if a bus is held up by traffic. The Command Centre is being developed as a privileged interface of communication between governments and local communities in the city.

The Bandung Command Centre also works as a data bank, storing information on traffic violations, road infrastructure conditions, safety performance, disaster frequency and locations, etc. It makes it possible to visualise the types of problems most frequently encountered in every district of the city, and make a performance assessment for each of them. In future, smaller operations centres will be opened in each district, in a strategy to decentralise smart city tool management. The Centre is being developed in three stages, only the first of which has been completed, and it is expected to cover management of other sectors in future.

Source: OECD (2016), *Green Growth in Bandung, Indonesia*, OECD Publishing, Paris, http://dx.doi.org/10.1787/9789264264113-en.

In addition, in order to boost the capacities of the observatory, local universities and the private sector should be active contributors, again through MCDCB / MCDA. The University of San Carlos for instance has significant research capacities and could support LGUs. In addition, local universities can indirectly support by raising capacities of the metropolitan administration itself. MCDCB has already linked up with two universities through the signing of a Memorandum of Understanding, including the University of San Carlos (USC) and the University of San Jose Recoletos, to research on capacity building needs in LGUs among other topics. A good recent example is USC's co-operation with Cebu Province and MCDB in the development of the province wide multi-hazard suitability map. The local university is also instituting a professional planning curriculum intended to build professional planning capacity. Such policies could be expanded and aligned with green growth objectives, in particular. MCDCB / MCDA could systemise and structure collaboration through Memoranda of Understanding (MoU) with some key universities and research institutes. MCDCB has already developed a MoU with USC to provide training programme to young people on urban development and disaster risk reduction, but the creation of MCDA with more extended power and resources should be an opportunity to create a more ambitious and effective co-operation for urban green growth. MCDCB / MCDA should take the example of Metro Vancouver's initiative to tap on the local research capacities more substantially and coherently (Box 4.8).

Box 4.8. Metro Vancouver's MOU with University of British Columbia

Metro Vancouver and UBC have a strong history of working together on a variety of projects within Metro Vancouver's areas of service. In most instances, collaboration has brought together researchers and students from the University's key faculties and research centres, with staff from Metro Vancouver's line departments. Collaboration has also focused on operational issues involving UBC's main campus operations and Metro Vancouver's departments. A compendium of joint initiatives put together by Metro Vancouver staff identified over 80 past and current joint projects between Metro Vancouver and UBC. Building upon the success of this relationship, in late 2014, senior staff from UBC and Metro Vancouver met to discuss the respective goals and needs of their organisations, as well as the range of opportunities for further collaboration. Through these discussions the concept of a 'Strategic Collaboration Memorandum' arose and prompted staff from both organisations to work together on a model that would explore and expand upon opportunities for future partnerships.

The *Strategic Collaboration MOU* is a non-binding document that expresses the shared commitment of Metro Vancouver and UBC "to the principles of sustainability and to the belief that the long-term liveability, prosperity and sustainability of the region – indeed the entire planet – require approaches to problem-solving that are characterised by innovation, creativity, entrepreneurship and collaboration". The MOU is a framework document within which the parties will identify and pursue joint initiatives. The scope of the MOU focuses the parties' efforts on developing initiatives under three areas of collaboration:

- **Research, Learning and Innovation**: under the MOU, the parties would endeavour to identify new opportunities to share knowledge and research findings, jointly undertake research to further individual and shared goals, and collaborate in the development of approaches designed to address important regional and global sustainability challenges. The parties would also regularly hold discussion forums and workshops to bring together staff and researchers from the two organisations. Information on best practices, innovations, technologies and approaches would be shared at these events, as would ideas for new initiatives and ongoing collaboration. Finally, the parties would seek ways to better engage UBC students in specific projects identified by Metro Vancouver.
- **Operations**: through their respective servicing responsibilities and activities, Metro Vancouver and UBC face a range of operational issues, some of which are best addressed collaboratively. In past years, collaboration on these issues has been largely reactive and inconsistent. Through the MOU, the parties would endeavour to proactively identify issues on which joint approaches for action can be considered.
- **Regional Prosperity:** the MOU would bring the parties together, as part of broader

Box 4.8. **Metro Vancouver's MOU with University of British Columbia** *(continued)*

> multi-party initiatives, on efforts to address a wide range of topics related to prosperity. Such efforts may focus on actions to reduce regional greenhouse gas emissions, adapt to climate change, align the management of growth in the region with viable transportation strategies and investment, and promote the conditions for a competitive metropolitan economy.

The MOU is managed by a Joint Steering Committee co-chaired by a senior staff member from each organisation. One of the key roles for the Steering Committee is to monitor and, where possible, co-ordinate the various initiatives pursued under the MOU. The Steering Committee also ensures that the regular discussion forums and workshops, so important to the exchange of ideas and development of collaboration opportunities, occurred as envisioned under the MOU. The proposed MOU with UBC may serve as a template for similar framework documents with other institutions, and can be viewed as the first in a series of strategic collaboration initiatives. Metro Vancouver staff has had preliminary discussions on the topic with representatives of Simon Fraser University, for instance.

Source: Metro Vancouver (2015), "Greater Vancouver Regional District Inter-government and Finance Committee", held on Thursday 26 November 2015.

Main policy recommendations

- Create a **national policy framework in the water supply and sanitation sector**. Devolve more responsibilities to LGUs and metropolitan forms of governance (MCDCB / MCDA) in the management of local resources, and reinforce mechanisms for technical assistance and outreach to build local capacities.
- **Involve national line ministries and agencies in the future MCDA** to align the Metro Cebu Roadmap with national development plans. Explore a stronger relationship with the Regional Development Council (RDC) of the Central Visayas to ensure proper co-ordination, policy complementarity and coherence across all sectors.
- Strengthen the role of provinces in facilitating inter-LGU co-operation on issues that affect multiple LGUs, like modelling local climate change impacts and flood early warning in shared river basins.
- Make greater use of economic instruments such as **charges and tariffs** (e.g. water extraction fees) in order to raise own revenue and encourage green behaviours. Align better national fiscal transfers with green growth objectives.
- **Loosen FDI restrictions** in critical opportunity areas for green growth and create incentives for green finance such as sustainability standards in infrastructure investment markets. Use MCDA as a means to facilitate PPP at the metropolitan level.
- **Channel down official development assistance more efficiently** to Cebu through good co-ordination between national government and MCDCB / MCDA. Build capacities at national and local levels to apply to international climate funds.
- Create a **Metropolitan Urban Observatory** to collect and monitor data on urban green growth and to identify the functional urban area, as well as ensure connection with policy makers, local universities and the private sector.

Notes

1. This figure excludes the municipality of Cordova, so only integrates 12 LGUs.
2. www.dof.gov.ph/index.php/tax_watch/lgu-2/ (accessed 11 May 2016).
3. In December 2014, the Board of the Asian Development Bank approved a direct loan of USD 75 million to the GMR Megawide Cebu Airport Corporation (SPV).
4. Volume 2 is entitled "Development of PPP projects for Local Government Units" and Volume 3 is entitled "Utilising LGU Project Templates and Bid Documents"
5. All the figures related to official development finance given in this chapter are expressed in 2013 constant prices.
6. Bilateral ODA activities targeting environmental objectives can be identified in a dataset accessible through the OECD statistical website and from the CRS database. This dataset contains commitment data on aid in support of environment sustainability and aid targeting the objectives of the Rio Conventions (biodiversity, climate change mitigation, climate change adaptation and desertification). Multilateral ODA activities and other official flows (OOF) targeting environmental objectives can be identified in the CRS database accessible through the OECD statistical website. The main approach to identifying projects committed to urban areas was based on a word search of their purpose name (e.g. "urban development and management"). For all other projects whose purpose name did not make it possible to determine whether the project was urban, the "urban" character was identified by examining at each project description. Similarly, the main element used to identify projects committed to rural areas was their purpose name ("rural development"). A second step, if the purpose name was not conclusive, was to look at the titles and a short description of the projects. Agricultural, fishery and forestry projects were classified as rural. The remaining rural projects were identified based on their long description. Unspecified projects refer to all other projects, with no detailed description, no details on the geographical scope or inconclusive geographical scope.
7. The total cost of the project is estimated at USD 228 million.
8. This current project cannot be integrated in Figure 4.8 because the data for the entire country for 2014 and 2015 is not available. However, it was integrated in Figure 4.9.
9. For instance, in 2014, an Environmental Development project (USD 239 million) and a Credit Line for Energy Efficiency and Climate Protection in the Philippines (USD 37 million) were committed as ODA to the national government (NEDA, 2015).

References

APEKSI (2012), *Best Practices of Indonesian Cities*, 8th Edition, Jakarta, Indonesia.

Climate Bonds Initiative (n.d), "The Swedes come marching in… just out Gothenburg 6yr, SEK1.8bn ($273m) Green City Bond. Earlier in the month new issuers Stockholm Lans Landstring SEK870m ($167m) and Rikshem green property SEK100m ($15m) joined the charge", 30 May, https://www.climatebonds.net/2014/05/swedes-come-marching-just-out-gothenburg-6yr-sek18bn-273m-green-city-bond-earlier-month-new (accessed 27 June 2017).

Corfee-Morlot, J. et al. (2009), "Chapter 2: Cities and climate change: Harnessing the potential for local action" in *Competitive Cities and Climate Change*, OECD, Paris, www1.oecd.org/gov/regional-policy/50594939.pdf.

Department of Finance (2015), "LGU Taxation and Revenue Practices", Bureau of Local Government Finance, Manila.

KPMG Philippines (2015), "Infrastructure In-depth: Philippines", *2015 Investment Guide*, www.kpmg.com/PH/en/PHConnect/ArticlesandPublications/ThoughtLeadershipPublications/Pages/InfrastructureIn-depthPhilippines.aspx (accessed March 2015).

Republic of the Philippines (2015), *Mega Cebu Development Authority Act of 2015*, Quezon City.

Llanto, G.M., A.M. Navarro and Ma.K. Ortiz (2015), "Development Finance and Aid in the Philippines: Policy, Institutional Arrangements and Flows", *PIDS Discussion Paper Series*, No. 2015-10.

Metro Vancouver (2015), "Greater Vancouver Regional District Inter-government and Finance Committee", held 26 November 2015.

National Economic Development Authority (NEDA) (2015), "ODA Portfolio Review, CY 2014", presented in March 2015.

OECD (2016a), *Green Growth in Hai Phong, Viet Nam*, OECD Publishing, Paris, http://dx.doi.org/10.1787/9789264260207-en.

OECD (2016b), *Subnational governments in OECD countries: Key data* (brochure), OECD, Paris, www.oecd.org/regional/regional-policy.

OECD (2015a), *Green Growth in Bangkok, Thailand*, OECD Publishing, Paris, http://dx.doi.org/10.1787/9789264237087-en.

OECD (2015b), "The Philippine PPP Framework and Programme", an OECD Review in Collaboration with the Government of the Philippines and the Department of Trade Affairs of Australia.

OECD (2015c), *Revenue Statistics in Asian Countries 2015: Trends in Indonesia, Malaysia and the Philippines*, OECD Publishing, Paris, http://dx.doi.org/10.1787/9789264234277-en.

OECD (2014a), *Southeast Asia Investment Policy Perspectives*, OECD Publishing, Paris.

OECD (2014b), *Recommendation of the Council on Effective Public Investment Across Levels of Government*, OECD, Paris, www.oecd.org/gov/regional-policy/Principles-Public-Investment.pdf.

PPP Centre (2012), *Developing Public-Private Partnerships in Local Infrastructure and Development Projects, A PPP Manual for LGUs: Understanding PPP Concepts and Framework*, Volume 1, Quezon City, Philippines, https://ppp.gov.ph/wp-content/uploads/2012/07/PPP-Manual-for-LGUs-Volume-1.pdf.

UNEP (2015), “Towards a Sustainable Financing System in Indonesia”, in partnership with IFC and AsRIA, Geneva Switzerland.

ORGANISATION FOR ECONOMIC CO-OPERATION AND DEVELOPMENT

The OECD is a unique forum where governments work together to address the economic, social and environmental challenges of globalisation. The OECD is also at the forefront of efforts to understand and to help governments respond to new developments and concerns, such as corporate governance, the information economy and the challenges of an ageing population. The Organisation provides a setting where governments can compare policy experiences, seek answers to common problems, identify good practice and work to co-ordinate domestic and international policies.

The OECD member countries are: Australia, Austria, Belgium, Canada, Chile, the Czech Republic, Denmark, Estonia, Finland, France, Germany, Greece, Hungary, Iceland, Ireland, Israel, Italy, Japan, Korea, Latvia, Luxembourg, Mexico, the Netherlands, New Zealand, Norway, Poland, Portugal, the Slovak Republic, Slovenia, Spain, Sweden, Switzerland, Turkey, the United Kingdom and the United States. The European Union takes part in the work of the OECD.

OECD Publishing disseminates widely the results of the Organisation's statistics gathering and research on economic, social and environmental issues, as well as the conventions, guidelines and standards agreed by its members.

OECD PUBLISHING, 2, rue André-Pascal, 75775 PARIS CEDEX 16
(85 2017 02 1 P) ISBN 978-92-64-27798-4 – 2017

www.ingramcontent.com/pod-product-compliance
Ingram Content Group UK Ltd.
Pitfield, Milton Keynes, MK11 3LW, UK
UKHW051502290926
15471UKWH00008B/1354

9 789264 27798